Do Running
Mates Matter?

Do Running Mates Matter?

THE INFLUENCE OF VICE PRESIDENTIAL CANDIDATES IN PRESIDENTIAL ELECTIONS

Christopher J. Devine
and
Kyle C. Kopko

University Press of Kansas

Published by the University Press of Kansas (Lawrence, Kansas 66045), which was organized by the Kansas Board of Regents and is operated and funded by Emporia State University, Fort Hays State University, Kansas State University, Pittsburg State University, the University of Kansas, and Wichita State University.

Library of Congress Cataloging-in-Publication Data

Names: Devine, Christopher, 1984– author. | Kopko, Kyle C., 1984– author.
Title: Do running mates matter? : the influence of vice presidential candidates in presidential elections / Christopher J. Devine and Kyle C. Kopko.
Description: Lawrence : University Press of Kansas, 2020. | Includes bibliographical references and index.
Identifiers: LCCN 2020004183
  ISBN 9780700629695 (cloth)
  ISBN 9780700629701 (paperback)
  ISBN 9780700629718 (ebook)
Subjects: LCSH: Presidents—United States—Election. | Vice-Presidential candidates—United States. | Voting research—United States.
Classification: LCC JK528 .D48 2020 | DDC 324.973—dc23
LC record available at https://lccn.loc.gov/2020004183.

Printed in the United States of America

10 9 8 7 6 5 4 3 2 1

The paper used in this publication is recycled and contains 30 percent postconsumer waste. It is acid free and meets the minimum requirements of the American National Standard for Permanence of Paper for Printed Library Materials z39.48-1992.

To our newest running mates—
Madison and McKinley Devine
Clara Grace Kopko

The decision you make as a presidential candidate on who your running mate is going to be is the first presidential-level decision that the public sees you make. It's the first time you're making a decision that you're going to have to live with. It gives the public a chance to watch you operate and see what you think is important, what kind of individual you choose to serve as your running mate, what are the criteria.

And I think the single most important criteria [sic] has to be the capacity to be president. That's why you pick them. Lots of times in the past that has not been the foremost criteria [sic]. It really varies [from] administration to administration. As you watch the talking heads out there now, they're talking about, "Well, gee, you better get a woman or you better get a Hispanic or you better pick somebody from a big state." Those are all interesting things to speculate about, but it's pretty rare that an election ever turns on those kinds of issues.

It's much more likely to turn on the kind of situation where they'll judge the quality of your decision-making process based on whether or not this individual is up to the task of taking over and serving as president of the United States should something happen to the president.

—FORMER VICE PRESIDENT DICK CHENEY, INTERVIEW, APRIL 23, 2012

Contents

Figures and Tables

FIGURES

TABLES

Acknowledgments

In early September 2008, the two of us—then graduate students in political science at The Ohio State University—set out on a road trip from Columbus, Ohio, to Columbia, South Carolina. Before we crossed the border into West Virginia, our conversation had turned to what was on every political junkie's mind that week: John McCain's selection of Sarah Palin, the heretofore unknown governor of Alaska, as his running mate. One frequent criticism of this selection, in particular, caught our attention—that McCain should have picked someone from a battleground state such as Ohio, where we lived, who could "deliver" its electoral votes in November. As budding political scientists, our first instinct was to ask whether this conventional wisdom about the vice presidential "home state advantage" had any basis in fact. "Does anyone know if that's actually true?" one of us wondered. The other one responded: "How would you even measure it?" With hours left to drive and the internet out of reach on our primitive flip phones, we spent the rest of the trip obsessing over these questions. By South Carolina, we had planned out our next research project. That's how it all started.

One decade, one book, and several journal articles later, the study of vice presidential candidates still fascinated us. Indeed, answering our initial questions about this topic only seemed to raise more, and more interesting, questions. Following the publication of our first book, on the vice presidential home state advantage, we recognized that our initial question really was just one piece of a larger puzzle. That puzzle is the subject of this book. It is, in fact, the most fundamental question about our chosen topic. It is the question that we have been asked most often but never quite knew how to answer. It is a question to which no one, surprisingly, has provided a comprehensive answer. And it is the question that we have (really) been asking all along: *Do running mates matter?*

Over the past decade—from the time that we first asked this question to now, when (hopefully) we have answered it, at last—many people have contributed to this work and to our lives in ways that we cannot adequately recognize here. But we'll try anyway. And we know where to start. First and foremost, we thank our wives, Trudy Devine and Sarah Kopko, who—in so many ways—made it possible for us to write this book. And we thank our children—Hayes, Wilson (aka Miles), Madison, and McKinley Devine; Mary and Clara Kopko—three of whom have joined us since our work on this book began. No matter the status of our current project, our families provide a daily reminder of who we really are and what really matters. They bring joy and fulfillment to our lives that no professional achievement can match—not even close. We are profoundly grateful for their love, support, patience, and faith. Our highest aspiration is to return it all.

Our respective institutions—the University of Dayton and Elizabethtown College—and our colleagues there also have made vital contributions to this work. In terms of institutional support, the University of Dayton funded our research on chapters 1, 2, and 4 of this book, via Research Council Seed Grants in the summers of 2017 and 2019. Our thanks go to Jon Hess, John Leland, Danita Nelson, and Jennifer Speed, for their help in securing this funding. For their invaluable guidance and support over the past several years, we thank our department chairs and colleagues, including Grant Neeley, Natalie Florea Hudson, Dan Birdsong, Nancy Martorano Miller, April Kelly-Woessner, Fletcher McClellan, Oya Dursun-Özkanca, and Betty Rider. Finally, for their help in sharing our research with the public, we thank our respective media relations departments and, in particular, Meagan Pant and Keri Straub.

Truly, we could not have done much of the analysis in this book but for the generous assistance of fellow scholars. In particular, we are grateful to Janet Box-Steffensmeier, David Darmofal, and Christopher "Kit" Baum, for graciously taking the time to answer our many questions regarding vector autoregression; Gabriel Lenz, regarding his three-wave test of panel data; and Wendy Mansfield, of GfK, regarding the 2008 Associated Press–Yahoo! News Panel survey. Part II of this book makes extensive use of these methodologies and data sources. We hope our work reflects well on these scholars' contributions, and we claim any shortcomings as our own. The introduction and first chapter of this book incorporate archival research conducted at the Gerald R. Ford Library in Ann Arbor, Michigan. We thank John O'Connell and Geir Gundersen for their assistance in conducting this research, and William Adler for his helpful advice as we prepared to visit the Ford Library. We also benefited from participating in a panel on vice presidential research at the 2017 Midwest Political Science Association's annual conference, with William Adler, Julia Azari, David Schultz, and Stacy Ulbig.

Also, we are grateful to those scholars who provided essential feedback on our book manuscript, or elements of it, prior to publication. Stacy Ulbig, Jody

Baumgartner, and William Mayer generously gave of their time to share insightful reviews of our book proposal and draft chapters. Herb Weisberg—a valued friend, mentor, and department chair during our time at The Ohio State University—reviewed a draft of Part I of this book and provided many helpful comments, as always. Joshua Darr provided excellent feedback on an early version of chapter 3 while serving as our discussant at the annual conference of the Midwest Political Science Association in 2018. Finally, we thank the up-and-coming scholars from the University of Dayton's American Presidency course, in Spring 2019, who read and critiqued our manuscript's introduction and first chapter—with special instructions to take revenge on Professor Devine and write comments all over his work. You did a great job, and we thank you for it. Now you can see that it paid off, too—in table 1.1 (Sarah); in the "conflicted," rather than "ambivalent," state of opinion described in the introduction (Nate); and in many, many other places (looking at you, Bo).

We are grateful to have found the perfect home for our book, too, at the University Press of Kansas—a publisher that has become synonymous with first-rate scholarship on the US presidency and vice presidency, which we have admired and enjoyed for many years now. It is an honor to publish with UPK and to work with our outstanding editor, David Congdon. Throughout this process, David has encouraged but also challenged us—exactly as a good editor must do. This book is all the better for his constructive and insightful feedback, and we thank him for it. We also extend our thanks to Larisa Martin and Susan Ecklund for their careful copyediting of this manuscript.

Last, but not least: Where would we be without Mark Kopko and Lamar Benton? Your unwavering support for political science research has been an inspiration.

Introduction

In January 2015, there were no declared candidates for the next presidential election. It was just too early. Yet the veepstakes already had begun. Rumor had it that Ohio's senior US senator, Sherrod Brown, was a leading contender for the Democratic vice presidential nomination. On paper, he was the perfect running mate: an experienced, two-term senator from a key battleground state, a vigorous campaigner, and a bona fide progressive who also could appeal to blue-collar swing voters. Many Democrats wanted Brown to run for president, in fact. But, like so many other credible candidates who doubted that Hillary Clinton could be defeated for the party's nomination, he declined. So, speculation shifted to the next best thing: a slot on the presidential ticket, as Clinton's running mate. There was one problem: Brown didn't want it. Not at all. In his words: "I have zero interest in being vice president" (Terris 2015).

WHO WANTS TO BE THE VICE PRESIDENT?

Brown's proclaimed disinterest in serving as vice president was not surprising. Throughout US history, the vice presidency has been derided as a dead-end job for ambitious politicians whose talents are spent on helping the presidential candidate to get elected rather than helping the president to govern once in office. In the words of one former vice president, Walter Mondale, "The office is handmade for ridicule and for dismissal. In the nature of it, you always look like a supplicant, a beggar, a person on a string" (Woodward and Broder 1992, 196).

Vice Presidential Power(lessness)

The vice presidency owes its unenviable reputation—notwithstanding many informal expansions of power since the 1970s (see Goldstein 2016)—to its institutional design. Indeed, the US Constitution grants few formal powers to the vice president. These include, first, presiding over the US Senate (a power that Harry Truman's vice president, Alben Barkley, last exercised with regularity; see Goldstein 2016, 22);[1] second, casting tie-breaking votes in that body (rarely);[2] third, in the presence of the US House and Senate, opening the sealed certificates containing each state's votes in the Electoral College, and then overseeing the electoral vote count;[3] fourth, and most important, assuming the office of president of the United States upon the president's death (eight times in US history), resignation (once), removal from office, or incapacitation,[4] and when a presidential election remains unresolved at the time that a new presidential term is scheduled to begin.[5]

Dismissing the Vice Presidency

No one has been more critical of the vice presidency, or so eager to make jokes at its expense, than the vice presidents themselves. Take, for example, John Nance Garner's dismissal of the vice presidency as being "not worth a bucket of warm spit"—or the favorite tale of several vice presidents, including Thomas Marshall (Milkis and Nelson 2011, 486), Alben Barkley (Smith 2008, 177–178), and Hubert Humphrey (Unger and Unger 1999, 255): "A mother has two sons; one goes off to sea, the other becomes vice president. Neither is heard from again."

The first vice president, John Adams, famously called it "the most insignificant office that ever the invention of man contrived or his imagination conceived."[6] Lyndon Johnson, who served for nearly three years as John Kennedy's vice president, said of his tenure: "I detested every minute of it" (Baker 2013, 60). Gerald Ford, who briefly served as Richard Nixon's vice president, reportedly described this as "the worst eight months of [my] life" (60). And Nelson Rockefeller, who was nominated and confirmed to the office following Ford's succession to the presidency, often referred to the vice president as mere "standby equipment." He explained: "I did not want to be Vice President. I'm a doer by nature, an activist. And I always felt, and I told Dick Nixon that in 1960 when he asked me to [be his running mate, allegedly], that it was standby equipment and I just wasn't cut out for it."[7] Rockefeller added: "I've known all the Vice Presidents since Henry Wallace. They were all frustrated, and some of them were pretty bitter."[8] Dick Cheney, one of Rockefeller's successors, later would concur: "I'd never met a vice president who was happy."[9]

Conflicted?

Yet many of the same vice presidents and potential running mates who have dismissed the office as ridiculous at other times have betrayed a more con-flicted—or, at least, a more nuanced—view of the vice presidency. In a fol-low-up interview to the one excerpted earlier, Nelson Rockefeller offered a very different assessment of the office:

> I totally disagree with John Nance Gardner [*sic*]. I think the office is a very important one, depending on the relation between the President and the Vice President and at least during the first 2/3rds–3/4ths of the time I was Vice President I've never been busier—heading commissions, undertaking special projects for the President and traveling at home and abroad. It's a very useful function in terms of both ceremonial activities that relieve the President and which are interesting and important, plus, depending on the experience of the individual, the opportunity to use that experience to undertake assignments for the President.[10]

Dick Cheney, who initially resisted entreaties to run alongside George W. Bush in 2000, and bluntly recalled the unhappy fate of previous vice presi-dents, nonetheless said at the end of his two terms in the office: "I don't regret it for a minute. It's been a tremendous experience" (Malcolm 2008).

And then there is John McCain. After failing to win the Republican Par-ty's presidential nomination in 2000, McCain brushed off speculation that he would join the ticket as George W. Bush's running mate. "The vice pres-ident has two duties," he scoffed. "One is to enquire daily as to the health of the president, and the other is to attend the funerals of third world dictators. And neither of those do I find an enjoyable exercise."[11] Four years later, amid speculation that John Kerry would ask him to run for vice president on the *Democratic* ticket, McCain joked: "I spent seven years in a North Vietnamese prison camp, in the dark, fed with scraps. Do you think I want to do that all over again as vice president of the United States?" (Halbfinger 2004).

Yet in 1996, when Bob Dole reportedly weighed selecting him for the Re-publican ticket, McCain expressed a more sober, reverential view of the vice presidency. "John Nance Garner described the office as not being worth a bucket of warm spit, but I hold the office in higher regard than that," McCain said. "It is certainly prestigious and would be a wonderful opportunity for some" (Pittman 1996). Then, in 2008, while once more—and this time successfully—seeking the Republican Party's presidential nomination, McCain said in a debate that "the vice president of the United States is a key and important issue, and must add [*sic*] in carrying out the responsibilities of the President of the United States."[12]

Playing the Vice Presidential Game

It is a good indication of the vice presidency's *actual* value that—jokes and public disavowals of interest notwithstanding—plenty of qualified individuals are willing to be selected as the running mate and undergo an intensive vetting process for that purpose. In fact, many ambitious politicians actively lobby for their selection, behind the scenes.

Take Dan Quayle, for example. George H. W. Bush's decision to name Quayle as his running mate in 1988 came as a shock to nearly everyone, including many Bush campaign staffers. But Quayle had been plotting, along with two of his top Senate aides, to secure a slot on the Republican ticket since the day after Bush won New Hampshire's Republican presidential primary, six months earlier (Woodward and Broder 1992, 15). This "sub rosa campaign" was designed to raise Quayle's profile nationally, and with Bush in particular. In early 1988, Quayle began delivering more speeches in the Senate, issuing more press releases, and writing more newspaper op-eds, particularly on issues of national defense, than at any point during his previous seven years in office. Quayle also tried to make himself more visible to Bush and his inner circle by increasing contact with senior campaign advisers, more regularly visiting the vice president's office in the US Senate, and taking a more vocal role at the weekly Senate Republican lunches that Bush attended, as vice president. To anyone witnessing these efforts, Quayle's intentions were clear. As one Republican Senate colleague, William Cohen of Maine, said: "It looked like there was a game plan to get Bush's attention because Quayle thought he had a shot [at being chosen as Bush's running mate]" (21).

Yet Quayle would not readily acknowledge his campaigning for the vice presidential nomination, even four years later while serving as vice president. He did so only reluctantly, after *Washington Post* reporters Bob Woodward and David Broder presented Quayle with irrefutable evidence of his efforts. Why play coy? Because, Quayle acknowledged, "You don't run for vice president."

Rather, to avoid the stigma of failure if passed over—and, probably, to avoid alienating the presidential candidate by seeming overly ambitious—"you keep expectations down and do things as quietly and subtly as possible" (Woodward and Broder 1992, 15–16).

In fact, Quayle had designs on the vice presidency ever since being elected to Congress in 1976, at the age of twenty-nine. At that time, he explained in a 2002 interview, "Obviously you're thinking about running for President or Vice President. It's there." But, he cautioned, "You don't do it overtly. It's something you have in the back of your mind and you set out a path to do it." Quayle followed that path to the US Senate, from where, he observed, most recent vice presidents had come. He described this as a "stepping-stone" to the vice presidency, and ultimately the presidency. "I was positioning myself to eventually run for President," Quayle explained. "Now, obviously, the Vice Presidency was a stepping-stone to that. I mean, *that's why people want to be Vice President* [emphasis added]."[13]

Joe Lieberman also wanted to be vice president, in 2000—but he, too, could not say so. "You're not supposed to campaign for the vice presidential nomination," he explained later. "You can't even acknowledge that you are under consideration for it" (Lieberman and Lieberman 2003, 11). When Al Gore's campaign asked to vet Lieberman for the nomination that year—a process so invasive that Lieberman likened it to "a colonoscopy without anesthesia" (9)—the prospective running mate consented and then, with the help of a close friend, "developed a strategy not simply for surviving the vetting, but for pursuing the nomination" (11). That strategy included "reach[ing] out, in a very discreet way, to a very few people who we thought might be talking to Gore about this selection" (12), as well as key constituency groups within the Democratic Party. In all cases, "These contacts were to be made subtly, quietly" (13).

Lieberman also sought out advice from Chris Dodd, a fellow senator from Connecticut and his most trusted colleague. Dodd counseled, "You should make sure you do everything you can so you will never look back to this time and say, 'If I had done just one more thing, I might have been the vice presidential nominee.'" But, Dodd acknowledged, "Of course I understand that you can't go out and campaign for it" (Lieberman and Lieberman 2003, 14).

Even after being selected, Lieberman would disclaim any ambition to the vice presidency. Wondrously, he recalled someone telling him, "This is like the ministry. You're called to the ministry, you don't seek it" (Barstow with Seelye 2000). But, of course, Lieberman *had* sought the vice presidential nomination—enthusiastically and methodically. He wanted to be the vice president. He just could not say so publicly at that time.

Quayle and Lieberman are only two examples, but they illustrate what seems to be a well-known strategy among politicians aspiring to the vice presidency: publicly deny that you are interested—better yet, laugh off the idea as ridiculous—all the while privately working with associates and campaign contacts to cultivate interest in your candidacy. Then, after the selection is made and the election is over, you can publicly admit it: yes, of course, I wanted to be the vice president. I *really* wanted it, in fact.

And that brings us back to Sherrod Brown.

Zero Interest?

In July 2017, Sherrod Brown gave another interview to Ben Terris, the *Washington Post* reporter to whom he had protested two-and-a-half years earlier: "I have zero interest in being vice president." A lot had changed since that time. In the summer of 2016—despite reiterating that April, "I've made it clear [that] I don't really want the job" (Raju and Schleifer 2016)—Brown agreed to be considered for selection as Hillary Clinton's running mate. He even participated in a vetting process that Connie Schultz—his wife, and a Pulitzer Prize–winning columnist—described as "excruciating." Brown was a finalist for selection; in fact, according to two highly placed sources, he was the first runner-up to Virginia senator Tim Kaine, whom Clinton selected only after initially favoring Brown (Terris 2017; but see, e.g., Allen and Parnes 2017; Baumgartner 2016). Perhaps the biggest strike against Brown was that, if elected, his replacement in the closely divided US Senate would be appointed by Ohio's Republican governor, John Kasich.

For a man who had expressed "zero interest in the vice presidency," being passed over for the position should have come as a relief. But Brown was disappointed—devastated, in fact. "By the end," he admitted, "I really wanted it." Brown wanted it so badly that he envisioned, in Terris's words, "liv[ing] out of a bus" and barnstorming across the Midwest throughout the fall campaign. Might this have changed the election's outcome? In Terris's article—titled "Sherrod Brown Thinks He Could Have Helped Democrats Win in 2016. But What about 2020?"—Brown answered cautiously: "I don't pretend that my being on the ticket would have made [Clinton] win. I don't know. I mean, if I had gone to Wisconsin and Michigan a lot, anything would have changed those two states." But then, perhaps to cover this tracks, he added: "My wife thinks we would have won. She thinks we would have won Ohio." Of course, Donald Trump won Ohio instead—helping him to become the next president of the United States. And Brown was left to wonder whether he could have made the difference in the Electoral College, apparently haunted by the regret that he did not get that chance.

As it turns out, Sherrod Brown really wanted to be vice president.

A FUNDAMENTAL TENSION

The preceding examples illustrate a fundamental tension in public opinion about the vice presidency as a governing institution. On the one hand, everyone is aware of the office's institutional weakness and its beleaguered reputation. This makes it easy to dismiss the vice presidency as a joke, and to belittle or reject the prospect of seeking that office. Yet many of the news or opinion articles that repeat those jokes—including, almost invariably, a reference to Garner's metaphorical "bucket of warm spit" (and, just as invariably, a caveat noting that he probably used more graphic language)[14]—or report a potential running mate's lack of interest in auditioning for the role, ironically, if not hypocritically, also engage in fevered speculation about the vice presidential selection process or the running mate's likely effect on the presidential race.[15] And, as we have seen, many of the vice presidents or prospective running mates who have disparaged the office or foresworn interest in seeking it at other times have celebrated its significance or actively campaigned for selection behind the scenes.

We do not argue that every such dismissal of the vice presidency or the prospect of running for it is insincere. Indeed, it is entirely possible that Sherrod Brown's initial denials of interest in the vice presidency were genuine, and that later he had a change of heart—or that, in Terris's (2017) words, "Sherrod Brown never wanted to be vice president, until one day he did." Nor do we contend that a vice president plainly contradicts himself when he is quoted both lamenting and praising his experiences in that office. For example, Nelson Rockefeller truly might have felt like "standby equipment" at some times and like someone serving "a very useful function" at others. Such inconsistency, we argue, is indicative not of insincerity but of a pervasive conflict—or

a "fundamental tension"—in attitudes toward the vice presidency, among political elites and within the mass public generally. In short, the vice presidency's public image—truth be told—is not that of an inconsequential institution
or an immensely powerful one (at least by its design); rather, it is an institution characterized by obvious strengths and weaknesses, the relative weight of
which is difficult to calculate and often context-dependent.

John Adams provided perhaps the most profound articulation of this truth
when he said: "I am vice president. In this I am nothing, but I may be everything" (Milkis and Nelson 2011, 486). Here he was referring to the possibility
of succession to the presidency. In the era of the "modern vice presidency"
(Goldstein 2016), when the power of that institution remains constitutionally
stagnant but informally expansive, the tension between viewing the vice presidency as powerless and powerful is that much greater.

WHO CARES ABOUT THE RUNNING MATE?

This book is about vice presidential *candidates*, not *vice presidents*. But the
two roles are intertwined—and not just because, barring extraordinary circumstances, serving as the former is a prerequisite to serving as the latter. It is
also because the (perceived) weakness of the vice presidency, as a governing
institution, has shaped perceptions of the vice presidential candidate, as an
electoral institution. Given the vice president's limited constitutional powers,
and the remote possibility of presidential succession, running mates tradition-
ally have been selected (by party conventions and then, starting in the 1940s,
by presidential candidates) on the basis of electoral considerations, typically in
order to provide geographic, demographic, or ideological "ticket balancing"
(Baumgartner 2012; Baumgartner with Crumblin 2015; Goldstein 2016). Even
so, most voters have had little incentive to weigh the running mate's credentials when voting in presidential elections, at least not to the extent of casting a
vote on that basis, since only the president is guaranteed to exercise substantial
power once in office. Recent expansions of vice presidential power might have
altered that equation somewhat, but—as indicated by the evidence presented
earlier, and by the predominant caricature of vice presidents in popular cul-
ture as buffoonish incompetents—for the most part, the office's unenviable
reputation is engrained and enduring.

A Fundamental Tension (Continued)

It is, therefore, no mystery that the same fundamental tension that characterizes attitudes toward the vice presidency also extends to vice presidential candidates. On the one hand, political observers and practitioners recognize the limited powers of the vice presidency, and so they are duly cautious about overstating the running mate's (likely) influence on presidential voting. Often, they do so by repeating well-worn aphorisms to downplay veepstakes speculation—referring to it merely as a "parlor game," for instance. Or they cite the conventional wisdom that "Vice presidential candidates can't help you, they can only hurt you,"[16] and that "People don't vote for a vice president, they vote for a president."[17] We do not argue that such folk wisdom is wrong, necessarily; in fact, some of the empirical evidence that we present in this book would tend to support these claims. Nor do we contend that expressing such skepticism is insincere or contradictory, on its face. But it is important to recognize that these sentiments often exist in tension with other statements or behaviors that directly express or clearly imply a perception that running mates *are* electorally significant and potentially helpful—even decisive. In chapters 1 and 2, we provide evidence of such tension in the attitudes expressed by presidential candidates and voters, respectively. For now, consider one prominent and consequential example.

When asked to describe his criteria for selecting a running mate in July 2008, Republican presidential nominee John McCain said: "First, you want to make sure you have a candidate that's not going to hurt the ticket" (J. Mason 2008). In 1996, when discussing then-Republican nominee Bob Dole's selection of a running mate, McCain expressed essentially the same view by saying that the selection process sometimes "brings you the person who might not necessarily help you the most, but hurt you the least" (Pittman 1996). At the same time, he indicated that a running mate might confer significant electoral benefits by suggesting that Dole select someone who appealed not only to Republican voters but also "to those that make the difference between winning and losing campaigns"—presumably, Independents.

Yet, when it came time to select *his* running mate, in 2008, McCain passed over the quintessential "do no harm" candidate, in Minnesota governor Tim Pawlenty (the runner-up), and instead accepted his campaign advisers' recommendation to choose a risky but potentially "game-changing" vice presidential candidate, in Sarah Palin. McCain made this choice after meeting the

Alaska governor only for the second time, and following a rushed seventy-two-hour vetting process (see chapter 1). This hardly fulfilled his top criterion: "mak[ing] sure you have a candidate that's not going to hurt the ticket." In fact, following her rocky vice presidential campaign, Palin was widely perceived as hurting the ticket in exactly the way that McCain previously had warned against—a perception validated by subsequent empirical analyses (e.g., Court and Lynch 2015; Elis, Hillygus, and Nie 2010; Knuckey 2012).

McCain illustrates the fundamental tension apparent in many people's—including presidential candidates'—expressed views regarding running mates' electoral significance. He repeatedly stated, and he genuinely might have believed, that the overriding principle of vice presidential selection is "First, do no harm." But, as is the case with matters of public opinion more generally (Zaller 1992), McCain's judgments on the matter seem to have drawn on a mix of considerations. Thus, when pressured by campaign advisers to adopt an alternative approach, he sampled from those conflicting considerations to arrive at a decision fundamentally opposed to his oft-stated conviction. In other words, no matter how confidently McCain stated this conviction in public, and when discussing vice presidential selection in the abstract, to some extent he also believed that it was possible—*maybe just in these special circumstances*—that a running mate could yield transformative electoral benefits, and that the chances of this happening in 2008 were good enough to justify picking Sarah Palin.

What to Believe?

It is ironic that McCain, of all people, would stand out as the presidential candidate who most obviously threw a "Hail Mary" pass, with his choice of a running mate, in order to win an election. Yet, because he at least entertained principles directly in conflict with his oft-stated, and quite possibly genuine, philosophy of vice presidential selection, we suspect that McCain is not a hypocritical outlier but an exemplar of the fundamental tension that characterizes much of public discourse regarding vice presidential candidates and their electoral significance.

Indeed, McCain's is the same type of conflicted opinion that we see in the journalist (Chris Cillizza) who declares that "the vice presidential pick—viewed through the lens of history—has almost no broad influence on the fate of the ticket and, to the extent the VP choice has mattered, it's been in a negative way"—yet, when ranking veepstakes contenders, regularly dangles the prospect of a decisive home state advantage (Devine and Kopko 2016, 14). Or the scholar (Stuart Rothenberg) who scorns veepstakes speculation as "a game" to be played at "cocktail parties or around the kitchen table" before condescending to remind readers that this year's election actually is between two *presidential* candidates—yet in other writings, indeed in the same year, plays precisely that game by rating contenders largely on the basis of their ability to deliver swing states or the party's base (13). Or the presidential candidate (George W. Bush) who writes, "I believe voters base their decision on the presidential candidate, not the VP"—yet also speculates that several other vice presidential finalists on his list might have delivered their home state in the general election (see chapter 1).

Like McCain, these actors state their convictions about running mates' electoral effects definitively—with little, if any, hint of nuance. And, like McCain, it is entirely possible that they have expressed their convictions sincerely. (Bush, for example, *did* choose a running mate with little electoral appeal and no prospect of delivering a swing state.) But there is also good reason to believe that they, like many other actors in the electoral process that we analyze in later chapters, are more conflicted about running mates' electoral significance than they let on. In reality, they probably entertain a mixture of views and therefore, under a particular set of circumstances (e.g., a close election, a popular governor, a divided party), might draw on considerations that conflict with their prevailing philosophy to determine that a (potential) running mate really could make a difference in the election—*maybe this one time.*

That is why one must be careful not to take the conventional wisdom about vice presidential candidates at face value, no matter how frequently or confidently it is publicly pronounced. As is true of the vice presidency itself, evaluations of the running mate's electoral significance are complex, and often they reveal, on close inspection, quite a bit of internal conflict, especially when moving from the abstract to the particular.

In this book, we take nothing about running mates' electoral significance for granted. Whatever our preconceptions about their effects on presidential voting—and it would be fair to describe us as skeptics—our commitment is to let the empirical data speak for themselves.

DO RUNNING MATES MATTER?

Recognizing the fundamental tension in public attitudes toward vice presidential candidates, described earlier, in this book we ask: Do running mates matter? That is to say, do they influence voting in presidential elections? And, if so, how? Do running mates influence voters, in general, or only targeted subsets of the electorate? Do they, in fact, "deliver" their home state or region? Affiliated demographic groups? Ideological allies? And, to the extent that running mates influence elections, is this because voters actually cast votes for (or against) a vice presidential candidate? Or is it because running mates help to shape voters' perceptions of the presidential candidate who selected them, thereby exerting an indirect effect on vote choice?

To emphasize the practical significance of this research, and the manner in which we present it, our fundamental research question may be reformulated as follows: Do running mates do what people—namely, presidential candidates and voters—*think* they do, electorally speaking? Our objective is to answer this question, by testing perceptions of the running mate's (potential) electoral significance against the relevant empirical data. To do this, we divide our research into two essential and integrally related parts. In the following, we briefly describe each chapter's methods of analysis and its empirical results.

Part I: Perceptions of Running Mate Effects

Part I (comprising chapters 1 and 2) analyzes *perceptions* of the running mate's electoral significance. In particular, we evaluate, first, whether, and to what extent, presidential candidates and voters believe that running mates influence vote choice in presidential elections; and, second, what criteria—particularly in terms of electoral versus governing considerations—they use to evaluate (potential) vice presidential candidates. The purpose of this analysis is to set the agenda for the empirical analyses that follow in part II. In other words, we seek to establish—based on systematic evidence, rather than mere assumption—*that it is relevant to ask whether running mates matter in the first place.* Moreover, we seek to identify the nature of these perceived electoral effects. Having done so, in part II we can test whether running mates matter in the way that people—particularly, those who *select* and *elect* them—think they do.

Chapter 1: (Why) Do Presidential Candidates Think That Running Mates Matter?
In this chapter, we use qualitative evidence from the 1976–2016 elections (i.e., the era of the modern vice presidency) to evaluate presidential candidates' perceptions of running mate effects. In particular, we seek to determine whether, and why, presidential candidates think that running mates have the potential to influence election outcomes. We have gathered evidence for this analysis from a diverse range of sources, including public speeches and interviews, media coverage, personal memoirs, oral histories, and archival materials from presidential or other public libraries.

Our analysis indicates that most presidential candidates perceive vice presidential candidates to be electorally consequential—and, in some cases, determinative—but in public they downplay or deny such considerations, so as to focus on governing qualifications. In fact, presidential candidates in nearly all recent elections have publicly communicated a remarkably consistent set of selection criteria: that running mates must be qualified to serve as (vice) president, first and foremost; next, they must be personally and politically compatible with the presidential candidate; finally, as something of a bonus, they may provide a modest electoral advantage. But privately, or in subsequent public comments, many presidential candidates emphasize electoral considerations quite a bit more, and governing considerations less, than they do in public during the campaign.

While we cannot generalize across all selection processes, it is fair to say that most presidential candidates think that running mates matter, electorally speaking, and might even prove decisive in a close race. Such perceptions have the potential to influence the actual selection of a vice presidential candidate—and, in turn, who serves in office as vice president.

Chapter 2: (Why) Do Voters Think That Running Mates Matter?
In this chapter, we analyze public polling data on vice presidential selection, mostly from the 2000–2016 presidential elections. The purpose of this analysis is to determine, first, whether voters think that running mates influence *their* votes, or election outcomes more generally, and second, what criteria voters use to evaluate (potential) running mates, such that we might characterize the nature of their electoral appeal.

Our analysis indicates that voters have mixed, or conflicted, perceptions of running mate effects. Generally, survey respondents affirm the importance of vice presidential selection, in the abstract, and in many cases they report being more or less likely to vote for a given presidential candidate based on his or her choice of a running mate. Yet, at the same time, respondents rate vice presidential selection as less important than nearly all other electoral considerations; fewer than one in ten respondents say that a running mate *ever* has changed their presidential vote; and when given the opportunity to explain, in their own words, why they support or oppose a particular presidential candidate, few, if any, respondents cite the candidate's choice of a running mate.

Also, voters seem not to have fixed criteria in mind when evaluating (potential) vice presidential candidates. However, they do prefer running mates who balance a given ticket by compensating for the presidential candidate's perceived deficiencies. This is evident with respect to attributes of professional experience, in particular, but not demographic characteristics. Indeed, voters seem to value the running mate's qualifications very highly, and for the most part they do not give credence to electoral considerations.

Part II: Evidence of Running Mate Effects

Part II (comprising chapters 3–5) tests perceptions of the running mate's influence, as established in part I, against the relevant empirical evidence. Essentially, our objective in these chapters is to evaluate whether running mates matter in the way that relevant political actors *think* they matter. Each chapter examines a distinct—but not mutually exclusive—process whereby running mate effects might occur: first, by directly influencing vote choice among voters, in general (chapter 3); second, by directly influencing vote choice among targeted subsets of voters (chapter 4); third, by indirect means—that is, by influencing voters' evaluations of the presidential candidates, which, in turn, directly influence vote choice (chapter 5). For this analysis, we use a diverse range of data sources and research methods. Indeed, the depth and breadth of our analysis of vice presidential candidates' electoral influence are unprecedented in the political science literature.

Chapter 3: Direct Effects

In this chapter, we evaluate the running mate's direct effect on voting, generally. First, we do so by providing descriptive statistics on presidential versus vice presidential candidate preferences, based on data from the 1968–2016 American National Election Studies (ANES). Next, using the same data, we estimate the relative influence of vice presidential versus presidential candidate evaluations on vote choice, via logistic regression analyses. Finally, and for the first time in the literature, we test the causal effects of *dynamic* changes in running mate evaluations (i.e., favorability ratings) on intended vote choice, as well as presidential candidate evaluations, over the course of a campaign. We do so using time series (i.e., rolling cross-sectional) data from the 2000 and 2004 National Annenberg Election Survey (NAES).

Our analyses indicate that running mates do, in fact, directly influence vote choice, but only to a limited extent. Indeed, vice presidential candidate evaluations have much less influence on vote choice than do presidential candidate evaluations. Furthermore, our vector autoregression analysis indicates that while running mates can influence intended vote choice during a campaign, in most cases their effects last only for a few days. This analysis also indicates that presidential and vice presidential candidate evaluations are interdependent (or endogenous) over time. Such direct evidence of interdependent intraparty candidate evaluations is important because it shows that running mates are not just shadows of the presidential candidate. Rather, voters view vice presidential candidates, in part, as a reflection on the presidential candidate—such that reevaluating the former may cause them to reevaluate the latter.

Chapter 4: Targeted Effects

Perhaps, then, running mates are most effective at influencing vote choice among particular groups of voters that presidential campaigns may wish to "target" in order to win an election. To evaluate this possibility, in chapter 4 we examine running mates' "targeted effects" on vote choice among groups of voters with whom they share a salient geographic (i.e., home state or region), demographic (i.e., gender, religious), or ideological (i.e., liberal, conservative) identity. For example, we assess whether women were more likely than in other years to vote for the Democratic ticket in 1984 or the Republican ticket in 2008, both of which featured a woman running mate (Geraldine Ferraro and Sarah Palin, respectively). Our analysis draws on three distinct, high-quality data sources—the American National Election Studies (1952–2016), the National Annenberg Election Studies (2000–2008), and The American Panel Survey (2012–2016)—and estimates running mate effects by using a multimethod approach that includes linear or logistic regression analyses, for cross-sectional data, and an adaptation of Lenz's (2012) three-wave test, for panel data.

We find little evidence of targeted running mate effects. For instance, cross-sectional data indicate that Catholics were no more likely to vote for the Democratic Party in 2016, when Tim Kaine was the vice presidential nominee, than in previous elections. And panel data indicate that the effect of Catholic identification on intended vote choice did not change from the period before versus after Kaine's selection. Likewise, we observe no significant change in women's voting behavior in response to the Ferraro or Palin selections. The only clear evidence of a targeted effect comes from 2012, when conservative support for the Republican ticket significantly increased following Mitt Romney's selection of Paul Ryan as his running mate, and ultimately influenced vote choice. In all other cases, we see no such effects at any point during the campaign, or, at best, a temporary increase in support that fades away by Election Day.

Chapter 5: Indirect Effects

In chapter 5, we expand the scope of our analysis to include *indirect* running mate effects—or the effects of vice presidential candidate evaluations on presidential candidate evaluations, which, subsequently, influence vote choice. This, we argue, is the most realistic conception of running mate effects. Yet indirect effects have gone almost entirely unexplored in the scholarly literature, to date (two exceptions are found in Kenski, Hardy, and Jamieson [2010] and Romero [2001]; but see chapter 5, note 6). In this chapter, we provide an unprecedented analysis of indirect running mate effects, using data from the ANES (1968–2016), NAES (2000–2008), and Knowledge Networks (2008), and a multimethod approach comprising logistic regression analyses and structural equation models (cross-sectional data), vector autoregression (rolling cross-sectional data), and an adaptation of Lenz's (2012) three-wave test (panel data). Moreover, we evaluate indirect effects based on a diverse range of candidate evaluations, including ones pertaining to ideology, experience, and various professional or personal attributes, as well as general favorability.

Our analysis of more than two hundred statistical models provides overwhelming evidence that running mates influence voters' perceptions of the presidential candidate who selected him or her. We also present structural equation models demonstrating that running mate evaluations indirectly influence vote choice. In other words, running mates have indirect, as well as direct, effects on voting—although the former appear to be much stronger than the latter. To provide one example of such an effect, in 2008 respondents were significantly more likely to approve of John McCain's judgment if they believed that his choice of a running mate, Sarah Palin, was ready to be president. Specifically, respondents who rated Palin as "extremely" ready to be president, versus "not at all," rated McCain's judgment 2.2 points higher on a scale of 0 to 10. This, in turn, decreased the respondent's likelihood of voting for the Democratic ticket by 7 percentage points, according to our structural equation models. Nor are these effects limited to perceptions of judgment. Indeed, we find strong and consistent evidence that respondents' perceptions of the presidential candidate—across a wide range of attributes relating to leadership skills, trustworthiness, and competence—are shaped by their evaluation of the running mate, in terms of overall favorability or experience.

Chapter 6: Why Does This Matter?
This book's final chapter emphasizes the practical implications of our research findings by discussing several key takeaway points that may help to better inform future deliberations over vice presidential selection among political practitioners, journalists, and the public at large. We present these takeaway points as five recommendations to presidential candidates and their campaigns, when engaging in vice presidential selection. Our recommendations are as follows:

1. Pick someone who can be a good *vice president.*
2. Don't just say it; mean it.
3. Ask whether the running mate will matter *enough.*
4. Don't expect the running mate to "deliver" a key voting bloc.
5. Don't just take our word for it.

In each case, we summarize the research findings that inform our recommendation and discuss their implications for vice presidential selection, presidential campaign strategy, and presidential administration. In the course of this discussion, we also consider the limitations of the present research, opportunities for future research, and the role that vice presidential candidates may play in the 2020 election.

SO, WHAT IF RUNNING MATES MATTER?

To be sure, we are not the first scholars to analyze the electoral significance of vice presidential candidates. The existing literature on "running mate effects," in fact, attests to the importance of a subject that easily can be mistaken as insignificant or even frivolous. And this literature provides valuable perspective—in terms of theory, methodology, and substantive conclusions—that helps to guide our research, while also raising questions that we hope to answer, with a greater measure of clarity, in the pages that follow.

Scholarly Literature

Numerous studies examine running mates' effects on elections generally (e.g., Adkison 1982; Burmila and Ryan 2013; Devine and Kopko 2016, chap. 8; Grofman and Kline 2010; Ulbig 2010; Wattenberg 1984, 1995; Wattenberg and Grofman 1993), and with respect to specific considerations such as party identification (Court and Lynch 2015), ideology (Court 2012; Krumel and Enami 2017), demography (Jelen 2018), and geography (J. Campbell 1992; J. Campbell, Ali, and Jalalzai 2006; Devine and Kopko 2011, 2013, 2016, 2019; Dudley and Rapoport 1989; Garand 1988; Heersink and Peterson 2016; Holbrook 1991; Kahane 2009; Mixon and Tyrone 2004; Morini 2015; Rosenstone 1983; Schultz 2016; Tubbesing 1973). We review these literatures in the relevant chapters to follow. Also, many studies examine secondary matters that we reference in this book, including media coverage of vice presidential candidates (e.g., Ulbig 2010, 2013) and the vice presidential selection process (e.g., Baumgartner 2012, 2016; Hiller and Kriner 2008; Sigelman and Wahlbeck 1997). But the existing literature has two significant limitations.

First, many of these studies narrowly focus on one aspect of running mate effects, such as geography (e.g., Devine and Kopko 2016) or media coverage (e.g., Ulbig 2013). Second, other more comprehensive studies analyze *vice presidential candidates*, as an electoral institution, within the broader context of the *vice presidency*, as a governing institution, and with a predominant focus on the latter (e.g., Baumgartner with Crumblin 2015; Goldstein 2016). Such studies represent tremendous contributions to scholars' understanding of the vice presidency, which we make no attempt to challenge or to significantly revise here. However, these studies do not provide a comprehensive, empirically driven analysis of running mates' electoral effects, along the lines of what we present in this book.

In fact, no book to date has been devoted exclusively to the subject of vice presidential candidates' effects on presidential voting, in general or along several dimensions at a time, such as ideology, geography, and demographics.[18] Also, ours is the first study to systematically examine voters' perceptions of vice presidential candidates' electoral influence and their criteria for vice presidential selection (chapter 2). Finally, ours is the first study to analyze how voters' perceptions of a *vice presidential candidate's* characteristics (e.g., readiness to be president) influence their perceptions of the *presidential candidate's* characteristics (e.g., judgment), as well as how these perceptions may influence vote choice (chapter 5).

Running Mates and the Vice Presidency

A clarification of terms is in order, also, before proceeding with this analysis. The title of this book, and our central research question, asks: Do running mates matter? We are not asking whether *vice presidents* matter. Goldstein (2016), in particular, has answered that question rather definitively, and in the affirmative. Although vice presidents have little constitutional power, since the inception of the "modern vice presidency," under Jimmy Carter, they have wielded significant and growing power as a result of informal institutional changes. In particular, as Goldstein explains, this power comes from serving as a senior adviser to, and troubleshooter for, the president, with the support of extensive personal access and in-house resources. Indeed, many of the most recent vice presidents—including Al Gore, Dick Cheney, and Joe Biden—have played a major role in shaping administration policy on foreign and domestic matters, and in advancing the president's agenda through their work with Congress and foreign leaders.

Unfortunately, we think, it is all too common—particularly among journalists—to treat the terms "vice president" and "vice presidential candidate" interchangeably. Needless to say (but we will, anyway), the two roles are different, and they coincide only when an incumbent vice president is seeking re-election. In fact, we see the study of vice presidential candidates, as an electoral institution, as quite distinct from the study of vice presidents, as a governing institution (although there is good reason to draw relevant connections between the two at times, in the same way that, say, studying judicial nomination and confirmation processes is connected to, but distinct from, studying judicial behavior). That is why, as noted previously, we explicitly characterize our work as a study of vice presidential *candidates*, not *vice presidents*. And it is why, in hopes of limiting confusion about our subject matter and research objectives, we emphasize that distinction by framing our title, research question, and much of the language to follow in terms of "running mates."

This discussion also provides a useful reminder as to why it is important to know whether, and in what ways, running mates matter. Regardless of their electoral influence, running mates ultimately matter because, if successful, they become vice presidents. And, as the research cited earlier demonstrates, vice presidents are highly, and increasingly, influential actors in American government. If it is the case that presidential candidates (at least sometimes) misjudge the nature of running mates' effects on presidential voting—perhaps by overestimating their ability to "deliver" a home state or an affiliated demographic group—then they might select someone who is unqualified, or at least less qualified than other credible alternatives, to serve as a partner in government and next in the line of presidential succession, simply because an electoral consideration tipped the scales. This may seem like a remote possibility, but—perhaps depending on one's political views—it is not difficult to think of a time when it nearly happened or actually did (e.g., Dan Quayle, John Edwards, Sarah Palin).

To the extent that our research validates some perceptions of running mate effects, perhaps it will help to inform presidential candidates, their campaigns, and members of the news media when gaming out viable electoral strategies. But, to the extent that our research challenges errant or oversimplified perceptions of running mate effects, then perhaps it will help to divert attention away from illusions of electoral advantage and redirect it toward efforts to identify the person best qualified to serve as vice president.

PART I
Perceptions of Running Mate Effects

Our objective in this book is to test perceptions of the vice presidential candidate's electoral significance—or what we call "running mate effects"—against the empirical evidence. Essentially, we ask: Do running mates matter in the way that people *think* they matter? To fulfill this objective, first we must demonstrate that the perception of running mate effects actually exists, and that it is common among those actors who directly influence the selection and election of vice presidential candidates.

Such an analysis is necessary because, as the evidence from this book's introduction indicates, many actors relevant to the electoral process—including voters, journalists, presidential candidates, and other political elites—frequently, if not reflexively, express skepticism about the significance of vice presidents and vice presidential candidates. At the same time, many of these actors' comments and behaviors betray a more complex set of attitudes that we have characterized as conflicted, or marked by a "fundamental tension" rooted in the institutional weakness of the vice presidency. It would be presumptuous, we think, merely to dismiss these actors' expressions of skepticism and proceed to our empirical analysis, based on limited evidence that it is a relevant question to ask, in the first place, whether running mates matter. Instead, we begin by establishing, on an empirical basis, that the perception of running mate effects is prevalent, and potentially influential, enough among the most relevant political actors to merit further analysis.

In the next two chapters, we examine perceptions of running mate effects among those actors who directly determine the *selection* and *election* of vice presidential candidates: presidential candidates (chapter 1) and voters (chapter 2), respectively. While the perceptions of other actors (e.g., journalists, party officials, campaign donors, issue advocates) also are important, and worthy of similar analysis elsewhere, we focus on presidential candidates and voters because their perceptions have the most direct implications for vice presidential selection, campaign strategy, and electoral outcomes.

First, presidential candidates' perceptions of running mate effects are important because these individuals must weigh numerous considerations when selecting a vice presidential candidate, and when deciding how to utilize him or her during the campaign. If a presidential candidate believes that running mates have little or no effect on voting behavior and election outcomes, then he or she is likely to make a selection strictly based on governing considerations (e.g., qualifications, personal compatibility). If, however, a presidential candidate believes that running mates significantly influence voting behavior, among the electorate in general and/or among key electoral subgroups, then this perception might influence the vice presidential selection process and various strategic choices made during the general election campaign (e.g., campaign messaging, advertisements, allocation of campaign visits). In extreme circumstances—particularly when clearly behind in the polls and apparently headed for defeat—the presidential candidate even might make a risky, if not reckless, choice of a running mate in hopes that he or she will prove to be an electoral "game changer."

Second, voters' perceptions of running mate effects are important because voters constitute the primary audience for presidential campaign activity. If, on the one hand, voters believe that the running mate will have little or no effect on how they and others vote, then they are unlikely to devote much attention to vice presidential selection or the candidate's performance during the campaign; quite simply, this would seem to be irrelevant. Furthermore, voters' (professed) indifference may help to dissuade presidential candidates from making a selection that is, at least to a significant degree, based on electoral considerations. If, on the other hand, voters believe that the running mate is likely to influence how they and others will vote, then it stands to reason that they will devote significant attention to vice presidential selection and the candidate's performance during the campaign. Perhaps more important, by signaling that a vice presidential candidate is likely to influence their vote, or that a certain type of running mate (e.g., a historic first or someone who "balances the ticket") would be particularly appealing, voters' expressed perceptions might encourage the presidential candidate to make a selection based on electoral considerations. Voters' responses to the selection of an actual running mate also might influence other aspects of presidential campaign strategy. For instance, if the running mate proves to be popular, and voters indicate that his or her selection has increased their likelihood of voting for the presidential ticket, the campaign might respond by making the running mate more visible on the campaign trail and even scheduling more joint appearances with the presidential candidate.

In part I of this book, we use qualitative and quantitative methods of analysis to evaluate presidential candidates' and voters' perceptions of running mate effects, respectively. First, for presidential candidates, in chapter 1 we present a content analysis of their public and private statements about vice presidential selection, focusing on the era of the "modern vice presidency" (1976–present). Evidence for this analysis comes from a wide range of sources, including public speeches, media coverage, interviews, personal memoirs, and archival materials from presidential or other public libraries. Our objectives in this analysis are to determine the following: first, whether, and to what extent, presidential candidates perceive the vice presidential candidate to be electorally consequential; second, which criteria presidential candidates perceive to be most relevant to vice presidential selection, broadly speaking (i.e., electoral vs. governing considerations) and in more specific terms (i.e., geographic, demographic, ideological characteristics).

Of course, this analysis is complicated by the fact that presidential candidates often choose not to publicly reveal their internal deliberations, or they edit their opinions for public consumption, particularly when trying to project to voters a favorable image during a campaign. For instance, a presidential candidate probably would resist saying that he or she chose a running mate in order to win the election, or to win a particular state, even if this were true. Such admissions might come later, or in private, if at all. Recognizing this limitation, we draw the reader's attention to discrepancies between statements made by presidential candidates for public consumption during a campaign and other statements made by them or their close associates either in private, as reported later, or outside of the immediate campaign context.

Second, to evaluate voters' perceptions of running mate effects, in chapter 2 we present quantitative analyses of public polling data, primarily focusing on the 2000–2016 presidential elections. While we would prefer to analyze the entire era of the modern vice presidency (1976–present), as in chapter 1, it is not practical to do so given the limitations of the available polling data. That is to say, since 2000 it has become much more common for pollsters to solicit opinions on the vice presidential selection process and vice presidential candidates more generally.[1] For instance, many polls ask whether voters are more or less likely to vote for a presidential ticket based on the selection of a given running mate. A small number of polls directly ask voters if they ever have voted for or against a presidential candidate on the basis of vice presidential selection, or which criteria a particular presidential candidate should use when selecting a running mate.

Polling data therefore provide considerable insight into voters' perceptions of running mate effects. However, an important limitation is that most of these polls directly ask respondents to evaluate the electoral significance of vice presidential candidates, and in doing so they provide an implicit cue to the respondent that the choice of a running mate *should* be important, or at least that it is sufficiently important to other voters as to merit the inclusion of such a question in that survey. To address this limitation—while also expanding the scope of our analysis to include a wider range of elections than what the traditional polling data allow—we also analyze open-ended response data from the 1952–2004 American National Election Studies (ANES) surveys.[2] Specifically, these surveys ask respondents to list their reasons for liking or disliking the major party presidential candidates in that year's election, with multiple response codes indicating references to a vice presidential candidate.

Our analysis indicates that most presidential candidates and voters are, in keeping with the theme of this book's introduction, conflicted when it comes to evaluating the electoral significance of vice presidential candidates. For presidential candidates, it has become almost ritualistic to forswear electoral considerations when publicly discussing vice presidential selection, and to assure voters that their first, and perhaps only, objective is to choose someone who is qualified to become president. Yet many of the same presidential candidates reveal privately, or publicly at another point in time, that they perceive the vice presidential candidate to be an electoral asset, or that their selection of a running mate was motivated, at least partially, by electoral considerations. Even those presidential candidates whose selections clearly were not motivated by electoral considerations in many cases indicate that their evaluation of other potential running mates was influenced by perceptions of running mate effects.

Voters' perceptions of running mate effects seem to be conflicted, as well. Generally, when responding to public opinion polls, voters affirm the importance of vice presidential selection, in the abstract, and in many cases they report being more or less likely to vote for a given presidential candidate based on his or her choice of a running mate. Yet, at the same time, survey respondents tend to rate vice presidential selection as less important than most other electoral considerations; few respondents report that a running mate ever has changed their presidential vote; and rarely do respondents mention the running mate when given the opportunity to freely explain their evaluation of a particular presidential candidate. Also, while voters apparently do not use fixed criteria to evaluate running mates, they do seem to prefer ones who "balance the ticket" by compensating for the presidential candidate's perceived deficiencies. This is particularly evident when it comes to attributes of professional experience, but much less so for demographics. Indeed, voters seem to care a great deal about the running mate's qualifications, while largely dismissing electoral considerations.

To provide a succinct summary of the evidence from chapters 1 and 2: presidential candidates and voters alike generally think that running mates *can* influence vote choice—but they resist the notion that this has been, or should be, a factor in *their* decision-making process.

1. (Why) Do Presidential Candidates Think That Running Mates Matter?

Do presidential candidates think that running mates matter? That is to say, do presidential candidates believe that they can gain votes, or even win an election, based on their choice of a running mate—perhaps by increasing the ticket's appeal to voters, in general, or by targeting voters who belong to a particular geographic, demographic, or ideological group?

If so, then this perception has significant implications for vice presidential selection and the vice presidency. Specifically, the expectation of electoral advantage might influence a presidential candidate's formulation of a vice presidential shortlist; evaluation of vice presidential finalists; selection of a running mate; strategic choices about the running mate's role in the presidential campaign; and, ultimately, who becomes the next vice president of the United States.

Previous research indicates that electoral considerations do influence vice presidential selection, but their effects are limited or inconsistent. Sigelman and Wahlbeck (1997), Hiller and Kriner (2008), and Baumgartner (2016), most notably, use logistic regression models to predict who, from the short list of vice presidential finalists, was selected in the 1940–1996, 1940–2004, and 1960–2016 elections, respectively. Two of these studies provide evidence of ticket balancing by age, home state size, or having been a rival for that year's presidential nomination, while one indicates ticket balancing by demographics (i.e., gender/race/ethnicity). However, none of these studies finds systematic evidence of ticket balancing by region, ideology, or political insider-versus-outsider status.[1]

Hiller and Kriner (2008) also compare predictors of vice presidential selection before and after the 1972 McGovern-Fraser Commission reforms, which effectively shifted control of the presidential nomination process from party leaders at national conventions to party voters in state primaries. While presidential candidates already had established the prerogative to select a running mate by the 1940s, the McGovern-Fraser reforms' allowance for securing the party's nomination well ahead of its national convention transformed the selection process. Specifically, it gave the presidential nominee-to-be enough time to conduct a thorough vetting of potential running mates and the freedom to choose a running mate without regard to winning over convention delegates. As Hiller and Kriner (2008, 418) explain:

> Presidential candidates no longer need to use the vice presidency to strengthen their grip on the nomination. And with weakened parties, less coherent factions, and candidate-centered campaigns, nominees feel less pressure than before to award the second spot to a regionally or ideologically distant individual to mollify a disgruntled party wing or court key state and local party leaders needed to orchestrate the general election campaign. Rather, because of the lingering specter of the [Thomas] Eagleton debacle [in 1972, when the vice presidential nominee withdrew from the race following reports of his prior treatment for mental illness,] changing public expectations for vice presidential credentials over time, presidential nominees in the modern era have increasingly relied on an individual's prior experience in government when choosing a running mate.

Indeed, Hiller and Kriner find that electoral considerations such as regional balancing and home state competitiveness were significant predictors of vice presidential selection prior to 1972, but not afterward. Conversely, political experience emerged as a significant predictor of selection in the modern era, whereas this had not been the case prior to McGovern-Fraser.[2]

Yet perceptions of running mate effects need not *determine* vice presidential selection, as a general matter or in a particular case, in order to be consequential.[3] As long as a given presidential candidate believes that his or her choice of a running mate can influence the election's outcome, or is likely to do so, then this perception has the *potential* to influence vice presidential selection. In other words, it becomes a consideration that the candidate might draw on when making his or her selection. And its relative salience depends on a variety of factors, such that even presidential candidates who do not select running mates primarily based on electoral considerations still might have done so under different circumstances.

For instance, a presidential candidate—guided by his or her instincts, or under pressure from campaign advisers—might give greater weight to electoral considerations, including potential running mate effects, when clearly trailing an opponent and in need of a "game changer." This appears to have been the case for John McCain in 2008 (as described in the introduction and later in this chapter). Conversely, this consideration might be less salient, and thus less influential, for a candidate who seems to have the electoral advantage.

Table 1.1. Presidential Candidates and Their Running Mates, 1976–2016

Year	Presidential Candidate	Political Office	Home State	Running Mate	Political Office	Home State
			DEMOCRATS			
1976	Jimmy Carter	Former governor	Georgia	Walter Mondale	Senator	Minnesota
1980	Jimmy Carter	President	Georgia	Walter Mondale	Vice president	Minnesota
1984	Walter Mondale	Former vice president	Minnesota	Geraldine Ferraro	Representative	New York
1988	Michael Dukakis	Governor	Massachusetts	Lloyd Bentsen	Senator	Texas
1992	Bill Clinton	Governor	Arkansas	Al Gore	Senator	Tennessee
1996	Bill Clinton	President	Arkansas	Al Gore	Vice president	Tennessee
2000	Al Gore	Vice president	Tennessee	Joe Lieberman	Senator	Connecticut
2004	John Kerry	Senator	Massachusetts	John Edwards	Senator	North Carolina
2008	Barack Obama	Senator	Illinois	Joe Biden	Senator	Delaware
2012	Barack Obama	President	Illinois	Joe Biden	Vice president	Delaware
2016	Hillary Clinton	Former secretary of state	New York	Tim Kaine	Senator	Virginia
			REPUBLICANS			
1976	Gerald Ford	President	Michigan	Bob Dole	Senator	Kansas
1980	Ronald Reagan	Former governor	California	George H. W. Bush	Former CIA director	Texas
1984	Ronald Reagan	President	California	George H. W. Bush	Vice president	Texas
1988	George H. W. Bush	Vice president	Texas	Dan Quayle	Senator	Indiana
1992	George H. W. Bush	President	Texas	Dan Quayle	Vice president	Indiana
1996	Bob Dole	Former senator	Kansas	Jack Kemp	Former secretary of HUD	New York
2000	George W. Bush	Governor	Texas	Dick Cheney	Former secretary of defense	Wyoming
2004	George W. Bush	President	Texas	Dick Cheney	Vice president	Wyoming
2008	John McCain	Senator	Arizona	Sarah Palin	Governor	Alaska
2012	Mitt Romney	Former governor	Massachusetts	Paul Ryan	Representative	Wisconsin
2016	Donald Trump	None	New York	Mike Pence	Governor	Indiana

Note: Political offices listed are those held at the time of a given election, or the most recent office held prior to that election.

For example, McCain's opponent, Barack Obama, chose a highly qualified running mate, with no obvious electoral appeal, in Joe Biden. But this hardly proves that Obama was impervious to considerations of running mate effects or that he did not believe in them. Nor does it prove that McCain readily embraced them. Rather, it is entirely plausible that, had the electoral dynamics been reversed, Obama might have made a riskier choice in hopes of gaining votes (e.g., Hillary Clinton), and McCain a safer choice with minimal electoral implications (e.g., Tim Pawlenty).

In that case, our objective in this chapter is not to find out whether electoral considerations determine vice presidential selection, generally, or did so in each particular process herein described. Instead, it is to find out whether—and, if so, why—presidential candidates believe that running mates *can* influence voting, such that this consideration at least had the potential to influence vice presidential selection. Moreover, we seek to identify the specific electoral considerations that might have influenced a particular presidential candidate's selection calculus.

To these ends, we present a qualitative analysis of presidential candidates'—and, in some cases, campaign advisers'—statements regarding vice presidential selection, from 1976 to 2016. We begin by analyzing statements made in the immediate context of a presidential campaign, when the candidates are most likely to discuss their vice presidential selection criteria but also least likely to do so transparently. Then, in order to more reliably assess presidential candidates' perceptions of running mate effects, we examine statements made outside the immediate context of the presidential campaign. To guide readers through the analysis that follows, in table 1.1 we identify the presidential candidate and his or her running mate in each of these elections.

THE VP FORMULA

Do presidential candidates have electoral considerations in mind when picking a running mate? There is a simple way to find out: ask them. In fact, presidential candidates regularly are asked to describe their vice presidential selection criteria, while on the campaign trail. In February 2016, for example, Donald Trump was asked by an audience member at a Liberty University presidential candidates' forum, "What are the most important qualities you're going to look for in a vice presidential candidate . . . ?" He answered:

Look, the main quality that you want is somebody that can be a great president, if something happens to you. That's got to be—don't you think? That's got to be number one. And then I would want somebody that could help me with government. So most likely that would be a political person because, you know, I'm business. . . . The most important thing is you have to have somebody that can be a great president. But after that, you want somebody that can help you with legislation, getting it through, etc., etc.[4]

In other words, Trump's principal criterion when selecting a running mate was to choose someone who could succeed him as president, if necessary. Beyond that, Trump sought someone who could compensate for his lack of political experience—but this was in order to help him govern, not to help him win over skeptical voters.

In July 2016, Hillary Clinton gave a similar response when asked about her vice presidential selection process during an appearance on *The Charlie Rose Show*. She explained her criteria as follows:

Would this person be a good president? You know, I am afflicted with the responsibility gene, and I know what it's like being president. I've seen it up close, I've worked for one, I've had that experience. So for me there is nothing more important than my rock-solid conviction that the person I choose literally could get up one day and be the president of the United States. . . . I'm looking for someone who can be a world-class president of the United States, and who can help me govern, because I think they go hand in hand.[5]

Clinton later affirmed these criteria when introducing Virginia senator Tim Kaine as her running mate: "Now, there's no doubt in my mind—because I'm here with him—that Tim is so qualified to be vice president, and as I have said many times, the most important qualification when you are trying to make this really big choice is can this person step in to be president."[6]

It is striking that Trump and Clinton, despite their many differences, essentially cited the same selection criteria: the running mate must be someone who is qualified to serve as president, if necessary, and to help govern as vice president. But, in doing so, they were not so much agreeing with each other's ideas as simply reading from the same script. That is to say, their comments on this subject echoed every other presidential candidate in the era of the modern vice presidency, by citing selection criteria so familiar—indeed, so conventional as to make affirmations forgettable and material deviations remarkable—that we refer to this as the "VP Formula."

How do we know this? By way of evidence, consider how presidential candidates since 1976 have described their vice presidential selection criteria in public.

- Gerald Ford, 1976: "First, the nominee must be a person of character and experience, capable of leading the country. Second, the nominee must articulate and support the principles of the Republican Party and be disposed to work in full harmony with the Chief Executive. Finally, the nominee must be an asset in the November campaign and a major contributor to governing the country in these next four years."[7]
- Jimmy Carter, 1976: "The first [criterion] . . . is who would be the best person to lead this country if something should happen to me. Secondly, I would choose someone who was politically compatible with me on my basic philosophy and on the major issues—not completely subservient, of course. And the third reason would be quite the remotest in importance, some sort of geographical or other balancing."[8]
- Ronald Reagan, 1980: "I think your choice should be based on who do you feel could be a President if he had to be" (Shirley 2009, 335).
- Walter Mondale, 1984: "My choice will be guided by the need to select someone totally qualified to assume the office of the President should that be necessary" (Weinraub 1984).
- George H. W. Bush, 1988: "Look, the fundamental criterion [is] who best to take over if something happens to the president. . . . [Also,] *some* compatibility. . . . I would want a certain philosophical compatibility to be there. . . . Then I will do what all politicians do, throw a little bit of seasoning in there for geography—and I think that's less important than it is used to be, historically."[9]
- Michael Dukakis, 1988: "The single most important criteria [*sic*] has to be whether or not that person would be a first-rate President if something were to happen to the President" (Weinraub 1988).
- Bill Clinton, 1992: "[First,] I said I wanted a vice president who really understood what had happened to ordinary Americans in the last twelve years. Someone who was committed to making government work again for average, hardworking American families. [Second,] I said I wanted a vice president who would complement me and my own experiences and bring other experiences,

knowledge, and understanding to our common endeavor. And, above all, I said I wanted a vice president who would be ready, should something happen to me, to immediately assume the office of President of the United States."[10]

- Bob Dole, 1996: "I would select someone who pretty much fit my views. I want a conservative running mate, somebody who's prepared to take over on day one, if necessary. Somebody who's had the experience, somebody who understands Bob Dole, somebody I can work with" ("Text of GOP Candidates" 1996).
- George W. Bush, 2000: "I'll name somebody who can be the president. That ought to be the main criterion for any one of us who has the opportunity to pick a vice president. . . . It's going to be, can that person serve as president of the United States? I also am going to ask the question, will the person be loyal? There's nothing that can be worse than to have a vice president be disloyal to the president. And of course I would expect that person to share my conservative views."[11]
- Al Gore, 2000: "I'll tell you what I'm looking for is someone who can become president on a moment's notice should that become necessary, someone with whom I can have a great relationship and someone who shares my values" (Glover 2000).
- John Kerry, 2004: "I believe what's important is that I've picked somebody with the character, with the judgment, with the values to be able to take over as a president, lead this nation if something were to happen to me."[12]
- John McCain, 2008: "The fundamental principle behind any selection of a running mate would be whether that person is fully prepared to take over and share your values, your principles, your philosophy, and your priorities. I think that's the first and only real criteria [*sic*] for the selection of a running mate" (Quaid 2008).
- Barack Obama, 2008: "Obviously, the most important question is, is this person prepared to be president? The second most important question from my perspective is, can this person help me govern? . . . And the third criteria [*sic*] for me I think was independence. I want somebody who is going to be able to challenge my thinking and not simply be a 'yes' person when it comes to policymaking."[13]
- Mitt Romney, 2012: "Well, by far, the most important factor is whether this is a person who could lead the country if that were necessary. . . . [T]hat's the most important element—would the American people and would I see this person as someone who could lead in that kind of eventuality?"[14]

Indeed, presidential candidates since 1976 have been remarkably consistent when publicly describing their vice presidential selection criteria. Adhering to what we describe as the VP Formula, these candidates emphasize that their foremost, and perhaps only, objective is to find a running mate who is qualified to serve as president and one who can help to govern as vice president given his or her political experience and/or personal and philosophical compatibility with the presidential nominee. Some candidates also reference electoral considerations—in general, or with respect to specific characteristics such as geography. But when deviating from the standard script in this way, candidates invariably downplay electoral concerns as something of a "bonus" that may, if only by fortuitous coincidence, attend their selection of the most qualified running mate.

The message to voters is clear: when selecting a running mate, the presidential nominee's principal and most legitimate objective is to find someone who can help him or her to govern, not someone who can help to win the election. Even if a running mate can gain votes for the ticket, factoring this into the selection process is either inappropriate or so trivial as to be nearly irrelevant.

At least, that's what presidential candidates tell us, publicly. But should we believe them?

WHAT DO PRESIDENTIAL CANDIDATES REALLY THINK?

Presidential candidates often describe vice presidential selection as "the most important decision" to be made during the campaign—even, in Michael Dukakis's words, "the first Presidential act" ("Comments from Dukakis" 1988). Why? Because, as George W. Bush writes, "The vice presidential selection provides voters with a window into a candidate's decision-making style. It reveals how careful and thorough he or she will be. And it signals a potential president's priorities for the country" (Bush 2010, 66–67). Barack Obama, as a candidate in 2008, concurred: "This is one of the most important decisions I can make and I think it will signal how I want to operate my presidency."[15] Indeed, presidential candidates who make a poor decision, or conduct the search process in such a way as to demonstrate incompetence or irresponsibility, invite unfavorable inferences about their likely performance as president.

George McGovern's ill-fated selection of Thomas Eagleton as his running mate in 1972—at the end of a chaotic, last-minute search process—is a case in point. Eagleton's withdrawal from the race, after eighteen days of controversy stemming from his previously undisclosed treatment for mental illness, prompted *Newsweek* ("A Crisis Named Eagleton" 1972, 12) to observe: "Selecting Eagleton in the first place after only the most slapdash screening reflected badly on McGovern's staff and finally on the nominee himself." A Republican quoted in the same article scoffed: "The people want a President who at least gives the appearance of having done his homework" (14).

In the same way, voters might conclude that a presidential candidate who makes important campaign decisions based on political calculations (i.e., how to win the election) also will make important decisions as president that are based on political calculations (i.e., how to win reelection or boost his or her approval ratings).[16] For this reason, it makes little sense—indeed, it would be naive—to rely on public statements made during the campaign to determine whether, and to what extent, presidential candidates expect the selection of a running mate to influence voting, and factor this consideration into their selection process and subsequent campaign strategies. To better evaluate presidential candidates' perceptions of running mate effects, then, we must analyze evidence from outside of the immediate campaign context. Such evidence includes the candidate's public statements about vice presidential selection made before and after running for president, particularly in media interviews and in personal memoirs. Also, it includes private conversations or memoranda later made public via interviews with, or the writings of, their close advisers; journalists' accounts; and presidential or other public library archives. In short, we seek evidence of what the candidates and their campaign strategists say about vice presidential selection *absent the threat of electoral sanction.*

To be clear, it has not been our expectation, nor is it our conclusion, that all vice presidential selection processes secretly are driven by naked electoral calculations.[17] In fact, many vice presidential candidates—particularly in recent years—have been highly qualified and clearly were not selected primarily for the purpose of delivering electoral advantages (e.g., Dick Cheney, Joe Biden, Mike Pence). But this does not mean that presidential candidates, generally or in these particular cases, necessarily rejected the possibility of running mate effects as illusory or irrelevant and would not have given them greater weight under different circumstances (e.g., when facing certain loss absent a dramatic change in campaign dynamics, or when in need of a tiebreaker between two otherwise equally attractive vice presidential finalists). What's more, we *do* find strong evidence that electoral considerations were decisive in some cases—particularly those in which the presidential candidate seemed headed for defeat and in need of a game changer. In other cases, these considerations played a more ambiguous role.

Regardless of whether, or how often, electoral considerations have decided vice presidential selection, our overarching conclusion is that most presidential candidates think that running mates *can* influence the outcome of a presidential election—either dramatically so or just at the margins. To the extent that this perception has the potential to influence future selections—*even just once*, given the enhanced power of the modern vice presidency and the possibility of presidential succession—the following evidence illustrates why it is important to determine, as we try to do in this book, whether running mates actually matter.

Gerald Ford, 1976

In 1976, Gerald Ford could not have been clearer about his vice presidential selection criteria. In fact, by the time that he selected Kansas senator Bob Dole as his running mate in August, Ford must have been sick of repeating himself. At a July 19 White House press conference, for instance, Ford described the same criteria that he would repeat two weeks later, in the statement cited earlier in this chapter. Still, one reporter insisted on asking: "Mr. President, can you tell us some of the criteria that you will be using in selecting a Vice President? You have said here today that you will consider the Vice Presidential nominee only on the basis to become President should something happen to you, but will there be other criteria as well?"[18] Ford responded: "That is the principal one, of course, and any other criteria would have to be secondary to that. But, other criteria might be age, compatibility with my own philosophy, the experience both in domestic and international affairs. There are a whole raft of potential criteria that I think have to be put into that formula."[19] He would reiterate the same criteria, yet again, when meeting with the Virginia delegation to the Republican Party's national convention later that month.[20]

But internal memoranda from Ford's White House and presidential campaign suggest that electoral considerations dominated his vice presidential selection process. One undated memo located in the papers of its likely author, special counsel to the president Michael Raoul-Duval,[21] at the Gerald R. Ford Library, outlined a strategy for selecting the running mate and then utilizing

VICE PRESIDENT

I.   Qualities Needed

    A.   Must have strong, positive appeal to swing voters.

    B.   Able to carry key state or region (border states, northeast, etc.).

    C.   Aggressive campaign style.

    D.   Attractive media candidate.

    E.   Must be acceptable to most elements of the Party.

    F.   Must not run counter to mood of country or image of strategy (experience, and active, responsible change).

II.   Prenomination Strategy

    A.   Must keep all options open so as :

       1.   Not to alienate any region.

       2.   Not to alienate any ideological segment.

       3.   Not to alienate any potential aspirants.

       4.   Not to reveal general election strategy.

III.   Role in Campaign.

    A.   Veep nominee will be most active campaigner.

    B.   May need to visit areas President does not cover.

    C.   Must concentrate on key states.

    D.   Will be in traditional campaign mode.

    E.   Must help (perhaps with Rockefeller) to unify Party.

Figure 1.1. Internal White House memorandum regarding Gerald Ford's 1976 presidential campaign strategy and vice presidential selection (page 1 of 2). *Source*: Folder "Vice Presidential Selection," Box 24—Election Campaign Papers, Michael Raoul-Duval Papers, Gerald R. Ford Library.

him or her during the campaign (figure 1.1). The first section of this memo lists six "Qualities Needed" in a running mate, each of which (e.g., appeal to swing voters, delivering a home state or region) exclusively pertains to how he or she would help Ford to win the election. Remarkably, the memo makes no explicit reference to the running mate's qualifications—only requiring that the candidate's experience not conflict with the "image of [the campaign's] strategy." It goes on to describe the campaign's "Prenomination Strategy" for vice presidential selection, and the running mate's "Role in [the] Campaign." Here, too, there is no mention of qualifications or governing capacity—only electoral considerations, such as ensuring party unity, attacking the opposition, and not alienating any voting blocs or political rivals.[22]

Also, in an August 16 "Memorandum for the President," campaign pollster Robert Teeter reported the results of a national telephone poll—conducted at White House chief of staff Dick Cheney's request (Cheney with Cheney 2011, 100)—that was designed to gauge the electoral implications of vice presidential selection. The poll found little evidence that Ford's choice of a running mate would influence voters; as Teeter concluded, "The differences between the five candidates tested are not great. I think we can continue to assume you would run better alone than with any specific individual." But more interesting, for our immediate purposes, is a series of questions asking respondents to evaluate the importance of various vice presidential selection criteria. Specifically, the poll asked, "Do you agree or disagree that the following characteristics would be good qualities for President Ford's running mate to have?" Five of the six characteristics pertained to balancing Ford's ticket: age ("Should be under 50 years of age"); gender ("Should not be a woman"); outsider status ("Someone not connected with Washington politics"); and ideology ("Someone who is more liberal than Ford" or "Someone who is more conservative than Ford"). Only one characteristic pertained to qualifications: "Someone who has held elective office before." Interestingly, this item received the strongest endorsement, by far (65 percent "Agree," with the age item second at 46 percent).[23]

But how do we know that electoral considerations influenced Gerald Ford *himself*, when selecting a running mate and developing his campaign strategy? Because Ford said so. In a 1990 interview with his biographer and former White House staffer, James Cannon, Ford candidly recalled:

> The selection of Dole was purely a pragmatic political one. We analyzed and came to the conclusion—this is [campaign adviser] Stu Spencer and Teeter—we were not going to carry any southern states. To offset the southern states, we had to carry every state west of the Mississippi and then had to gamble we would carry our share of states, New England, Central Atlantic, Middle West. And Bob Dole was the person who would be most helpful to implement that pure political strategy.

Ford continued, in reference to other vice presidential finalists:

> Howard Baker [the US senator from Tennessee] could not change any of the significant southern states. He might have carried Kentucky, but he would have had no real impact in the western agricultural states, which we had to carry, where Dole's strength was. [William] Ruckleshaus [the former Nixon administration official, from Indiana] would not have added anything either in the south, he might have helped in the Middle West, but not in the far west. Anne Armstrong [the US ambassador to the United Kingdom, from Texas] would have been a big, big gamble, which I did not think we were as a country prepared to take [because she was a woman].[24]

Ford judged Dole's selection as a success—recalling, with evident satisfaction: "I was sure pleased that the strategy of having Dole on the ticket gave us the West except for Texas."[25]

Campaign officials later confirmed that Ford had selected Dole for strategic reasons. "President Ford picked Bob Dole in 1976 to win back the Farm Belt, Ford adviser Stuart Spencer said," in a 2008 interview with *USA Today* (S. Page 2008). And Dole reached the same conclusion; going into the 1976 convention, he and his closest campaign advisers suspected that Ford might give him the nod because, as Dole recalled, "We were thinking, 'Well, you know, he's got trouble in the Farm Belt, veterans,' all that stuff."[26] Sure enough, in a 1995 interview with Bob Woodward, of the *Washington Post*, Dole salvaged the memory of his admittedly lackluster vice presidential candidacy by noting, "But I was important from the standpoint of agriculture and veterans" (Woodward 1996, 346).

In his 1990 interview, Gerald Ford lamented: "I think it is unfortunate that too often Presidents when they pick Vice Presidents don't get the most qualified person they can get as a running mate."[27] Ironic, isn't it? That wasn't Ford's priority, either.

Jimmy Carter, 1976

After choosing Walter Mondale as his running mate—following a thorough and deliberative selection process that has set the precedent for every subsequent presidential campaign (see Goldstein 2016)—Jimmy Carter reflected on the (in)significance and (im)practicality of ticket balancing:

Had [Mondale] come from a metropolitan area and had he been a Catholic, that
would probably have been an asset. But, you know, I can't balance the ticket
geographically, and between me and the Congress, and between an aggressive
campaigner and a more dormant campaigner and in a religious way. I just
can't balance a ticket all that kind of ways [*sic*]. And I finally just eliminated
that process and I came to the conclusion . . . that if I took a person that I felt
would be the best President or Vice President regardless of race or location or
background or religion, that I was making the right political decision.[28]

But Carter later acknowledged being influenced by geographic considerations when asked about Bill Clinton's decision to select a fellow southerner,
Al Gore, as his running mate in 1992. "Well, you know, even 16 years ago,
when I was nominated . . . *I had to consider geography*, because at that time the
South was a condemned region. It was looked down upon by the rest of the
country" ("A Conversation" 1992 [emphasis added]).

Mondale also seemed to believe that regional balancing played a role in his
selection. In a 2007 interview, historian Richard Norton Smith asked: "How
did you get to be on the Democratic ticket?" Mondale responded: "I fit what
[Carter] needed. I could help him in the North, where he was having some
troubles, and in the Midwest."[29]

More generally, Carter has endorsed the notion that a running mate may
cost the presidential candidate votes. When asked whether Barack Obama
should select Hillary Clinton in 2008, Carter responded:

I think it would be the worst mistake that he could make. . . . If you take that 50%
who just don't want to vote for Clinton and add it to whatever element there
might be who don't think Obama is white enough or old enough or experienced
enough or because he's got a middle name that sounds Arab . . . you could have
the worst of both worlds. (Freedland 2008)

Ronald Reagan, 1980

Ronald Reagan, who made his mark in Republican politics as an uncom-
promising conservative, rejected the notion of ideological ticket balancing
as "cynical" (Shirley 2009, 335) and "hypocritical" (Raum 1980) during his
campaign for the Republican nomination in 1980. But in 1976 he had named

a liberal Republican, Pennsylvania senator Richard Schweiker, as his running mate in what seemed to be a play for the support of Pennsylvania's convention delegates, and in 1980 he would select a well-known moderate, in George H. W. Bush.

Reagan said very little, publicly or privately, to explain whether ideological balancing, or other electoral considerations, played a role in his decision to select Bush. But journalistic accounts suggest that an internal campaign poll, conducted by Richard Wirthlin, influenced his decision first to seriously explore the possibility of selecting former president and rival Gerald Ford as his running mate, and then to select Bush. The poll—much like the one conducted four years earlier, by the Ford campaign—asked voters about their vice presidential preferences and the importance of attributes including age, ideology, region, religion, and gender (Cannon 1980a). The only potential running mate who seemed to help Reagan was his rival for the 1976 presidential nomination, former president Gerald Ford. According to *Washington Post* reporter, and later Reagan biographer, Lou Cannon: "The best thing for Reagan, the poll said, would be to run alone. Since he couldn't do that, the next best thing was to take Ford as his running mate" (Cannon 1980b). Cannon suggests that these results dictated Reagan's next moves: "Reagan read the poll literally. If Ford really was the best, Reagan seemed to believe, why not go out and get him?" After negotiations with Ford, who wanted to establish something of a "co-presidency," broke down, Reagan turned to Bush, who, after all, possessed the attributes—including congressional experience, relative youth, and close but not exact agreement with Reagan on the issues—that rated most highly in Wirthlin's poll (Meacham 2015, 243–244).

Thus, there is reason to suspect that Reagan's selection was influenced by electoral considerations—specifically, in terms of which potential running mate or type of running mate polled best among voters. But, clearly, the evidence is not as definitive for Reagan as for other recent presidential candidates—including his Democratic opponent in the 1984 election.

Walter Mondale, 1984

Heading into the 1984 Democratic convention, Walter Mondale was trailing Ronald Reagan, the incumbent president, by about 25 percentage points in the latest polls. So, Mondale later recounted, "I told the staff that during [the convention] we would have to do something dramatic while we had the nation's attention. That's when we started thinking about the choice of a running mate" (Mondale with Hage 2010). It was not just the choice itself that mattered to Mondale; as he said, "I also wanted to use the selection process to send . . . a message about opening doors." To that end, he vetted—and invited to his Minnesota home, for well-publicized, one-on-one meetings—a diverse group of potential running mates, including multiple women and people of color.

Mondale ultimately selected New York congresswoman Geraldine Ferraro as his running mate. It was a historic decision, since Ferraro would be the first woman vice presidential nominee on a major party ticket. She was also Catholic and an Italian American. Why pick Ferraro? "First," Mondale explains in his 2010 memoirs, "I thought she would be an excellent vice president and could be a good president." But, he acknowledges, "She also brought a lot of political strengths to the ticket." How so?

> The Democratic constituency was shrinking and the departure of the Reagan Democrats was killing us. I had worked hard in the ethnic communities to try to reconnect with them, and Ferraro's biography helped make that connection. She came from Queens, New York. She was a Catholic and a mother. And she had a lot of fire. I also knew that I was far behind Reagan, and that if I just ran a traditional campaign, I would never get in the game.

He would not directly acknowledge that Ferraro's gender played a role in the decision, instead attributing this consideration to his wife: "Joan, too, urged me to choose a woman." In part, this was because "she also believed the women's vote had a considerable new and unappreciated strength that we could tap" (Mondale with Hage 2010).

Mondale acknowledged the political calculations behind Ferraro's selection more frankly in a 2016 interview. "She filled a lot of holes for me," he explained. "We were losing with ethnic Americans, and she was a good Catholic." But he denied that Ferraro's gender also played a role. "This is not identity politics, where you're just gonna say, 'Well, I got a woman, vote for me,'" Mondale scoffed. "That was not it. I'm looking at a talented candidate, who happened to be a woman."[30]

Yet, in a 2006 interview, Mondale indicated that gender *had* played a role—in fact a decisive role—in Ferraro's selection. And he framed the decision explicitly in electoral terms:

We were looking for running mates who could help us, and we were looking at polls. We were down 10–15 points, and another white male wasn't interesting the public an awful lot. So there was this very strong movement in America and in the Democratic Party, saying that the time had come to include women on the ticket. . . . So we started exploring that. We decided to pick Ferraro.[31]

George H. W. Bush, 1988

Indiana senator Dan Quayle hardly struck voters and political observers as being someone who met George H. W. Bush's "number one criterion" for a running mate, which was "will this person be capable of taking over if something happened to the president?" (Raum 1988). Quayle's poorly organized vice presidential rollout (see Goldstein 2016, 228–229) contributed to this impression. But, even beforehand, Bush had anticipated that Quayle might not come across as presidential. "He wouldn't get instant credibility," Bush conceded in a diary entry on July 27, several weeks before Quayle's introduction. However, hinting at electoral considerations, Bush added, "It would make a generational difference. He's smart, bright, a good speaker." Also, "He comes from the Midwest, and that would be good" (Meacham 2015, 337).

Quayle's youth, at forty-one, and his fresh, energetic image seemed to play a decisive role in Bush's decision to select him. Bush's campaign manager, James Baker, later said: "I think it was a generational thing. I think that's the main reason that Quayle was selected, and Quayle was being pushed pretty hard by [campaign advisers] Roger Ailes and Bob Teeter."[32] Ailes, for his part, later explained: "A youthful-looking Quayle would make Bush seem the fatherly, senior figure. And Quayle had a good record, so that, plus the 'casting dimension,' if you will, put him in the mix" (Meacham 2015, 336).

Michael Dukakis, 1988

Geographic and ideological considerations seemed to influence Massachusetts governor Michael Dukakis's selection of Texas senator Lloyd Bentsen as his running mate in 1988. Indeed, these appear to have been the dominant concerns for Paul Brountas, whom Dukakis liked to describe as "a committee of one to run my vice presidential selection process."[33] Brountas later recounted:

"I had thought of, from a strategic point of view, for Dukakis to pick somebody not from the northeast, but somebody from somewhere else, and maybe less, I mean more conservative than he. Because he was very liberal, maybe he could balance the ticket. And somebody who was older." To that end, Brountas broached the subject of a vice presidential run with Bentsen at a meeting to discuss other potential candidates, by asking: "Senator Bentsen, what about you?" He explained: "You come from a conservative area, Texas; they're not for Dukakis, and Dukakis is considered a liberal, but I think you could really help the campaign." When asked whether geographic considerations caused him not to seriously consider selecting Maine senator George Mitchell, Brountas responded: "That was the key, is when, you know, how to balance the ticket, because Dukakis was perceived to be so liberal that maybe, well this is a guy that picks somebody who isn't that liberal, and so he's comfortable with Bentsen."[34]

Given Brountas's central role in the selection process, his emphasis on geographic and ideological considerations probably reflects Dukakis's mind-set, as well. But Dukakis cited only the VP Formula when explaining his decision in later years: "The first and most important criterion for that selection was whether or not my running mate was ready to be president if, God forbid, something happened to me" (Dinan 2008). Yet in a 1976 interview on NBC's *Meet the Press*, Dukakis had indicated that other considerations, including geography, were relevant to vice presidential selection. "I would think that it would be helpful to [that year's Democratic presidential nominee, Jimmy Carter] to have somebody who in a sense, uh, complements him. Perhaps from a different region of the country. Perhaps with a different area of expertise."[35]

Bill Clinton, 1992

Bill Clinton's decision to select Al Gore as his running mate in 1992 clearly was not motivated by ticket-balancing concerns. Indeed, Gore—a fellow young, southern, centrist Democrat—struck many observers as something of a Clinton clone. As such, his selection did much to reinforce the campaign's message. Clinton—who often faced criticism as a presidential candidate, and later as president, for being driven by polling rather than personal convictions—took pride in bucking ticket-balancing conventions and choosing a running mate who embodied the VP Formula. "I did my country right on my first big decision," he said in a 2004 interview. "And that's more important than what state [the running mate comes] from or any of this other stuff. If [a presidential candidate] feels good, if he feels I did right by my country with this decision, that will help him more politically than anything else."[36]

But Clinton did not altogether reject the notion that a running mate could help to win votes. In his memoirs, Clinton recalled: "I also thought [Gore's] selection would be good politics in Tennessee, the South, and other swing states" (Clinton 2004, 414). His perception of running mate effects was even more evident when he was evaluating other vice presidential finalists. For instance, Nebraska senator Bob Kerrey "was a figure who could attract Republican and independent voters." And Florida governor Bob Graham "would almost certainly bring Florida into the Democratic column for the first time since 1976" (413).

Bob Dole, 1996

Bob Dole's belief in running mate effects is apparent from comments that he made during, or about, past campaigns. For instance, in the 1995 interview with Bob Woodward cited earlier, he credited himself with helping Ford in 1976 to win votes from farmers and veterans as a vice presidential candidate. Dole also emphasized electoral considerations when discussing Ronald Reagan's selection of a running mate in 1980: "Reagan is strong in the South and West, so you would think he probably wouldn't go either place [for a running mate], but he might." A midwesterner, Dole suggested, might provide more of an advantage: "If there should develop a real race in the farm belt then he is going to need somebody . . . who would be helpful" (Nelson 1980). Of course, it may not be coincidental that Dole, who wanted to be named as Reagan's running mate, seemed to be describing himself.

Dole sounded a similar note in 1988 when describing the type of running mate that George H. W. Bush, his presidential rival from earlier in that year's primaries, should select: "Someone who can get him elected, first. Secondly, someone who can help him after he is elected—someone like myself. I know Congress fairly well." He hastened to add, "And probably, most important, someone who could be president" (Taylor and Dewar 1988).

Dole's self-interest in each of these cases makes it difficult to evaluate whether, or how well, they reveal his thought process when selecting former

New York congressman Jack Kemp as his running mate in 1996. But Bob Ells-
worth, who headed the vice presidential search process that year, makes clear
that Kemp's selection was motivated by ideological considerations, saying that
the selection of Kemp "had to do with Dole's sense of what would enthuse
the conservative base in the party at the time, which it did at the Convention."[37] According to Dole's campaign manager, Scott Reed, the campaign
also wanted to generate excitement by announcing a bold, unexpected pick
that would help to change the unfavorable dynamics of the race at that time:

We envisioned that arrival ceremony [at the Republican Party conven-
tion] in San Diego, where you had twelve, fourteen thousand people outside,
screaming, excited to see Dole and excited to see his running mate, and every
time we put the other faces in that picture, we just didn't get that excitement.
So we thought [Dole-Kemp] was the right type of combination, again had an
element of surprise, again reinforced our issues that we were going to run on,
and also we thought it would be something that could help us win.[38]

George W. Bush, 2000

George W. Bush explicitly rejected the notion of running mate effects. "I believe voters base their decision on the presidential candidate, not the VP," he
wrote in his memoirs (Bush 2010, 69). Bush's decision to select Dick Cheney
as his running mate in 2000, and the search process that led to it (which, ironically, Cheney presided over), did nothing to cast doubt on the sincerity of this
statement or his articulation of the VP Formula during the campaign. Bush
recalled, "I hadn't picked him to be a political asset; I had chosen him to help
me do the job" (87). And Cheney confirmed this account: "I . . . believed that
he was serious, that he was looking for somebody of consequence to do the job
and he wasn't just worried about the Electoral College" (Baker 2013, 61). Bush
even rejected an impassioned plea from his campaign manager, Karl Rove,
not to select Cheney because he lacked electoral appeal. According to Rove,
"Bush called me the next day and said, 'All of those political problems, you are
right; go solve them. But I am looking at this as a prospective president and
[Cheney] would be a great partner to me in the Oval Office.'"[39]

Like Bill Clinton, though, Bush seemed to think that other potential running mates could have provided an electoral advantage. He said that former
Missouri senator John Danforth, the runner-up in that year's veepstakes, "was

a principled conservative who could also appeal across party lines," and "As a dividend, he might help carry Missouri, which would be a key battleground state" (Bush 2010, 67–68). Likewise, Senator Bill Frist, Senator Fred Thompson, and former governor Lamar Alexander—all from Tennessee—"were fine men, and they might help me pull off an upset in Tennessee, the home state of the Democratic nominee, Vice President Al Gore" (67). And Arizona senator Jon Kyl "was a rock solid conservative who would help me shore up the [Republican Party's] base" (67).

Al Gore, 2000

Al Gore's decision to select Connecticut senator Joe Lieberman as his running mate, in 2000, was historic in that it made Lieberman the first Jewish nominee on a major party's presidential ticket. Many observers also interpreted Lieberman's selection as a calculated attempt to distance Vice President Gore from President Clinton's sex scandals and related impeachment, given Lieberman's very public criticism of the president on these issues and his reputation for moral rectitude. Gore denied making any such political calculations. He later said about the vice presidential selection process: "If you focus on [selecting a qualified running mate] you will automatically cover a lot of other considerations. Ultimately, voters will ask the same question, so selecting a capable running mate will cover many political bases, too" (Hiller and Kriner 2008, 418).

But an August 2000 analysis of Gore's selection process, published in the *New York Times*, painted a very different picture. Based on interviews with numerous participants in that process, it concluded: "Again and again, Mr. Gore's search was shaped by gritty political concerns that had little bearing on what he had repeatedly described as his single most important criterion for choosing a running mate: someone possessed of the experience and ability to assume the presidency if necessary" (Barstow with Seelye 2000). For instance, this report alleged that Gore's emphasis on qualifications for the most part was a strategic response to Bush's vice presidential announcement: "On . . . the day before Mr. Bush announced his selection of Mr. Cheney, Mr. Gore told reporters that Mr. Bush's pick probably would not have an effect on his selection. But behind the scenes, advisers believed that Mr. Cheney's experience had to be accounted for, and that dynamic favored Mr. Lieberman, 58" (Barstow with Seelye 2000). To his credit, Gore reportedly refused to allow polling on the likely electoral impact of selecting a Jewish running mate. According to Warren Christopher, who led the vice presidential search, "Gore said: 'That's not part of me. That's not part of my thinking. I exclude that'" (Barstow and Seelye 2000). But electoral considerations may have motivated this decision as well; Gore reportedly feared that a leak would occur, which would then provide Republicans with evidence to support the charge that his decision-making process, like that of President Clinton, was poll-driven.[40]

Bob Shrum, a top adviser to the campaign, affirms that electoral considerations played a major role in Gore's vice presidential selection process: "He was intrigued with the unexpected, the unconventional, the breakthrough idea. He didn't want to make the 'usual' vice-presidential choice, and he didn't think he could afford to. . . . [H]e was far behind. He sensed the need to throw a long ball and I could tell he relished the chance" (Shrum 2007, 343). By Shrum's account (which is questionable in some respects, including his assertion that Gore was far behind Bush at that point in the campaign), this is why North Carolina senator John Edwards "nearly got the nod" despite having only two years of political experience at that time (343). But, Shrum recalls: "Gore was bothered about the press reaction if he chose someone so inexperienced" (344). Geographic considerations also played a role in the decision, according to Shrum. For instance, Gore seriously considered selecting Massachusetts senator John Kerry, "But Kerry came from a state we were going to carry anyway, Gore calculated" (344). Given that the same could be said for Lieberman's home state of Connecticut, though, it seems unlikely that geography played a decisive role in Gore's decision.

John Kerry, 2004

John Edwards was a freshman senator when John Kerry selected him as his running mate in 2004. But Edwards also had been one of Kerry's top rivals for the Democratic nomination that year, and he was relatively popular with the general public. According to Bob Shrum, also a top adviser to the Kerry campaign that year, electoral considerations greatly influenced the Democratic nominee's evaluations of potential running mates. With respect to New York senator Hillary Clinton and Missouri congressman Dick Gephardt, Shrum (2007, 453) writes: "Kerry was ready to partner with Clinton if it was the way to win, but he doubted it was. He liked Gephardt, was confident he was up to the job of being president, and hoped he might help carry Missouri, which could make the difference in a close election. But both he and [his wife] Teresa [Heinz-Kerry] worried that Gephardt was a gray choice who wouldn't light any fires."

Shrum also writes that Kerry was "uneasy" with Edwards, on a personal level, and later regretted selecting him: "Kerry said that he wished he'd never picked Edwards, that he should have gone with his gut" (Shrum 2007, 456; see also Kerry 2018). So why *did* Kerry pick him? Obviously, Edwards was not the most qualified person for the job, and it is debatable whether he was even sufficiently qualified. It seems likely that electoral considerations—such as Edwards's relative popularity and the impressive campaign skills that he had demonstrated during that year's primaries—played an important role in Kerry's decision. More concretely, geographic considerations appear to have influenced Edwards's selection, or at least the campaign's subsequent strategic choices.

Indeed, the Kerry campaign began airing its first television advertisements in North Carolina on the day after Edwards was introduced as Kerry's running mate. Tad Devine, a top Kerry campaign adviser, explained: "The advertisements in North Carolina reflected the campaign's calculation that the presence of Mr. Edwards on the ticket would allow Mr. Kerry to compete in Southern states like North Carolina, Arkansas, and Louisiana" (Devine and Kopko 2016, 41). Kerry and Edwards even capped off their postannouncement tour four days later with a major rally in North Carolina, replete with references to Edwards's roots in the state. Also, it is apparent that the Kerry-Edwards campaign regarded North Carolina as more competitive than their Republican counterparts did. According to Daron Shaw (2006), a political scientist who worked as a Bush campaign strategist in 2004, the Kerry-Edwards campaign rated North Carolina as "Leans Republican" and "worth watching," while the Bush-Cheney campaign rated it as "Base Republican." The reason for Democrats' optimism was clear: "North Carolina . . . emerged as [a] pickup possibilit[y] in the early summer . . . due to the presence on the ticket of Tar Heel senator John Edwards" (Shaw 2006, 65).[41]

In his recent memoirs, Kerry says all the right things about the importance of selecting a qualified running mate—but then provides no real substantive justification for picking Edwards, the freshman senator, over other, far better qualified vice presidential finalists. In fact, Kerry spends much more time on describing his personal discomfort with Edwards and his shortcomings as a running mate than on making any affirmative case for this risky, and ultimately disappointing, selection. One thing that does come through clearly in Kerry's discussion of the vice presidential selection process is his belief in targeted geographic effects. Among the "compelling reasons" for crossing party lines to select John McCain, Kerry writes, is that "John could potentially have changed the electoral map, I believe, putting Arizona and Colorado in play" (Kerry 2018, 273). As for Dick Gephardt, "Many people suggested he could have made the difference in Ohio and they may well have been right" (274). Bob Graham, the other vice presidential finalist, "brought southern credentials to the table" (274). So did Edwards, of course. Kerry even notes that "with John Edwards on the ticket," the campaign could "possibly make a run in North Carolina" (277). In fact, others would make that case even more boldly—John Edwards, for one. According to Kerry, "Edwards promised to deliver his home state" (277).

At a Democratic primary debate in January 2004, John Kerry was asked, "Senator, how do you plan to broaden the [party's] base and reach out to those voters, particularly Southern white voters who no longer even consider Democratic candidates?" Kerry responded by citing his military and political experience, as well as issues of particular concern to southern voters. He concluded: "And in the end, if I'm the nominee, I could always pick a running mate from the South, and we'll do just fine."[42] Perhaps this was just a joke. Or perhaps it was a prophecy.

John McCain, 2008

John McCain's first choice for vice president in 2008 certainly was unconventional. But it was not Sarah Palin. It was Joe Lieberman—yes, Al Gore's Democratic running mate in 2000, but also a national security hawk and a close friend to McCain, whom he had endorsed during the Republican primaries. Lieberman fit McCain's publicly stated criteria for vice presidential selection: he was qualified to take over as president, if necessary, and he shared McCain's foremost political priorities and values (if not his ideology, as a whole). But Lieberman's selection also would be symbolically important. "Were Joe to join the ticket it would send a clear message of change," McCain wrote in his memoirs. "It would be an emphatic statement that I intended to govern collaboratively with an emphasis on problem solving not politics, which in 2008 would have been very good politics" (McCain and Salter 2018, 51). Indeed, he recalled that, going into the general election, "My biggest predicament was my difficulty convincing voters I was an agent of change. That was our principal concern as we assembled a list of potential vice presidents that summer" (49).

But McCain's campaign advisers feared that choosing Lieberman—who, aside from foreign policy, essentially was a liberal Democrat—would alienate the conservative Republican Party base that was rather skeptical of McCain already. Initial reactions to Lieberman's rumored selection seemed to confirm this. Indeed, one week before the party convention in late August, campaign pollster Bill McInturf reported that the selection of a pro-choice running mate would cost McCain votes among Republicans while making little difference to Independents (Heilemann and Halperin 2010, 358). With the deadline for announcing his selection fast approaching, McCain's advisers begged him to reconsider. Campaign manager Steve Schmidt, in particular, said that McCain needed a game changer. "Here's my view of the politics of it," Schmidt said. "In any normal year, [Minnesota governor] Tim Pawlenty's a great pick, a no-brainer. But this isn't a normal year. We need to have a transformative, electrifying moment" (359). And Schmidt had just the right candidate in mind: Alaska's governor, Sarah Palin.

McCain invited Palin to visit his ranch in Sedona, Arizona, for an interview and some last-minute vetting. He came away impressed. As McCain later explained, "Her profile as a reformer and as someone who managed to get important stuff done without years of experience or deferring to established interests was her main appeal. The fact that she was an accomplished woman succeeding in a male-dominated profession didn't hurt, either" (McCain and Salter 2018, 53). Indeed, he thought Palin could help in winning the election: "We felt, and polling confirmed, that there were moderate and conservative Democrats who had voted for Hillary Clinton [in the Democratic primaries] and might be persuaded to vote for a Republican presidential candidate with a record of working with both sides, and the female chief executive he had picked as his running mate" (53–54). But, contrary to McCain's oft-stated selection criteria, his campaign did little to confirm that Palin was ready to assume the vice presidency, let alone take over as president if something happened to the seventy-two-year-old former prisoner of war and cancer survivor. According to Heilemann and Halperin (2010, 361–362), McCain's advisers "asked her nothing to plumb the depths of her knowledge about foreign or domestic policy. They didn't explore her preparedness to be vice president. They assumed she knew as much as the average governor, and that what she didn't know, she would pick up on the fly."

With Palin waiting just outside, and the clock ticking, McCain met in his living room with Schmidt, Mark Salter, his most trusted adviser, and A. B. Culvahouse, who was leading the vice presidential search, to reach a final decision. Salter made the case for choosing Pawlenty, who McCain regarded as "a safe, conventional choice, solid on the merits, but not an outsider or a credible change agent" (McCain and Salter 2018, 50). And Salter warned against choosing Palin, who, he said, "was untested, would undermine the experience argument against Obama, and might damage McCain's status. 'This is your reputation,' Salter stressed," in closing (Heilemann and Halperin 2010, 363).

Then, it was Schmidt's turn. As McCain recalled:

> We had three opportunities, he argued, to stop the race from trending inevitably to the challenger in any environment where over 70% of voters believed the country was going in the wrong direction: my vice president selection, my convention speech, and the debates. If we failed to use any of those opportunities to convince voters we would bring change to Washington, we would lose. And Sarah was the biggest change message on the list of possible choices. (McCain and Salter 2018, 55–56)

Schmidt acknowledged that Palin might turn out to be a poor choice—she was a "high risk, high reward" candidate, in Culvahouse's words (55)—but on the other hand, Schmidt argued, Pawlenty would not deliver any votes. "If I were running," he said, "I'd rather lose by ten points trying to go for the win than lose by one point and look back and say [that] 'I should have gone for the win'" (Heilemann and Halperin 2010, 363).

McCain agreed: "I thought Schmidt made the better argument, probably because it echoed my own thoughts about Sarah and the challenges ahead" (McCain and Salter 2018, 56). That settled it. McCain called the meeting to a close, stepped outside onto his porch, and offered Sarah Palin the vice presidential nomination.

Barack Obama, 2008

Barack Obama's decision to select Delaware senator Joe Biden as his running mate, in 2008, seemed to be motivated by governing, rather than electoral, considerations. Biden had decades of Senate experience and presented little in the way of obvious electoral advantages. In a 2015 interview, Biden recounted: "I asked [Obama] why he wanted me to be vice president. And he said two things, in this order. Number one—one—you will always tell me the truth and be straight with me. There will be no varnish on what you say. Secondly, I need help governing. Thirdly [*sic*], your experience in foreign policy will be helpful."[43]

David Axelrod, a top campaign strategist, said that Obama "wasn't dismissive of the political considerations [of vice presidential selection], but . . . was intent on finding someone who could not only help us win the election, but also bring value to the administration. Above all, he wanted someone who would be ready to take over if disaster struck" (2015, 295). Whenever Axelrod recalled Obama's decision-making process, however, political considerations were at the top of the list—literally, as Joe Biden might say. Early in the process, when Obama first brought up the idea of selecting Biden, "Barack ticked off his reasons." First, in Axelrod's reconstruction: "A native of Pennsylvania who still had close ties there, Biden could help us in a must-win state that had given us problems." Next, "[Biden] had a strong connection to the struggling middle class, which was central to our economic message and our chances" (281–282). At the end of the selection process, "The favorite was still Joe Biden, for all the reasons Barack had laid out in May." What's more, as Axelrod hastened to add, "Biden had come through our polling project on top" (296).

Obama also was sensitive to what he perceived to be voters' preference for a balanced ticket. For instance, while his first choice apparently would have been Virginia governor Tim Kaine, Obama said, "The problem with Tim is that we're too much alike. I don't know how many young, liberal, Harvard-educated civil rights lawyers with very little Washington experience the market will bear" (Axelrod 2015, 299). Campaign polling and focus groups confirmed Obama's ticket-balancing concerns and perhaps even contributed to them. "Not surprisingly," Axelrod recounts, the campaign found that voters "wanted more of what Barack didn't have. . . . [F]olks were looking for someone with a little gray hair. They thought Obama represented sufficient change by himself, and preferred as his backstop a candidate with long experience in Washington and a deep résumé on national security" (295). Whether electoral considerations played into the decision or not—and we cannot know for sure—that is exactly what voters got in Joe Biden.

Mitt Romney, 2012

In an election postmortem, senior campaign adviser Beth Myers recalled Mitt Romney's instructions when tasking her to lead his vice presidential search in 2012: "He gave two simple criteria: someone who's immediately qualified to be president and someone whose background is not going to create such a distraction that the campaign would derail. He wanted to make his selection from a choice of qualified candidates" (Jamieson 2013, 122; see also Halperin and Heilemann 2013, 343). Myers also rejected the notion that geography influenced the selection process. "We very consciously said we were not going to make a decision about the vice president based on winning an individual state. . . . We never really said, 'If we pick this guy, we've got a better chance at this state'" (Jamieson 2013, 123).

But after Paul Ryan's selection in mid-August, the campaign began to target his home state of Wisconsin more aggressively than it had before (Devine and Kopko 2016, chap. 3). Indeed, the Badger State's share of national campaign advertising expenditures increased threefold following Ryan's selection. And, whereas Mitt Romney had visited Wisconsin only once prior to Ryan's selection, the Romney-Ryan ticket visited fifteen times thereafter—again, representing a threefold increase in percentage terms nationally. Ryan, the native son, made ten of these visits.

Perhaps this evidence indicates that geography played a role in Ryan's selection. Or perhaps Ryan's qualifications got him selected and *then* the Romney campaign decided to make the most of the (perceived) strategic opportunity that this presented in Wisconsin. Whatever the case may be, for our purposes this evidence is important because it suggests that the Romney campaign expected Ryan's selection to give it a better chance of winning in Wisconsin. In other words, the campaign behaved as if, geographically speaking, it thought that the running mate mattered.

Donald Trump, 2016

Donald Trump dismissed the notion that a running mate could help him win the 2016 election. "History has said nobody ever helps," he told the *Washington Post* in July of that year. "I've never seen anybody that helps." But he had, actually (or thought so, at least). In the same breath, Trump cited John Kennedy's choice of Lyndon Johnson in 1960 as one vice presidential candidate—indeed, the last one—that "truly mattered" (in the interviewer's paraphrase).[44] This, of course, happened when Trump was fourteen years old. Trump further contradicted his initial assessment of running mate effects when, in the same interview, he said that one of the factors guiding his selection process—in addition to political experience, personal chemistry, and party unity—was finding "someone who can help you win" (Cillizza 2016). Earlier that year, Trump also suggested that choosing the wrong running mate could cost a presidential candidate the election. In reference to Mitt Romney's selection of Paul Ryan in 2012, Trump said: "That was the end of the campaign, when they [*sic*] chose Ryan. . . . [T]hat was the end of the campaign" (Kertscher 2016).

Hillary Clinton, 2016

In 2016, Hillary Clinton was focused on selecting a well-qualified running mate with whom she could govern, if elected president. She paid little, if any, attention to electoral considerations. This, at least, is according to one (otherwise rather critical) inside account of the Clinton campaign (Allen and Parnes 2017). For instance, one potential running mate, Massachusetts senator Elizabeth Warren, "had precisely the sizzle Hillary was looking for to juice up the campaign, but Clinton wanted a governing partner, someone who saw the world in a similar way and could help her run the executive branch" (Allen and Parnes 2017, 256). Indeed, the *Washington Post* reported during the campaign that Clinton had decided not to select labor secretary Tom Perez or housing and urban development secretary Julian Castro because "both leading Hispanic contenders lack experience that Clinton has told friends and advisers she considers critical for the role: Neither has military or national security experience—considerable drawbacks in a time of heightened domestic and global strife" (O'Keefe 2016).

It is difficult to say whether Clinton believed that running mates simply had no effect on voters, or she did but rejected that consideration as inappropriate. In the 2008 presidential campaign, she seemed to think that Barack Obama's choice of a running mate could prove decisive. "'I think it's fifty-fifty whether he wins, right?' she said, noting that Obama's VP choice was critical" (Heilemann and Halperin 2010, 267). Also, her closest advisers—many of whom had served her for years and knew her mind quite well—seemed to view the selection process as an exercise in electoral coalition-building. In a private e-mail sent to Hillary Clinton in March 2016, and released by WikiLeaks that fall, campaign chairman John Podesta wrote: "Cheryl [Mills], Robby [Mook], Jake [Sullivan], Huma [Abedin], Jennifer [Palmeiri] and I also did a first cut of people to consider for VP." He added, "I have organized names in rough food groups." In what reads like a Republican parody of Democratic Party identity politics, Podesta's "food groups" included "Latinos," "Women," "White Men," "Black Men," "Military," and "Businesspeople,"—plus, in a class by himself, "Bernie Sanders."[45]

Summary

Notwithstanding their public articulations of the VP Formula during the campaign, most presidential candidates believe that running mates have the potential to influence voters and perhaps decide elections. This is not to say that presidential candidates' perceptions of running mate effects determine vice presidential selection, or that all candidates perceive these effects to be dramatic. Indeed, the qualitative evidence presented in this chapter indicates that candidates' perceptions, and the impact of those perceptions on the selection process, vary considerably. For some candidates, particularly in recent years, electoral considerations seem to have very little, if any, effect on their choice of a running mate. For instance, George W. Bush in 2000, Barack Obama in 2008, and Donald Trump and Hillary Clinton in 2016 each chose a highly qualified running mate who seemed unlikely to deliver any major electoral benefits. But other candidates, and particularly those who made their selection at a time when the campaign dynamics clearly were not in their favor, seemed to place a great deal of emphasis on electoral considerations. Specifically, Walter Mondale in 1984, Bob Dole in 1996, and John McCain in 2008 each chose his running mate with the apparent hope, if not the expectation, that it would prove to be an electoral "game changer."

Of course, the fact that Mondale, Dole, and McCain were expected to lose, and ultimately did so, might suggest that such acts of desperation are inconsequential, in that they do *not* determine who actually becomes the next vice president. But what about George H. W. Bush, in 1988? Bush was losing to Michael Dukakis by double digits heading into that summer, and his deficit grew larger after the Democratic convention in July (Meacham 2015, 331). Campaign adviser Roger Ailes recalled, "I could tell Bush was thinking, 'You know, they're right. We could lose this thing" (333). And so, according to biographer Jon Meacham, "Bush had an urge to shake things up, and he was interested in . . . Dan Quayle" (336). Quayle was much less qualified than other potential running mates, and Bush knew as much. Weighing the choice between Dole and Quayle, Bush wrote in his diary on August 13, just before making the selection, "Dole would be more instantly perceived as President, and Quayle is more exciting and new" (337). Had this been a closer race at the time, perhaps with Bush in the lead, it is quite possible, if not probable, that he would have chosen Dole instead. As it turns out, Bush went on to defeat Dukakis, decisively, and Dan Quayle became the next vice president of the United States.

This is why we argue that presidential candidates' perceptions of running mate effects are important, even when those perceptions are not decisive or the candidate chooses a highly qualified running mate. Quite simply, under different circumstances, the same candidate might have chosen a less qualified running mate in hopes of gaining an electoral advantage. Also, the candidates' and their campaign advisers' perceptions of running mate effects might influence strategic decisions made after the selection of a running mate, such as the allocation of campaign visits and advertisements. Indeed, John Kerry's selection of John Edwards in 2004 and Mitt Romney's selection of Paul Ryan in 2012 seem to have influenced the allocation of campaign resources to the running mate's home state.

This analysis also provides insight into *why* presidential candidates think that running mates matter. That is to say, we can assess which of the running mate's characteristics presidential candidates believe are likely to influence voters. Geographic considerations come up most often in our qualitative analysis (Gerald Ford, Jimmy Carter, George H. W. Bush, Michael Dukakis, Bill Clinton, Bob Dole, George W. Bush, John Kerry, Barack Obama, Mitt Romney). Multiple candidates, or their close advisers, also referenced ideological considerations (Michael Dukakis, Bob Dole, John McCain). And three candidates made explicit references to demographic appeals—ethnicity, religion, and gender for Walter Mondale; age for George H. W. Bush; and gender for John McCain. In other cases, the candidates indicated in more general terms that a running mate might add or subtract votes, or seemed to be influenced by polling or press coverage.

CONCLUSION

Presidential candidates almost always downplay or dismiss electoral considerations when publicly discussing their vice presidential selection criteria during
a campaign. Instead, they invoke what we call the VP Formula—by insist-
ing that their principal, if not sole, objective is to choose a qualified running
mate who is ready to serve as president, if necessary, and to help govern as
vice president, if elected. Is this because presidential candidates do not believe that running mates influence election outcomes, or because they fear
that acknowledging as much will lead voters to infer that they put politics over
principle and will do so once in office?

Our analysis indicates that most presidential candidates believe that running mates can influence voting, and under certain circumstances—namely,
when a candidate is trailing in the polls and desperate for an electoral advantage—this perception can influence vice presidential selection and subsequent
campaign strategy. But this does not mean that presidential candidates are
lying when they dutifully recite the VP Formula, and that vice presidential
selection merely is an exercise in electoral gamesmanship. Rather, we suspect
that most—if not all—candidates really do want to choose someone who will
be credible as a running mate and effective as a vice president. After all, if
elected, the vice president can be a valuable governing partner and potentially
someone who can carry on the president's legacy as a successor (via election
eight years later, or under unexpected circumstances beforehand).

However, it makes little sense to think of qualifications and compatibility
as the only standards for selection. Indeed, there are any number of persons—
members of Congress, governors, cabinet officials, and so forth—available in
a given election year who are reasonably qualified to serve as president. And
many of them are sure to be among the presidential candidate's political allies
and/or close friends. In that case, it makes more sense to think of qualifications and compatibility as *thresholds* for selection rather than *determinants*. In
other words, candidates need some other criteria to narrow down their choice
from a long list of individuals who would be qualified and compatible running
mates, as well as potential vice presidents. To the extent that a given presidential candidate believes that running mates can win votes for the party ticket,
and identifies an otherwise qualified, compatible candidate who meets his or
her electoral needs, this perception might influence vice presidential selection
and the campaign's subsequent strategic choices.

But do voters—who constitute the audience for such strategic appeals—share these perceptions of running mate effects? And, if so, what criteria do *they* use to evaluate vice presidential candidates? Answering these questions, as we do in the next chapter, further helps to set the agenda for our empirical analysis of running mate effects in part II of this book.

2. (Why) Do Voters Think That Running Mates Matter?

Do *voters* think that running mates matter? That is to say, do voters perceive vice presidential candidates to be influential in determining their presidential vote? And, if so, which of the running mate's attributes do they consider to be most important?

Public opinion polls provide a good indication as to how voters might respond to these questions. Indeed, many polls directly ask respondents to evaluate how the hypothetical or actual selection of a given running mate might influence their vote for president, or—less frequently—to evaluate the effect that running mates have had on their vote in a particular election, or in past elections more generally. Other polls provide insight into voters' vice presidential selection criteria, by asking them to rate the importance of various attributes that a potential running mate might possess.

In this chapter, we use public polling data—primarily from the 2000–2016 presidential elections—to evaluate whether, and in what ways, voters perceive vice presidential candidates to be influential in determining presidential vote choice. There is no dedicated database from which to draw such polling results; instead, we conducted an extensive search of relevant online resources in order to identify any polls that asked about perceptions of running mate effects.[1] The resulting data come from a variety of major polling organizations, via their websites or news reports summarizing their findings. Each of the polls included in our analysis employed representative sampling techniques. Most of the polls were conducted at the national level, but several were conducted in a single state or a small set of battleground states at one time. In terms of sampling, most of the polls included registered or likely voters, only, while a few of them included adults, generally. We note these sampling characteristics in the subsequent text or tables, whenever possible.

We divide this chapter's analysis into two sections. The first section analyzes various survey measures indicating whether respondents think that running mates influence their presidential vote, specifically by asking respondents to evaluate the electoral importance of vice presidential selection, generally; estimate the effect that vice presidential selection has had on their voting in past elections; and estimate how likely it is that the hypothetical or actual selection of a given running mate will influence their vote. Also, in this section, we evaluate voters' familiarity with several recent vice presidential candidates. Finally, we analyze open-ended responses from the 1952–2004 American National Election Studies (ANES), to determine how often respondents referenced vice presidential candidates' electoral significance absent a survey prompt to consider such effects.

The second section analyzes voters' criteria for evaluating (potential) running mates. Specifically, we capitalize on a limited number of polls that ask respondents how important it is for a presidential candidate—in the abstract, or in a particular case—to select a running mate who possesses various attributes, including some that pertain to demographics (e.g., age, gender, race/ethnicity) and others that pertain to political beliefs or experience. This analysis allows us to characterize not only which attributes voters—at least in the most recent elections—find most (or least) relevant to vice presidential selection, but also whether these criteria are fixed or dependent on the attributes associated with the presidential candidate making the selection. In other words, we can use this information to determine whether voters think it is important to "balance" the presidential ticket, and, if so, on what bases (e.g., personal vs. political attributes).

Our analysis indicates that public opinion about running mate effects is, in keeping with much of the preceding evidence, rather conflicted. For instance, many respondents say that the choice of a running mate is important to them, as an abstract matter or directly in relation to their intended presidential vote. Yet, vice presidential selection is quite unimportant when measured in relation to other electoral considerations, and few respondents can recall that it ever has changed their vote. Moreover, only a small percentage of respondents reference the vice presidential candidate when given the opportunity to discuss their vote in an open-ended fashion.

The evidence is clearer with respect to voters' criteria for evaluating vice presidential candidates. Voters generally prefer a running mate who balances the presidential ticket, particularly in terms of experience. In fact, their highest priority seems to be ensuring that the running mate is qualified to serve in office and capable of helping the president to govern effectively. It is striking, and probably not coincidental, that these criteria so closely correspond to the "VP Formula" that presidential candidates regularly cite during campaigns, when discussing vice presidential selection (see chapter 1). Indeed, presidential candidates' rhetoric may be designed to satisfy public expectations. Or perhaps the candidates' rhetoric has become so familiar as to coach the public on how to respond to such questions, whatever their actual preferences or their behavioral manifestations may be.[2]

VOTERS' PERCEPTIONS OF RUNNING MATE EFFECTS

In this section, we evaluate whether, and to what extent, voters believe that running mates influence presidential voting. Specifically, we analyze polling data in which survey respondents rated the running mate's electoral importance, in abstract or relative terms; evaluated the running mate's effect on their vote in past elections; and made projections about a hypothetical or an actual running mate's likely effect on their vote in the present election. Finally, we analyze respondents' open-ended explanations as to why they would or would not vote for a particular presidential candidate, using data from the 1952–2004 ANES, to determine how often they cited vice presidential selection as a contributing factor.

How Important Is the Running Mate?

In May 2016, Rasmussen Reports conducted a national poll of likely voters that asked: "In terms of how you will vote in the upcoming presidential election, how important is the vice presidential nominee to your vote?"[3] Nearly 80 percent of respondents answered "Very important" (33 percent) or "Important" (45 percent), while a small minority answered "Unimportant" (13 percent) or "Not at all important" (5 percent).[4] Coming from a nationally representative sample, in the most recent presidential election, these data provide a clear indication of how voters might respond to the question "Do running mates matter?" The answer, it seems, is a resounding "*Yes!*"

Unfortunately, few public opinion polls include the same measure or a close variant thereof. The only other examples we find come from a series of polls conducted in select battleground states during the 2008 presidential election. A pair of Quinnipiac University polls conducted in June of that year asked likely voters in Florida, Ohio, and Pennsylvania,[5] as well as in Colorado, Michigan, Minnesota, and Wisconsin:[6] "In deciding your vote for president, how important is the vice-presidential candidate?" In each state, the percentage of respondents answering "Very important" or "Somewhat important" ranged between 82 and 87 percent, with no more than 4 percent answering "Not important at all." A poll of likely voters in North Carolina that same month, conducted by Public Policy Polling (PPP),[7] yielded similar results, with 85 percent of respondents answering "Very important" or "Somewhat important." These results suggest that the Rasmussen Poll was not an aberration, or an artifact of a presidential election contested by two historically unpopular nominees (Enten 2016). If we are to take voters at their word, the obvious conclusion is that running mates matter.

The PPP North Carolina poll contained another, incomparably direct measure of perceived running mate effects. It asked: "How much of an effect do you think the vice-presidential nominee has on the race?" Nearly two-thirds of respondents (64 percent) said that the running mate has a "Strong effect," while 27 percent answered "Weak effect" and 9 percent answered "No effect at all." This question is valuable because it asks respondents to assess the running mate's likely impact on the electorate, generally, rather than on their own vote, specifically, or just in the present election. As such, it represents the purest available survey measure of perceived running mate effects. Of course, it bears repeating that these results come from a poll of likely voters in one state, North Carolina, and not a national sample. But, given how similarly respondents rated the running mate's importance to their vote in this poll, as compared with other state-level polls from 2008 and Rasmussen's national poll from 2016, it seems probable that a different state or national sample of respondents, or one surveyed in a different election year, largely would agree that the choice of a running mate has a "strong effect" on the presidential race.

Is the Running Mate More Important Than . . . ?

Another poll from 2008, conducted by the *Washington Post* and ABC News among a national sample of registered voters, provides valuable context for the preceding results.[8] Much like the polls described earlier, this one asked respondents to rate the running mate's importance to their presidential vote. However, this poll was unusual in that it also asked about the importance of several other factors (e.g., "The economy" or "Health care") that might influence vote choice—thereby allowing us to characterize perceptions of the running mate's *relative* importance to voters. This survey design should be particularly useful if, as we suspect, respondents are biased toward affirming an item's importance simply because pollsters ask about it in a survey. In other words, asking whether vice presidential selection, or any other factor, is important to their vote might cue respondents to think that they *should* find it important and, in turn, bias their responses upward. By presenting vice presidential selection as one in a series of possible electoral influences, this survey should help to account for such biases.

As in other polls, described earlier, more than 80 percent of respondents said that "The candidates' choices for vice presidential running mates" were important to their vote.[9] And yet, when comparing across items, the choice of a running mate seems exceptionally *unimportant.* Indeed, this item finished dead-last on every metric of importance—for instance, garnering the fewest "Extremely important" responses (by 12 percentage points) and the most "Less important than that" responses (by 8 percentage points).[10] This finding suggests that we should treat isolated ratings of the running mate's importance, such as those presented earlier, with a great deal of skepticism. While voters may claim that vice presidential selection is an important factor in deciding their vote, in reality its effects are likely to be crowded out by many other, more important considerations.

Perhaps the best evidence of vice presidential candidates' relative (un)importance comes from a postelection survey conducted by Gallup in 2004 (Jones and Carroll 2005). The respondent sample included 1,567 voters from the final CNN/*USA Today*/Gallup preelection poll, who agreed to participate in a follow-up interview after the election. Much like the *Washington Post*/ABC News poll described earlier, Gallup asked respondents to rate the importance of thirteen items potentially influencing their vote in the 2004 presidential election, including "His [the presidential candidate's] choice of a vice presidential running mate." Specifically, Gallup interviewers asked respondents who they voted for in that year's election, and later: "How important were each of the following as reasons why you voted for [this presidential candidate]?" After asking about the first item's importance, interviewers then asked: "How about [the next item]?" The thirteen items were rotated, randomly, by respondent.

Bush and Kerry voters rated the running mate's importance almost identically. Among Bush voters, 16 percent described Cheney's selection as extremely important; 34 percent, very important; 32 percent, somewhat important; and

18 percent, not important. Among Kerry voters, 18 percent described Edwards's selection as extremely important; 35 percent, very important; 33 percent, somewhat important; and 14 percent, not important. As always, we find that more than 80 percent of respondents ascribed some degree of importance to vice presidential selection.

But, in terms of relative importance, vice presidential selection ranks quite low. Among all respondents, it ranks ninth out of twelve items in terms of "Extremely important" responses—ahead of "His performance in the debate" (15 percent); "Because he is a [Democrat/Republican]" (14 percent); and "His convention speech" (12 percent).[11] Using combined "Extremely important" and "Very important" responses makes no difference; vice presidential selection (51 percent) again ranks ninth out of twelve items—ahead of "His performance in the debates" (43 percent); "Because he is a [Democrat/Republican]" (39 percent); and "His convention speech" (38 percent).

The fact that party affiliation ranks second to last in both cases suggests that voters may be misjudging the determinants of their presidential vote.[12] Indeed, partisanship is one of the most powerful determinants of vote choice in elections, generally (A. Campbell et al. 1960; Lewis-Beck et al. 2008). As an empirical matter, there is every reason to believe that the candidates' party affiliations should rank much higher on each list. By the same token, it is possible that respondents misperceived the running mates' actual influence on their vote. Our empirical analysis in part II helps to clarify whether these responses underestimated or overestimated the running mate's effect on vote choice.

Are You Voting for a Vice President, Too, or Just a President?

The relative importance measures, described in the previous section, provide our first indication that running mates might not be as important to vote choice as polls often suggest. Another indication can be found in a CBS News poll conducted just before the vice presidential debate in early October 2016 among registered voters, nationwide.[13] In a rather direct measure of the axiom that "people don't vote for a vice president, they vote for a president," this poll asked respondents: "Which of these statements comes closer to your opinion: The presidential candidates' choices for vice president will have a great deal of influence on my vote; OR, I will vote based mostly on the presidential candidates, not on whom they choose for vice president?" Here, the vast majority of respondents (84 percent) said that their vote would be for a presidential candidate, essentially, while only 14 percent said that the running mate would have a great deal of influence on their vote.

CBS included the same question in a July 2000 poll,[14] with nearly identical results: 81 percent reported essentially voting for a presidential candidate, while 15 percent ascribed a great deal of influence to the running mate. The fact that we observe so little variation across this sixteen-year period suggests that these results—and probably many others in this chapter—are not specific to a particular election year. Nor, for that matter, do we observe any meaningful variation in responses by party in the 2000 CBS poll; approximately 80 percent of Democrats, Republicans, and Independents said that they would be voting for a presidential candidate, only.

Has the Running Mate Ever Changed Your Vote?

Another unique indicator of perceived running mate effects comes from a July 2000 CNN/*USA Today*/Gallup poll (Saad 2000). This national poll of adults asked two questions directly assessing the running mate's impact on vote choice, in terms of the respondent's voting history. First, it asked: "Have you ever changed your mind and voted for a presidential candidate whom you would not have voted for otherwise because of that candidate's selection of a vice presidential running mate?" The vast majority of respondents, 88 percent, answered "No," while 9 percent answered "Yes," and 3 percent offered no opinion.

Second, the poll asked: "Have you changed your mind and not voted for a presidential candidate whom you would have voted for otherwise because of that candidate's selection of a vice presidential running mate?" The responses were almost identical, with 89 percent of respondents answering "No," 8 percent answering "Yes," and 3 percent offering no opinion.

Of course, a healthy dose of skepticism is in order when considering these results. First, as indicated in our earlier discussion of relative importance measures, voters often seem to misperceive the actual determinants of their votes. Second, when surveying a lifetime of presidential voting, many voters might forget an instance in which the running mate did, in fact, change their mind about a presidential candidate.

Yet these results provide valuable perspective, in two ways. First, to put it bluntly, they show that talk is cheap. As the evidence presented throughout this chapter indicates, in many cases survey respondents claim that the running mate is important to their vote, or that the choice of a particular running mate will make them more or less likely to vote for a given presidential ticket. But what matters, ultimately, is whether the running mate actually causes voters to vote differently; otherwise, running mates do not matter, electorally speaking, or their effects are perceptible only on the margins of electoral behavior (e.g., a voter's degree of activism in support of the candidate). If running mates actually change votes—or even change election outcomes—to any significant degree, surely more than one in ten adults would be able to recall a single instance in which a running mate ever changed *their* vote.

Second, these data put another familiar axiom about running mates' electoral influence to the test: that, as Joe Biden said years before taking on the role, "The only thing vice president[ial candidate]s can do is hurt you" (Rees 2000). If this were true, and if voters perceived it to be true, we should observe more variation between responses to the first item (which, essentially, asks whether a running mate ever has *won* the respondent's vote) and the second item (which, essentially, asks whether a running mate ever has *lost* the respondent's vote). Yet, again, the results nearly identical across both measures, with fewer than one in ten respondents reporting a decisive running mate effect.

To be clear, we do not regard these survey data as empirical evidence of running mates' *actual* electoral influence; we reserve such analysis for part II. Rather, in keeping with this chapter's objectives, we regard these data as valuable indicators of voters' *perceptions* of running mate effects. In other survey measures, voters provide speculative affirmations of the running mate's electoral influence. With these survey measures—which, unfortunately, we do not find replicated in any other election year—respondents provide a more concrete indication of that influence, or the lack thereof: with few exceptions, voters cannot recall an instance in which the vice presidential candidate ever changed their vote.

How Would You Vote If . . . Was on the Ticket?

Perhaps the most familiar way in which polls measure perceptions of running mate effects is to ask respondents how the hypothetical or actual selection of a given running mate will influence their presidential vote.

Table 2.1. Effect of Hypothetical Running Mates on Intended Vote for Donald Trump, 2016

Republican Running Mate	*More Likely* (%)	*Less Likely* (%)	*No Impact* (%)	*DK/No Opinion* (%)
MORNING CONSULT				
Chris Christie	17	21	43	19
Mary Fallin	11	13	49	28
Newt Gingrich	21	17	42	20
Mike Pence	12	12	47	28
Jeff Sessions	12	12	48	28
Average	14.6	15.0	45.8	24.6
MONMOUTH UNIVERSITY				
Chris Christie	20	28	49	—
Joni Ernst	7	15	66	—
Newt Gingrich	24	26	47	—
Marco Rubio	27	20	50	—
Sarah Palin	13	42	43	—
Jeff Sessions	9	17	63	—
Average	16.7	24.7	46.3	—

Morning Consult data come from a poll of US registered voters, July 8–10, 2016 (n = 2,001; margin of error ±2 percent). Available at https://morningconsultintelligence.com/media/mc/160701_topline_Topicals_VP_v2_AP.pdf (accessed January 2, 2018).

Morning Consult question: "If Republican Presidential candidate Donald Trump selected [insert name] as the Vice Presidential candidate, would you be more or less likely to vote for Donald Trump?"

Monmouth University data come from a poll of US registered voters, June 15–19, 2016 (n = 803; margin of error ±3.5 percent). Available at https://www.monmouth.edu/polling-institute/reports/MonmouthPoll_US_062316 (accessed January 2, 2018).

Monmouth University question: "I'm going to read you the names of some people who have been mentioned as possible Vice Presidential candidates for the Republican Party. For each one I read please tell me if you would be more likely or less likely to support the Republican ticket if Donald Trump picked this person as his running mate, or if this pick would have no impact on your vote either way?"

First, with respect to hypothetical running mates, in table 2.1 and table 2.2 we present data from two polls conducted among nationally representative samples of registered voters in 2016, by Morning Consult[15] and Monmouth University.[16] Each poll presented respondents with a list of potential running mates for Republican presidential candidate Donald Trump (table 2.1) or Democratic presidential candidate Hillary Clinton (table 2.2) and asked how a given selection would affect the respondent's presidential vote. Numerous

Table 2.2. Effect of Hypothetical Running Mates on Intended Vote for Hillary Clinton, 2016

Democratic Running Mate	More Likely (%)	Less Likely (%)	No Impact (%)	DK/No Opinion (%)
MORNING CONSULT				
Elizabeth Warren	21	19	39	21
Cory Booker	13	14	47	26
Sherrod Brown	12	13	48	26
Tom Perez	12	13	49	26
Julian Castro	13	13	48	26
Tim Kaine	11	13	49	27
Average	13.7	13.8	46.7	25.3
MONMOUTH UNIVERSITY				
Julian Castro	10	17	63	—
Elizabeth Warren	24	21	51	—
Bernie Sanders	39	20	39	—
Cory Booker	13	13	64	—
Tim Kaine	9	13	68	—
Al Franken	12	21	60	—
Average	17.8	17.5	57.5	—

Morning Consult data come from a poll of US registered voters, July 8–10, 2016 ($n = 2,001$; margin of error ±2 percent). Available at https://morningconsultintelligence.com/media/mc/160701 _topline_Topicals_VP_v2_AP.pdf (accessed January 2, 2018).

Morning Consult question: "If Democratic Presidential candidate Hillary Clinton selected [insert name] as the Vice Presidential candidate, would you be more or less likely to vote for Hillary Clinton?"

Monmouth University data come from a poll of US registered voters, June 15–19, 2016 ($n = 803$; margin of error ±3.5 percent). Available at https://www.monmouth.edu/polling-institute /reports/MonmouthPoll_US_062316 (accessed January 2, 2018).

Monmouth University question: "I'm going to read you the names of some people who have been mentioned as possible Vice Presidential candidates for the Democratic Party. For each one I read please tell me if you would be more likely or less likely to support the Democratic ticket if Hillary Clinton picked this person as his running mate, or if this pick would have no impact on your vote either way?"

polls, over the course of recent elections, have included similar items. We present these data as examples of voters' responses, particularly in recent elections.

On average, 45 to 58 percent of respondents in each poll said that choosing one of the potential running mates would have "No impact" on their vote. The Morning Consult poll also provided a "Don't know/No opinion" option, which one-quarter of respondents selected. This raises the share of unaffected respondents to more than 70 percent, for both parties. The remaining respondents, generally speaking, split evenly on whether a running mate's selection would make them more or less likely to support a given ticket. In fact, the "More likely" and "Less likely" percentages canceled each other out, on average, for both parties in the Morning Consult poll and for Democrats in the Monmouth poll. Only Donald Trump's running mates, according to Monmouth, would have had a net impact on voting—but this was an electoral *disadvantage*, whereby 25 percent of respondents became less likely to vote for the ticket, and 17 percent became more likely to do so, on average.

Sarah Palin's inclusion in the Monmouth poll is to blame for the exceptionally poor performance of Trump's potential running mates. By far, Palin was the most unpopular candidate tested in these polls, generating three times as many "Less likely" (42 percent) responses as "More likely" (13 percent) responses. But few running mates seemed to add votes. In fact, only five candidates—Newt Gingrich and Elizabeth Warren in the Morning Consult poll; Marco Rubio, Bernie Sanders, and Warren in the Monmouth poll—won more of the respondents' votes than they lost, and only Sanders posed a significant electoral advantage (39 percent more likely, to 20 percent less likely).

As it pertains to voters' perceptions of running mate effects, this evidence is mixed. In the affirmative, a nontrivial proportion of voters—one out of six or seven, on average, and two out of five in the most exceptional case—indicated that the choice of a running mate might positively influence their vote. While these respondents constituted a distinct minority, in a close election their votes could prove decisive.

Yet this evidence also warrants skepticism. Many survey respondents, if not a clear majority (depending on the response options provided), reported being no more or less likely to vote for a presidential ticket based upon vice presidential selection. And those who were affected usually canceled out each other's votes or represented an electoral disadvantage. Indeed, eighteen of the twenty-three running mate selections tested in these polls yielded no net advantage, or yielded a net disadvantage.

Furthermore, it is quite unclear that respondents who report being more (or less) likely to vote for a presidential ticket based on vice presidential selection are signaling an actual *change* in vote intentions. In most cases, these respondents probably plan to, or eventually will, vote for the same ticket regardless, as a function of their partisanship and other electoral "fundamentals" (see Sides and Vavreck 2013). If so, then claiming to be more (or less) likely to vote for a presidential ticket based on a hypothetical vice presidential selection probably serves more as a means of expressing support for (or opposition to) the running mate, as a political figure, than a valid indicator of actual changes in vote choice.

How Will You Vote Now That . . . Is on the Ticket?

Polls frequently include similar questions about the running mate's impact on vote intentions after an official selection has been made and throughout the ensuing campaign. For instance, immediately after Donald Trump selected Mike Pence as his running mate in July 2016, Monmouth University asked a national sample of registered voters: "Does Donald Trump picking Indiana Governor Mike Pence as his running mate make you more likely or less likely to support the Republican ticket, or does this have no impact on your vote either way?"[17] Responses to this question mirror those from other polls described earlier in this chapter: 76 percent of respondents reported that Pence's selection had "No impact" on their vote, while 11 percent reported being "More likely" to vote for Trump and 10 percent "Less likely." Again, the vast majority of respondents were unaffected by Pence's selection, while the remainder essentially canceled each other out.

Party affiliation clearly influenced these responses. Twenty percent of Republicans said Pence's selection made them more likely to vote for Trump, and only 5 percent said less likely. But Democrats exhibited the opposite pattern—19 percent said Pence's selection made them less likely to vote for Trump, and only 4 percent said more likely. Independents split nearly evenly, with 12 percent more likely to vote for Trump and 8 percent less likely to do so. Given many Republicans' and Democrats' dissatisfaction with that year's presidential nominees, and Pence's conservative reputation, these percentages may reflect actual changes in vote intention among members of both party's bases. But it is also possible, if not more likely, that most of these reported changes in vote intention really were partisan expressions of support for or opposition to Pence, and that the partisans who believed they were "coming home" to the party ticket as a result of Pence's selection eventually would have done so for other reasons, anyway (see Sides and Vavreck 2013, 155–161).

Perhaps the most important takeaway from these results is that three-quarters of respondents generally, as well as within each partisan category, said Pence's selection had no effect on their vote. Recall from the evidence presented earlier that, in May 2016, approximately 80 percent of respondents in a national sample said that the selection of a running mate would be "Very important" or "Important" in determining their vote for president. Yet, when Trump selected his running mate, nearly the same percentage said that it made no difference!

Lest one assume that Pence's selection was exceptionally ineffective at changing voters' minds—perhaps because Pence was relatively unknown at the national level, or because attitudes toward Trump's candidacy were fixed by July 2016—consider voters' reactions to Tim Kaine being selected as Hillary Clinton's running mate. A national CNN/Opinion Research Council (ORC) poll of registered voters, conducted immediately after Kaine's selection, asked: "Does having Tim Kaine as her running mate make you more likely to vote for Clinton in November, less likely, or will it not have much effect on your vote?"[18] The results were nearly identical: 78 percent, "Not much effect"; 13 percent, "More likely"; and 8 percent, "Less likely."[19]

Table 2.3 presents data from a series of *USA Today*/Gallup polls conducted in the immediate aftermath of the 2000–2016 vice presidential selections (see Saad 2016), in order to provide a summary of recent running mates' effects on intended vote choice. In each case, the survey asked respondents: "Does having [insert vice presidential candidate] as [his/her] running mate make you more likely to vote for [insert presidential candidate] in November, less likely or will it not have much effect on your vote?"

At least two-thirds of respondents in each poll said that the running mate would have "No effect" on their presidential vote. However, among respondents who reported a change in vote intention, there is consistent evidence of an electoral advantage. In each case, the running mate attracted more voters to the ticket than he or she repelled. John Edwards's selection in 2004 had the most positive impact, with 24 percent of voters saying this made them more likely to vote for the Democratic ticket, versus 7 percent who said they were less likely to do so. On average, almost twice as many respondents said that they were more likely to vote for a presidential ticket because of the newly announced running mate (16 percent) as said they were less likely to do so (9 percent). But, in many cases, these apparent advantages canceled out. For instance, Kaine netted a 3 percentage-point advantage for the Democratic ticket in 2016, according to the polling data, while Pence netted a 4 percentage-point advantage for the Republican ticket. The same was true in 2008 (Palin +7

Table 2.3. Effect of Running Mate on Intended Presidential Vote Immediately Following Selection, 2000–2016

Year	Presidential Candidate	Running Mate	Polling Date(s)	More Likely (%)	Less Likely (%)	No Effect (%)
2016	Hillary Clinton	Tim Kaine	July 23–July 24	12	9	77
2016	Donald Trump	Mike Pence	July 15–July 16	14	10	74
2012	Mitt Romney	Paul Ryan	August 12	17	13	68
2008	Barack Obama	Joe Biden	August 23	14	7	72
2008	John McCain	Sarah Palin	August 29	18	11	67
2004	John Kerry	John Edwards	July 6	24	7	66
2000	Al Gore	Joe Lieberman	August 7	16	4	76
2000	George W. Bush	Dick Cheney	July 24	14	10	72
Average			—	16.1	8.9	71.5

Source: Gallup News Service, "Tim Kaine VP Announcement and Republican Convention Reaction," July 25, 2016. Available at http://www.gallup.com /poll/193907/tim-kaine-matches-mike- pence-lackluster-initial-ratings.aspx (accessed January 10, 2020).

Note: All polling data included in this table come from nationally representative samples of registered voters.

Survey question: "Does having [insert name] as [his/her] running mate make you more likely to vote for [name of presidential candidate] in November, less likely or will it not have much effect on your vote?"

percent, Biden +7 percent). Only Joe Lieberman in 2000 (+12 percent) won significantly more initial support than his counterpart on the opposing ticket, Dick Cheney (+4 percent).

Who Is the Running Mate, Anyway?

At this point, we should pause to ask: Do voters know enough about the running mates, in the first place, to evaluate what effect, if any, they will have on vote choice? In other words, can we be sure that responses to survey questions about the running mate and his or her electoral significance actually reflect public *opinion*—or, for many respondents, do such questions merely elicit nonattitudes (see Asher 2017, chap. 4; Converse 1964)?

It is worth taking this concern seriously given that, for example, 30 percent of Americans could not identify Dick Cheney and Joe Biden as vice president of the United States during the George W. Bush and Barack Obama administrations, respectively (Gallup 2003; Romano 2011). It stands to reason that, in turn, an even higher percentage of Americans would not know who is *running* for vice president in any given election. Indeed, in a nationwide poll of adults, conducted just before the 2016 vice presidential debate, nearly half of all respondents, 46 percent, could not name Tim Kaine as the Democratic running mate, and 41 percent could not name Mike Pence as the Republican running mate.[20]

Many voters also do not know enough about the vice presidential candidates to have, or at least express, opinions of them. For instance, in another poll conducted just before the 2016 vice presidential debate, 57 percent of registered voters said that they "Haven't heard enough" about Kaine to rate him favorably or unfavorably, while 47 percent said the same for Pence.[21] Adding in "Undecided" and "Don't know/No answer" responses brings the percentage of respondents with no discernible opinion of the running mates to 69 percent and 58 percent, respectively.[22]

Historically speaking, it is typical for the majority of voters to express no opinion, one way or the other, about the running mate immediately following his or her selection. To illustrate this point, in table 2.4 we present evidence from the same set of Gallup polls used in table 2.3 to evaluate postselection changes in vote intention (see Saad 2016). These polls also asked respondents: "Do you have a favorable or unfavorable opinion of [the running mate], or

Table 2.4. Running Mates' Favorability Ratings Immediately Following Selection, 2000–2016

Year	Running Mate	Polling Date(s)	Favorable (%)	Unfavorable (%)	Never Heard Of (%)	No Opinion (%)
2016	Tim Kaine	July 23–July 24	24	15	41	20
2016	Mike Pence	July 15–July 16	21	18	44	18
2012	Paul Ryan	August 12	27	21	32	21
2008	Joe Biden	August 23	34	15	23	28
2008	Sarah Palin	August 29	22	7	51	20
2004	John Edwards	July 6	54	16	12	18
2000	Joe Lieberman	August 7	37	10	24	29
2000	Dick Cheney	July 24	51	11	7	31
Average		—	33.8	14.1	29.3	23.1

Source: Gallup News Service, "Tim Kaine VP Announcement and Republican Convention Reaction," July 25, 2016. Available at http://www.gallup.com /poll/193907/tim-kaine-matches-mike-pence-lackluster-initial-ratings.aspx (accessed January 10, 2020).

Survey question: "Do you have a favorable or unfavorable opinion about [the running mate], or have you never heard of [him/her]?"

have you never heard of [him/her]?" In all but two cases—Dick Cheney in 2000, and John Edwards in 2004—the majority of respondents either had no opinion, or else had not heard of the vice presidential candidate. On average, the majority of respondents (52.4 percent) answered either "No opinion" (23.1 percent) or "Never heard of" (29.3 percent).

This evidence suggests that we should be cautious when evaluating public opinion data on vice presidential candidacies. This is not just because many, and in some cases a majority of, respondents in various polls have no clear opinion of the running mates or do not know their names. It is also, and perhaps most significantly, because many of the same respondents apparently express substantive opinions of the running mate elsewhere in these polls, despite being logically disqualified from doing so.

Consider the Gallup poll conducted immediately after Tim Kaine's selection in July 2016 (see Saad 2016). When asked for their opinion of Kaine, 41 percent of respondents said that they had never heard of him, and 20 percent said that they had no opinion of him—for a total of 61 percent. This means that only 39 percent of respondents *did* have an opinion of Kaine, one way or another. Yet, when asked other questions about Kaine's vice presidential candidacy, a much higher percentage of respondents offered substantive opinions. For instance, when asked to rate Clinton's choice of Kaine as a running mate, only 15 percent of respondents admitted having "No opinion" while the remaining 85 percent did state an opinion—whether that was "Excellent" (13 percent), "Pretty good" (22 percent), "Only fair" (30 percent), or "Poor" (49 percent). Also, when asked whether Kaine was qualified to serve as president, if needed, 47 percent of respondents declared him qualified, versus 32 percent unqualified. Only 21 percent of respondents said that they had no opinion on Kaine's qualifications—despite the fact that twice as many *of the same respondents* said they had never heard of him (not to mention the 20 percent that had no opinion of him).

How could 85 percent of respondents have an opinion as to whether Kaine was a good choice for running mate, or 79 percent have an opinion on Kaine's qualifications to serve in the White House, if only 39 percent of the same respondents recognized and had an opinion of him to begin with? For that matter, what does it mean when 77 percent of these respondents say that Kaine's selection will have "No effect" on their presidential vote? Should consumers of public opinion read this as evidence of Kaine's ineffectiveness as a candidate? Or is this figure mostly attributable to voters' unfamiliarity with Kaine?

Whatever the right interpretation may be in any particular case, our take-away point is the same: voters' relative unfamiliarity with vice presidential candidates makes public polling about them, and their role in the campaign, inherently problematic. That is to say, when consuming public opinion data bearing on running mate effects, or perceptions thereof, one should expect that the percentages do not precisely reflect an actual and predictively meaningful *public opinion*. This is not to say that any measurement of opinion on the vice presidential candidate is meaningless. Rather, it is to say that one should be skeptical of any public opinion data showing large running mate effects. Whatever media coverage these data may attract, their plausibility is limited by a rather high level of public ignorance of, or indifference to, running mates, generally.

If You Don't Mention Running Mates, Will Voters Bring Them Up?

Given the opportunity to explain their presidential vote, *in their own words*, how many voters would even mention the vice presidential candidates? This is a fitting question with which to conclude our inquiry into perceptions of running mate effects, in general, and it follows directly from the analysis that precedes it. Indeed, our concern with respect to nonattitudes is that merely asking whether vice presidential candidates have an effect on voting might prompt many survey respondents for whom this is not the case to answer in the affirmative—perhaps because they infer that this factor should influence their vote, or must influence others' votes, if professional pollsters working under obvious time and space constraints have chosen to mention it in their survey. To address this concern, and to answer the question just posed, requires somehow measuring respondents' perceptions of running mate effects *without asking them about running mates*. Perhaps the best way of doing so is to analyze open-ended responses to questions about the presidential election, in order to see how many respondents reference the vice presidential candidates without any prompting. But such data are hard to come by; nearly all campaign polls use closed-ended responses because they are easier to code and their results are more intuitive to summarize (see Bradburn, Sudman, and Wansink 2004, chap. 5).

Fortunately, there is a solution—and, for political scientists, it comes from an unsurprising source: the American National Election Studies. The ANES

Cumulative File includes data from a series of open-ended questions asking respondents to list up to five things that they liked, as well as disliked, about the major parties' presidential nominees.[23] Specifically, respondents were asked: "Is there anything in particular about [the Democratic presidential candidate] that might make you want to vote for him?" If the respondent answered "Yes," then he or she was asked: "What was that?" And if the respondent provided a substantive response to the follow-up question, then he or she was asked: "Anything else [that you liked about this candidate]?" This continued until the respondent described five things that he or she liked about the Democratic presidential candidate, or it ended before that point if the respondent answered "No." Then, the same process was applied to ascertaining the respondent's *dislikes* about the Democratic candidate, starting with the question: "Is there anything in particular about [the Democratic presidential candidate] that might make you want to vote against him?" Finally, the entire process was repeated in reference to the Republican presidential candidate.

The Cumulative File combines responses from the 1972–2004 ANES into variables representing Democratic candidate "likes" (VCF0476a–VCF0480a) and "dislikes" (VCF0482a–VCF0486a), as well as Republican candidate "likes" (VCF0488a–VCF0492a) and "dislikes" (VCF0494a–VCF0498a).[24] Then, in the codebook's appendix, the ANES provides master codes for each variable, encompassing all valid responses.[25] Most important, for our purposes, several of the master codes directly pertain to vice presidential candidates, including: "Reference to vice-presidential candidate" (55); "Reference to the Eagleton affair [in 1972]; reference to physical or mental health of vice-presidential incumbent/candidate; emotional stability/state of V-P incumbent/candidate" (541); "Reference to vice-presidential incumbent/candidate, running mate" (542); "Mondale's selection of a woman for vice-president [in 1984]; reference to age/gender/race (ethnicity/ethnic background) of V-P incumbent/candidate" (543); "Mention of issues that V-P incumbent/candidate is identified with or has taken a leading role in promoting: 1992–Gore's position on environment" (544); "Party selection of a woman for vice-president [in 1984]" (729); and several codes naming a particular vice presidential candidate.[26]

We use these codes to characterize ANES respondents' perceptions of running mate effects. Specifically, for each presidential candidacy, we begin by calculating the total number of "(dis)like" responses that qualified for one of the vice presidential master codes just listed. Then we divide this number by the total number of respondents who provided a "(dis)like" response for

Democratic Candidates

Republican Candidates

% Likes   % Dislikes

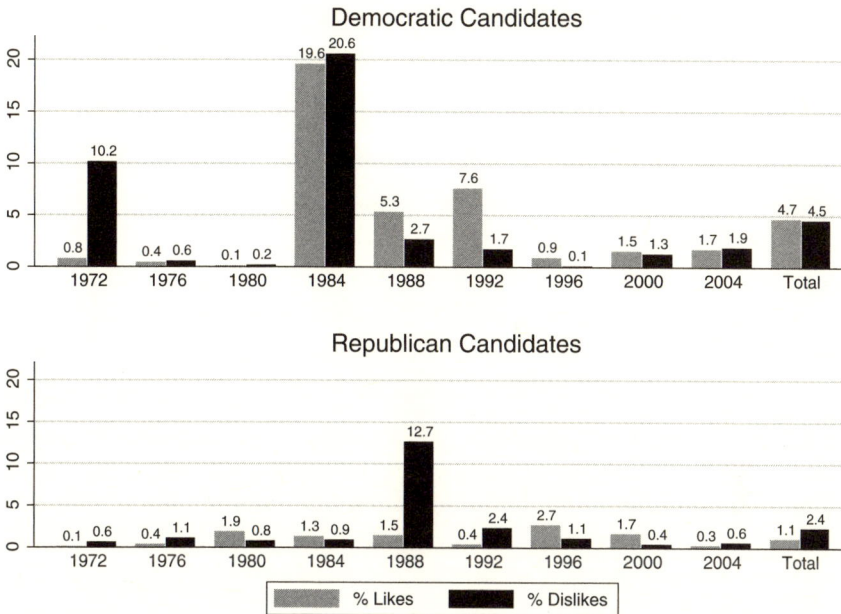

Figure 2.1. Referencing the vice presidential candidate to explain voting for (like) or against (dislike) the presidential candidate, 1972–2004 ANES. Survey question: "Is there anything in particular about [DEMOCRATIC/REPUBLICAN PRESIDENTIAL CANDIDATE] that might make you want to vote [for/against] him? What was that? Anything else [that you dis/liked about this candidate]?" (Up to five responses allowed).
Source: ANES Time Series Cumulative File (1948–2012). Available at https://election studies.org/data-center/anes-time-series-cumulative-data-file (accessed January 2, 2018).

the presidential candidate in question.[27] In other words, we calculate the proportion of respondents who, when asked what about a particular presidential candidate made them want to vote for (against) him, responded by invoking the running mate.

Figure 2.1 summarizes how often ANES respondents referenced vice presidential candidates when explaining their presidential vote, as a percentage of valid responses, for each presidential candidacy. The answer, in short: not very often. This is the case for Republican candidacies, especially: only 321 out of more than 18,000 valid like or dislike responses (1.8 percent) referenced the running mate. Dan Quayle, for one, did come up fairly often in 1988—more so as a reason for disliking (12.7 percent) rather than liking (1.5 percent)

the Republican presidential candidate, George H. W. Bush. In every other instance, fewer than 3 percent of like or dislike responses cited the Republican
running mate—and, except for Quayle in 1992 (dislikes) and Jack Kemp in
1996 (likes), fewer than 2 percent did so.

The Democratic running mates came up quite a bit more often as reasons
to vote for (4.7 percent) or against (4.5 percent) their party ticket, and in 822
out of 17,856 valid responses (4.6 percent), overall. Geraldine Ferraro's historic
1984 candidacy, when she became the first woman running mate on a major
party ticket, attracted the most references by far, at 20.1 percent (446 out of
2,217). Interestingly, respondents referenced her slightly more often as a reason to vote against Walter Mondale (20.6 percent), rather than for him (19.6
percent). Thomas Eagleton's short-lived 1972 candidacy, and his subsequent
replacement as running mate by Sargent Shriver, represents the other outlier
in these data; 10.2 percent of respondents referenced one or both of them as a
reason to vote against George McGovern, and only 0.8 percent as a reason to
vote for McGovern. Al Gore, in 1992, earned the most favorable references, on
balance, with 7.6 percent citing him as a reason to vote for, versus 1.7 percent
against, Bill Clinton. But Gore was much less salient four years later, attracting
0.9 percent and 0.1 percent of these references, respectively.

If the Democratic running mates' performance seems impressive, in comparison to that of their Republican counterparts, really it is not. Consider this
fact: 95 percent of the respondents who gave a valid response as to why they
were voting for or against any of the Democratic presidential candidates, from
1972 to 2004, *did not* mention their running mate. Even in Geraldine Ferraro's
case, more than 80 percent of these respondents explained their vote for or
against Walter Mondale without referencing her candidacy. And, of course,
the numbers are much greater for Republicans, although for reasons that are
not quite clear (but see Lewis-Beck and Rice 1983, 554). Fewer than two out of
every one hundred respondents included in this analysis cited the Republican
running mate as influencing their vote.

If voters really do consider vice presidential selection to be an important
factor in determining their vote—as more than 80 percent of survey respondents regularly report to be the case—then we should expect the running mate
to come up much more often when voters are given the opportunity to freely
express their reasons for supporting or opposing a presidential candidate.
Instead, our analysis of open-ended responses in the 1972–2004 ANES indicates that voters rarely think of the running mate's influence without being

prompted to do so. This evidence supports the interpretation that public opinion polls showing large running mate effects probably reflect nonattitudes, to a considerable degree, and should be treated with a great deal of skepticism.

Summary

The preceding analyses provide mixed evidence that Americans, in general, perceive vice presidential candidates to be influential in determining presidential vote choice. Approximately 80 percent of survey respondents say that vice presidential selection is important, to some degree, in determining their vote. But, in relative terms, respondents rate nearly all other electoral influences presented to them as more important. Many respondents also report being more or less likely to vote for a given presidential candidate based on his or her hypothetical or actual selection of a running mate. However, these respondents often—if not typically—cancel each other out, and in many cases they probably are not familiar enough with the subject to make such a judgment accurately. Further complicating this analysis is the fact that most survey measures of perceived running mate effects are framed prospectively. According to one of the rare retrospective measures available, which captures actual voting behavior, nine out of ten Americans cannot recall *ever* changing their vote for president based on positive or negative evaluations of the vice presidential candidate. Finally, when asked to explain why they would vote for or against a presidential candidate in that year's election, survey respondents very rarely invoke the running mate.

Perhaps the most appropriate conclusion to draw from our analysis is this: Americans generally affirm the importance of vice presidential selection, in abstract terms; however, the running mate's perceived influence all but disappears in the context of an actual voting decision, when the choice between presidential candidates and among the full spectrum of competing electoral considerations becomes concrete.

VOTERS' CRITERIA FOR VICE PRESIDENTIAL SELECTION

In this section, we examine voters' perceptions of the nature of running mate effects. In other words, we ask: If voters think that running mates matter, then what would it take to win their vote? Is there a specific set of criteria by which Americans evaluate vice presidential candidates? Or do their selection criteria vary depending on the presidential candidates' attributes, thus signaling a preference for "balanced" presidential tickets?

For this analysis, we identified several polls in which respondents were asked to rate the importance of various attributes that a vice presidential candidate might possess. We begin by analyzing the relative importance of such attributes in a generic context, to establish a baseline for understanding voters' perceptions of the relevant criteria for evaluating running mates. Then, to understand how ticket-balancing concerns affect voters' evaluative criteria, we analyze the relationship between a presidential candidate's attributes and the perceived importance of the attributes associated with his or her running mate.

In General, What Do You Look For in a Running Mate?

A June 2008 Associated Press–Yahoo! poll asked a national sample of registered voters what characteristics they valued in a vice presidential candidate— generally speaking, and not in reference to any particular selection process.[28] Specifically, it instructed: "Thinking about the qualities that a candidate for vice-president might have, please tell us whether each of the following qualities would make a stronger or weaker candidate." The poll presented respondents with six qualities, in randomized order, and asked them to state whether each quality makes the running mate "Much weaker," "Somewhat weaker," "Somewhat stronger," or "Much stronger," or whether it "Would make no difference." Three qualities pertained to the running mate's demographic attributes, including "Being a woman," "Being black," and "Being Hispanic." The other three qualities pertained to attributes of the running mate's professional experience, including "Having experience in Washington," "Having served in the military," and "Having experience in the business world." Table 2.5 presents a summary of responses for each criterion.

It is clear from this evidence that voters perceive experience to be more relevant than demographics when evaluating vice presidential candidates. Indeed, only about one-quarter of respondents said that it made no difference whether a running mate had federal governing experience (23 percent) or business experience (27 percent), and two out of five respondents said the

Table 2.5. Effect of Running Mate's Attributes on Perceived Strength of Presidential Candidacy

Running Mate's Attribute	No Difference	Much Weaker	Somewhat Weaker	Somewhat Stronger	Much Stronger	Refused/ NA
Being a woman	69%	5%	11%	10%	5%	1%
Being black	76%	7%	10%	5%	1%	1%
Being Hispanic	71%	9%	13%	5%	1%	1%
Having experience in Washington	23%	1%	4%	47%	25%	1%
Having served in the military	39%	1%	2%	41%	17%	1%
Having experience in the business world	27%	1%	2%	50%	19%	1%

Source: Associated Press–Yahoo! poll of US registered voters, June 13–23, 2008 (*n* = 1,507; margin of error ±2.5 percent). Available at http://surveys.ap.org/data/KnowledgeNetworks/AP_Election _Wave5_Topline_070208%20wrd%20codes.pdf (accessed January 10, 2020).

Question: "Thinking about the qualities that a candidate for vice-president might have, please tell us whether each of the following qualities would make a stronger or weaker candidate." Each quality was presented to respondents in randomized order.

same about military experience (39 percent). But at least two-thirds of respondents said that it made no difference whether the running mate was a woman (69 percent) or was black (76 percent) or Hispanic (71 percent).

Voters clearly prefer an experienced running mate. Majorities of respondents said that federal governing experience (72 percent), business experience (69 percent), and military experience (58 percent) made for a somewhat stronger or much stronger vice presidential candidate, while almost no respondents perceived these to be sources of weakness. On the other hand, very few respondents saw being black (6 percent) or Hispanic (6 percent) as a strength for vice presidential candidates, while a modest share of them (15 percent) said the same of being a woman. More often, respondents actually perceived that these attributes weakened a vice presidential candidacy.

Of course, it is not clear from the question wording—and perhaps intentionally so—whether respondents were making these judgments in reference to each attribute's effect on *their* vote, individually, or its presumed effect on the electorate as a whole. Much clearer is the conclusion to be drawn from this pattern of results: voters generally perceive experience to be an essential criterion when evaluating vice presidential candidates, whereas demographic considerations largely are irrelevant.

In This Election, What Are You Looking For in a Running Mate?

The preceding evidence, valuable as it may be, suffers from two important limitations. First, the AP/Yahoo! poll asks about vice presidential selection only in generic terms, but actual selections do not take place in a vacuum. Rather, specific presidential candidates make these selections, and the attributes associated with a given presidential candidate might influence which attributes voters perceive to be desirable for his or her running mate. For instance, voters might find it particularly reassuring for a relatively inexperienced presidential candidate (e.g., Donald Trump in 2016; Barack Obama in 2008) to select a more experienced running mate. Conversely, they might prefer to see an older, more experienced presidential candidate (e.g., Hillary Clinton in 2016; John McCain in 2008) select a young, "fresh face" for the vice presidency. In other words, it might be the case that what voters really want is a "balanced ticket." Thus, when evaluating voters' perceptions of relevant vice presidential selection criteria, it is better to use polling data that pertain to a specific presidential campaign, whenever possible.

Second, the AP/Yahoo! poll tests only two categories of vice presidential attributes: experience and demographics. This omits the two other attribute categories that are most associated with ticket balancing: geography and ideology. Indeed, previous analyses of vice presidential selection typically measure ticket balancing in terms of geography, demography, ideology, and governing experience. For instance, Sigelman and Wahlbeck (1997), as well as Hiller and Kriner (2008), model vice presidential selection as a function of geography ("Regional Balance" and "Size of State"); demography ("Gender/Race/Ethnic Balance," "Religious Balance," "Age Balance"); ideology ("Ideological Balance"); and governing experience ("Insider-Outsider Experience Balance").[29] Likewise, Goldstein (2016) divides his analysis of ticket balancing into categories including "Geographic Balance," "Demographic Balance" (e.g., gender, race, ethnicity), "Ideological Balance," and "Type of Government Experience," as well as two essentially demographic categories—"Religion" and "Age"—and a "Cross-Party Balance" category closely related to ideological balancing. Finally, Baumgartner with Crumblin (2015, 103–109) evaluate ticket balancing in the modern era based on "Region," "Diversity" (e.g., gender, race, ethnicity, religion), "Ideology," and "Experience," as well as a "Personal/Other" category partly based on demographic balancing by age. Therefore, it is more consistent with the literature on vice presidential selection to use polls that incorporate all four major attribute categories.

A Morning Consult poll of registered voters, conducted in April–May 2016, meets both of the standards just described.[30] First, it asked about the likely Democratic (Hillary Clinton) and Republican (Donald Trump) presidential nominees' vice presidential selections. Second, this poll asked about the importance of ten attributes that might be associated with Clinton's or Trump's running mate, at least one of which belongs to each of the four major ticket-balancing categories, including geography ("From a swing state"); demography ("A woman"; "A man"; "A minority"); ideology ("A moderate"; "A liberal," for Clinton; "A conservative," for Trump); and experience ("A current or previously elected official"; "From outside Washington, DC"; "A Washington insider"; "From a business background").[31]

Table 2.6 summarizes the relevant responses, first for Clinton's running mate (top) and then for Trump's running mate (bottom). Broadly speaking, these results reinforce our conclusion from the previous analysis that voters perceive experience to be particularly important, and demographics particularly unimportant, when evaluating vice presidential candidates. For Clinton and Trump, "From a business background" and "A current or previous elected official" rank among the two attributes most often cited as "Very important," as well as (combined) "Very important" or "Somewhat important." In fact, the top five items in terms of combined importance include three of the four experience attributes for Clinton and all four for Trump. Meanwhile, for each candidate, the lowest-ranked attribute is a demographic one ("A woman" for Clinton, and "A man" for Trump), and none of the three demographic attributes rank in their top five. The geographic attribute does not rank highly either, sixth for Clinton and ninth for Trump. At least one of the ideology attributes ("A moderate"), however, ranks in the top three for both candidates.

These results also suggest that voters prefer a balanced ticket. Indeed, many of the attributes that respondents perceived to be most important for the running mate to have were ones that the presidential candidate lacked. For Trump, whose liabilities included being politically inexperienced and in some respects ideologically extreme, respondents found it most important—in terms of combined "Very important" and "Somewhat important" responses—for him to select a running mate who was "A current or previously elected official" (46

Table 2.6. Perceived Importance of Running Mate Attributes, 2016

Attribute	Not at All Important	Not Too Important	Somewhat Important	Very Important	Don't Know/ No Opinion
	CLINTON'S RUNNING MATE				
A woman	28%	30%	13%	10%	19%
A man	24%	27%	17%	13%	19%
A minority	22%	29%	18%	11%	20%
A moderate	14%	23%	27%	15%	20%
A liberal	18%	23%	21%	17%	21%
From a swing state	18%	27%	19%	11%	25%
From outside Washington, DC	16%	25%	22%	16%	21%
A Washington insider	25%	27%	16%	11%	21%
From a business background	12%	20%	29%	21%	18%
A current or previous elected official	16%	23%	26%	17%	19%
	TRUMP'S RUNNING MATE				
A woman	24%	27%	17%	12%	20%
A man	25%	28%	14%	13%	20%
A minority	23%	25%	18%	14%	20%
A moderate	16%	21%	25%	18%	21%
A conservative	27%	23%	15%	14%	22%
From a swing state	19%	27%	17%	12%	24%
From outside Washington, DC	20%	25%	19%	16%	20%
A Washington insider	23%	23%	20%	14%	21%
From a business background	18%	20%	23%	20%	19%
A current or previous elected official	16%	19%	26%	20%	19%

Source: Morning Consult poll of US registered voters, April 29–May 2, 2016 ($n = 3,940$; margin of error +/−2 percent). Available at https://morningconsultintelligence.com/media/mc/160409_crosstabs_TOPICALS_v4_KD_stacked.pdf (accessed January 2, 2018).

Question: "If [Hillary Clinton/Donald Trump] is selected as the [Democratic/Republican] nominee for President, how important is it for [her/his] Vice Presidential running mate to be [insert attribute]."

percent), and next to select "A moderate" (43 percent). For Clinton, whose liabilities included being a Washington insider and either being too moderate (for liberals) or too liberal (for conservatives), respondents found it most important for her to select a running mate "From a business background" (50 percent). Ideological attributes also ranked highly, at third and fourth, but respondents were conflicted on whether it was more important for Clinton to select "A moderate" (42 percent) or "A liberal" (38 percent).

Conversely, many of the attributes that respondents perceived to be least important for the running mate to have were ones already associated with the presidential candidate. For instance, the lowest-ranked attribute for Clinton's running mate was being "A woman" (23 percent) and for Trump's running mate it was being "A man" (27 percent). Also, for Clinton, the second-least important attribute was being "A Washington insider" (27 percent). But this pattern does not always hold. In some cases respondents preferred that the candidate double down on his or her most distinctive characteristics. For instance, the second most important attribute for Trump's running mate was coming "From a business background" (43 percent), and for Clinton's running mate it was being "A current or previously elected official" (43 percent). Even so, the overall pattern of results quite clearly indicates that voters prefer running mates who balance the ticket, particularly in terms of experience.

Additional evidence helps to validate our conclusion that voters generally prefer balanced tickets. The first such evidence comes from a national poll of registered voters, conducted by NBC and the *Wall Street Journal* in July 2008.[32] This poll used a split-sample design to ask each respondent about either Barack Obama's or John McCain's impending vice presidential selection. Specifically, it included the following item: "I'm going to read you some qualities that a candidate for vice president might have. Of these qualities, which one or two do you think it is most important for [Barack Obama's/John McCain's] vice presidential choice to have?" Respondents selected among six qualities, including "Has experience in the business world," "Has served as a member of Congress," "Has served as governor of a state," "Is an expert in military or foreign affairs," "Is an expert on the economy," or "Is [conservative/liberal] on social issues."

In both cases, respondents most often selected a quality associated with the presidential candidate's perceived deficiencies. For Obama's running mate, 50 percent said it was important that he select someone with expertise in military or foreign affairs. For McCain's running mate, 60 percent said it was important that he select an expert on the economy. It is clear that these responses reflect a preference for ticket balancing, since in the same poll respondents were asked to identify their one or two greatest concerns about Obama and McCain. For Obama, respondents' greatest concerns pertained to inexperience and foreign affairs: 33 percent selected "He is too inexperienced and is not ready to be president," and 20 percent selected "He would not be strong and forceful enough in dealing with America's enemies." For McCain, two of the respondents' three greatest concerns pertained to economic issues, either directly or indirectly: 41 percent selected "It seems likely that he would continue George W. Bush's policies," and 22 percent selected "His economic policies would only benefit the wealthy."

Next, consider the results from a June 2016 poll conducted by Suffolk University and *USA Today*.[33] This poll asked a national sample of Republican and Democratic primary voters, respectively, whether Trump should choose a running mate who balanced him in terms of experience and whether Clinton should choose a running mate who balanced her in terms of ideology. Specifically, it asked Republicans: "Should Donald Trump choose a running mate with extensive experience in Washington or should he choose another 'outsider' like himself to shake up Washington?" And it asked Democrats: "Should Hillary Clinton choose a running mate with the sort of progressive politics of Bernie Sanders or Elizabeth Warren? Or should she choose someone with more centrist views?" In both cases, respondents decisively favored a balanced ticket. For Trump's running mate, 61 percent of respondents said "He should choose someone with Washington experience," while only 20 percent said "He should choose another outsider to shake things up," and 17 percent were undecided. For Clinton's running mate, 54 percent said "She should choose a progressive VP," while only 26 percent said "She should choose someone with more centrist views," and 17 percent were undecided.[34]

Finally, a June 2016 CNN/ORC poll of registered Republican voters, nationwide, asked: "What type of candidate would you most like to see Donald Trump select as his vice presidential candidate?"[35] The response options included: "Someone with experience in politics," "Someone with military experience," "Someone with experience in the business world," or "Doesn't matter." Nearly all of the respondents said that Trump should pick a running mate with military (47 percent) or political (43 percent) experience, both of which Trump lacked. Only 8 percent of respondents said that Trump should pick someone, like himself, with business experience.[36] These results reinforce the conclusion that voters prefer running mates who balance the ticket by complementing, rather than duplicating, the presidential candidate's attributes.

Why Is Experience So Important?

Our analysis, to this point, has emphasized the centrality of experience as a criterion by which voters evaluate vice presidential candidates. Indeed, attributes of the running mate's experience consistently rate as more important than geographic, demographic, or ideological attributes. And voters seem to favor running mates who balance the presidential candidate in terms of certain types of experience, such as governing versus business experience or experience inside versus outside the federal government.

So we must ask: *Why* is the running mate's experience so important to voters? The answer, we suggest, is that most voters have a basic grasp of, and appreciation for, the institutional role of the vice president. Most important, this role includes serving as a principal adviser to the president and being ready to succeed to the presidency, if necessary (see this book's introduction). Both responsibilities help to explain why it would matter to voters that, say, Barack Obama select a running mate with foreign policy experience, or that Donald Trump select a running mate with governing experience. That is to say, voters seem to intuit that, if elected, the vice president will be involved in the operations of government and in some cases he or she will be called upon to provide expertise or assistance in areas where the president is deficient. In that sense, this evidence goes to show that the American public does not consider the vice presidency to be a ridiculous or irrelevant institution after all. If this were the case, then voters would not care whether running mates were qualified for office in the first place; the very notion would not even make sense.

Yet the American public clearly expects vice presidential candidates to be qualified for office, and it cares about the nature of those qualifications. In addition to the evidence regarding experience, described in the previous section, consider the results of an August 2012 CNN/ORC poll that explicitly measured the importance of vice presidential qualifications among a national sample of Republican adults.[37] Specifically, it included the following item: "Now I'm going to read you a few phrases that might describe the person who Mitt Romney will choose as his vice presidential running mate. For each one, please tell me whether it would be very important to you, somewhat important to you, not very important to you, or not important at all for Romney to pick a running mate who has that quality." The poll then presented respondents with five qualities, including "Someone who is qualified to be president if necessary," "Someone who agrees with you on major issues," "Someone who believes that abortion should be illegal," "Someone who you currently know a lot about," and "Someone who comes from your state or the part of the country where you live."

Nearly every respondent (99 percent) said that it was important for the running mate to be qualified to serve as president, including 88 percent who answered "Very important" and 11 percent who answered "Somewhat important." Only 1 percent of respondents answered "Not important at all." Of course, this ranked first among the qualities presented to respondents. It was followed by agreement on issues (63 percent, "Very important"; 23 percent, "Somewhat important"); abortion policy (42 percent and 23 percent); familiarity with the candidate (29 percent and 37 percent); and geographic affiliation (12 percent and 18 percent). Evidently, each quality was important to some respondents. But only qualifications were *essential*.

CONCLUSION

The perception of running mate effects is pervasive—indeed, normative—among voters, according to our analysis of public polling data from 2000 to 2016. For example, more than 80 percent of survey respondents typically say that vice presidential selection is an important factor in determining their vote. But, on closer inspection, voters betray a sense of internal conflict that, we argue, shapes attitudes toward the vice presidency and vice presidential candidates more generally (see the introduction). Most notably, voters' perceptions of running mate effects seem to weaken when moving from abstract toward actual electoral decisions. For example, vice presidential selection is quite unimportant when measured in relation to other electoral influences; approximately 90 percent of survey respondents cannot recall ever changing their presidential vote on account of the vice presidential candidate; and 95 percent of ANES respondents, on average, do not mention the choice of a running mate when asked to explain, in open-ended fashion, why they like or dislike a given presidential candidate. We conclude that public perceptions of running mate effects are real, and potentially powerful, but also that they exist in tension with other considerations that render many, if not most, voters conflicted on the matter.

And what, specifically, do voters look for in a running mate? Which attributes do they think that a presidential candidate should prioritize when making his or her selection? Our analysis indicates that voters *do* use particular criteria when evaluating vice presidential candidates—but not fixed ones. Rather, voters adjust their criteria in relation to the presidential candidate's perceived deficiencies. In particular, they prefer running mates who "balance the ticket" in terms of professional experience (e.g., government, military, business). We note that this preference would make little sense if voters reject the vice presidency as patently ridiculous or irrelevant to governance. Instead, voters seem to perceive their interest in electing a vice president who can serve as an effective partner in government. Thus, voters' only fixed criterion for choosing a running mate may be that he or she is qualified to serve in office, if elected.

When it comes to evaluating perceptions of running mate effects, then, we can see significant points of commonality among presidential candidates (chapter 1) and voters (this chapter)—respectively, the individuals who are responsible for selecting and electing vice presidential candidates. Both sets of actors generally regard vice presidential selection as important, and potentially influential in determining the election's outcome. Moreover, both describe governing qualifications as the most important—if not the only truly essential—criterion for vice presidential selection, while also acknowledging the strategic importance of ticket balancing and adapting their criteria to the context of a particular candidacy. Yet presidential candidates and voters, alike, generally resist the notion that their decisions are based on, or even significantly influenced by, the running mate's electoral implications. That is to say, presidential candidates typically allow that the running mate *can* influence the election's outcome, but they cite other factors to explain their vice presidential selections. In similar fashion, voters typically allow that the running mate *can* be an important electoral consideration, but they cite other factors to explain their vote.

In short, presidential candidates' and voters' perceptions of running mate effects are best described as conflicted. Running mates *can* matter, they seem to be saying—but how often, by how much, or under what circumstances running mates actually influence vote choice is quite unclear. Indeed, it is questionable whether the running mate's potential for electoral influence is matched by any clear, systematic evidence of practical significance.

The political science literature provides only limited evidence by which to evaluate these perceptions of running mate effects, and to conclusively answer the question: Do running mates matter? Our objective in part II of this book is to provide such answers, based on a comprehensive analysis of the relevant empirical data. In particular, we examine three aspects of the running mate's (potential) electoral influence: direct effects on voters, generally (chapter 3), direct effects on targeted groups of voters (chapter 4), and indirect effects on voters' perceptions of the presidential candidates and subsequently on vote choice (chapter 5). We find that running mates do matter—but not necessarily in the way that many people, including presidential candidates and voters, might expect.

PART II
Evidence of Running Mate Effects

In part I, we establish that perceptions of running mate effects are prevalent among presidential candidates and voters. In part II, we ask whether these perceptions match reality. In other words, *do* running mates influence presidential voting? And, if so, how? Do voters, in general, factor in their evaluation of the *vice* presidential candidate when casting a vote for president? Or do running mates influence voting only among individuals with whom they share a salient social or political identity? Or, finally, do running mates *indirectly* influence vote choice, by shaping voters' perceptions of the presidential candidates who selected them?

Part II consists of three chapters, each of which separately analyzes a distinct (but not mutually exclusive) framework for understanding running mate effects—what we call "direct effects," "targeted effects," and "indirect effects." We present such a comprehensive analysis for two reasons. First, the existing literature on running mate effects does not rely on just one of these frameworks; indeed, it encompasses all three (albeit to widely varying degrees). Nor do we regard any of these frameworks as implausible—even if we do find indirect effects to be particularly important, for reasons that we address in chapter 5. By employing each of these frameworks, we maximize our ability to identify, and to properly characterize the nature of, vice presidential candidates' influence on presidential voting. Second, this method of analysis allows us to compare each framework's relative strengths and weaknesses. In other words, we can determine which one best, or most consistently, explains running mate effects. Since no previous study has used all three frameworks to estimate these effects, our analysis represents a distinct and important contribution to the relevant literature.

Chapter 3 evaluates whether running mates directly influence presidential voting, among voters in general (direct effects). Specifically, in this chapter we estimate the independent effect of vice presidential candidate evaluations on vote choice. For example, in 2016, if a voter had an unfavorable view of Tim Kaine, did that, in and of itself, make him or her less likely to vote for Hillary Clinton?

Chapter 4 evaluates whether running mates directly influence presidential voting, among strategically important subsets of voters (targeted effects). Specifically, in this chapter we estimate *changes* in the effect of a given social or political group identity on vote choice, following the selection of a running mate who shares that identity. For example, in 2012, did Mitt Romney gain support among midwesterners, Catholics, and/or ideological conservatives after picking Paul Ryan—a member of each of these groups—as his running mate?

Finally, chapter 5 evaluates whether running mates exert an *indirect* effect on vote choice, among voters in general. Specifically, in this chapter we estimate the effects of vice presidential candidate evaluations—in terms of overall favorability and various personal or political attributes—on same-party presidential candidate evaluations, which, in turn, influence vote choice. For example, in 2008, did perceptions of Sarah Palin's readiness to be (vice) president change perceptions of John McCain's judgment? And did McCain win or lose votes as a result?

Each of these chapters examines the causal relationship between an independent variable (e.g., vice presidential candidate evaluations) and a dependent variable (e.g., presidential vote choice). Methodologically, this raises two important points about the analyses that follow. First, in contrast to the qualitative research presented in part I, we use quantitative research methods to estimate the causal relationship between the variables of interest. That is to say, we must construct empirical models that allow us to quantify our level of confidence in these estimates while also controlling for the effects of potentially confounding variables.

Second, we must identify data sources that enable us to estimate each type of running mate effect, with appropriate precision. This is not as easy as it might sound. For one thing, most election-related datasets include few, if any, measures directly pertaining to the vice presidential candidate. For example, the American National Election Studies (ANES) did not include "feeling thermometers" (see chapter 3) for these candidates until 1968. And in most surveys since that time, it has included no other measures specific to the running mate. Also, most election-oriented surveys, including the standard ANES time series, are cross-sectional in nature—meaning that they provide a snapshot of respondents only at one point in time. Such datasets are appropriate for some of our purposes but not for others. For instance, when estimating indirect running mate effects, in chapter 5, we must be able to track *changes* in presidential candidate evaluations and intended vote choice over the course of the campaign, as a function of changes in vice presidential candidate evaluations. Likewise, when estimating targeted running mate effects, in chapter 4, we seek to determine whether voters shifted toward favoring a particular presidential ticket following the selection of a running mate who shared their geographic, demographic, or ideological group identity. Both analyses require the use of panel data, which derive from surveys that ask the same questions of the same individuals at multiple points in time. Finally, in chapter 3, we must disentangle the direct effects of presidential versus vice presidential candidate evaluations on vote choice. As we explain in that chapter, rolling cross-sectional data are most appropriate for this type of analysis.

This is all to say that our analysis of running mate effects requires a diverse range of data sources and quantitative research methods. In terms of data sources, we use cross-sectional data, from ANES (1952–2016); rolling cross-sectional data, from the National Annenberg Election Studies (2000–2008); and three-wave (or more) panel data, from Knowledge Networks (2008) and The American Panel Survey (2012–2016).[1] In terms of research methods, we use linear or logistic regression, for cross-sectional data; vector autoregression, for rolling cross-sectional data; and an adaptation of Lenz's (2012) three-wave test, for panel data.

By way of preview, what do we find? In short: the running mate's *direct* effect on voting behavior, among voters in general and within targeted subgroups, typically is quite limited. But there is strong evidence to suggest that running mates have a significant *indirect* effect on voting. It would appear that voters rarely see themselves as electing a vice president, in any meaningful sense; rather, they are electing a president, whose choice of a running mate says a great deal about whether he or she deserves to win.

3. Direct Effects

On October 4, 2016, vice presidential candidates Mike Pence and Tim Kaine met for their first—and only—debate, at Longwood University in Farmville, Virginia. That same night, twenty-seven undecided voters met in Cleveland, Ohio, to watch the debate and take part in a focus group led by pollster Frank Luntz, broadcast live on CBS. Luntz began the predebate session with what must have been a facetious remark, given the purpose for which he had gathered these undecided voters together: "What does this debate mean to you tonight? *It's only the vice presidential debate!*"[1]

The participants, taking their cue, responded in earnest. "I'm hoping it'll give us some more clarity on either one of the candidates," said one woman, "because—because we are—because I am so undecided. I'm hoping that one of them gives me *something* to go for one of the [presidential] candidates." Another woman interjected: "I'm hoping for *insight* into who these two [vice presidential] candidates are, because both of the [presidential candidates, Donald Trump and Hillary Clinton] are *so old*." Luntz seemed taken aback when most of the participants said that they actually preferred Pence to Trump, and Kaine to Clinton. "Oh my god," he exclaimed. "So this really matters to you!" To which the participants responded in a chorus: "Yes!"

In its postdebate session, the focus group was—per usual, for Luntz—virtually unanimous in proclaiming a winner: Mike Pence.[2] Why? "He appealed emotionally to a lot of undecided voters that are just tuning in," said one woman, giving the sense of the room. "For me[,] I just needed to see someone who was calm, and measured, and capable, and he *totally* gave me that." In contrast, as one man said, "Kaine came off as a jerk." After hearing several similar comments, Luntz cut to the chase. "So here's the question: Is this gonna change any of your opinions? Are any of you now more likely to vote for Donald Trump because of what you heard from Mike Pence?" Hands shot up across the room: "2, 4, 6, 8, 10," Luntz counted. "So *half* of you." Next question: "Will it actually change any of your votes?" He paused, looking around in silence. "Nobody!" Luntz seemed discombobulated. He turned toward the camera to begin wrapping up the segment but then—hopefully, even desperately—turned back to the audience. "Anyone," he implored, "last shot. Anyone change your minds because of what you saw this evening?" No, not one.

Another focus group met in Virginia that night, this one organized by the McClatchy news service and George Mason University's Schar School of Policy and Government (Lightman 2016). McClatchy's report on the event began as follows: "Jess Wetterau, a registered Republican, was leaning to Hillary Clinton. Then she watched Mike Pence in Tuesday's vice presidential debate." Indeed, Wetterau said, "I'm really impressed by Pence." As promising as this, and the audience's positive reaction to Pence's performance, might have sounded, Wetterau was the only focus group participant who reported being swayed by the debate. Yet, as McClatchy's report continued, somewhat confusingly, "She's not going to vote for Donald Trump." As it turns out, Wetterau only would say that she was undecided, now, because "Trump still gives her pause." After all, Wetterau explained, "He's the candidate, not Mike Pence."

This account of voters' reactions to the 2016 vice presidential debate illustrates a fundamental point that guides our analysis in this chapter, and in the ones that follow: voters cast their vote for a presidential *ticket*, not just a presidential candidate. That is to say, electing a president also means electing his or her running mate as vice president. Indeed, no person—whether spouse or surrogate or campaign operative—is more closely identified with the presidential candidate, during the campaign, than his or her running mate. It is the running mate, alone, whose name appears next to that of the presidential candidate on the ballot, as well as on campaign yard signs and bumper stickers (e.g., Trump/Pence, Clinton/Kaine). And only the running mates get to debate each other on behalf of the presidential candidates, in a prime-time media spectacle viewed by millions of voters and various focus groups whose purpose it is to answer one question: Will this change your vote?

In that case, one must ask: What is the voter's evaluative object, when deciding how to vote in a presidential election? Is it the presidential candidate, only? Or is it the presidential ticket—that is, the presidential *and* vice presidential candidate, together? If it is the latter, then to what degree, and in what ways, do evaluations of the vice presidential candidate influence vote choice? After all, voters have many opportunities to form attitudes about the running mates—from media coverage of their campaign activity, often including joint appearances with the presidential candidate, to high-profile campaign events, including the vice presidential announcement, party convention speech, and debate. Sure enough, voters are quite willing to share their opinions about the running mates. This is evident in the polling data from chapter 2, which shows that most respondents will evaluate a running mate's favorability and his or her qualifications to hold office, among other things, when asked to do so. And it is evident in voters' reactions to the 2016 vice presidential debate, as just described.

The question, then, is not whether voters bother to evaluate vice presidential candidates. They do. The question is whether these evaluations actually influence presidential vote choice. In other words, does it really matter whether Mike Pence came across to voters as "calm, and measured, and capable"—or Tim Kaine, as "a jerk"? Or do voters, even when (un)impressed by the running mate, ultimately reach the same conclusion that Jess Wetterau did—that "[Donald Trump's] the candidate, not Mike Pence"?

Our objective in this chapter is to determine whether vice presidential candidate evaluations directly influence presidential vote choice, among voters in general. In essence, we ask: Do (un)favorable evaluations of the running mate have a discernible, independent effect on actual or intended vote choice? And to what extent do voters even make meaningful distinctions when evaluating presidential versus vice presidential candidates who belong to the same ticket, such that their preferences might diverge in the first place?

METHODOLOGY

Many studies of presidential vote choice examine the effects of presidential candidate evaluations (e.g., Margolis 1977; Markus 1982; Markus and Converse 1979; B. Page and Jones 1979). It is far less common, however, for such studies to examine the effects of *vice* presidential candidate evaluations. This is not to say that scholars have discounted the running mate's influence entirely. In 1968, the American National Election Studies (ANES)—undoubtedly, the premier data source for research on American elections—included vice presidential candidate feeling thermometer measures for the first time.[3] Feeling thermometers, which we use for much of this chapter's analysis, require survey respondents to place an evaluative object (e.g., Mike Pence) on a scale, usually ranging from 0 to 100,[4] with lower scores indicating more negative, or cold, feelings toward that object, and higher scores indicating more positive, or warm, feelings. For example, the voters quoted earlier in the chapter perhaps would rate Pence at 90 or 100, and Kaine at 0 or 10. Presumably, the

ANES began including vice presidential candidate feeling thermometers because its designers believed that doing so might better inform scholars' understanding of elections and voting behavior. Indeed, the ANES has included vice presidential candidate feeling thermometers in every iteration of that survey since 1968.

Several studies have used presidential *and* vice presidential candidate evaluations as independent variables when constructing empirical models to predict presidential vote choice (e.g., Brox and Cassels 2009; Burmila and Ryan 2013; Devine and Kopko 2016; Kenski, Hardy, and Jamieson 2010; Ulbig 2010, 2013; for analyses that incorporate like/dislike measures, see Knuckey 2012, 2013; Wattenberg 1995). Each of these studies differs, to some degree, in terms of its methodology and the time frame for its analysis, depending on when the study was conducted. But each study yields a similar conclusion: while the magnitude of the effect varies from year to year, generally vice presidential candidate evaluations have a statistically significant and positive effect on vote choice—albeit to a much lesser degree than presidential candidate evaluations. Specifically, according to some estimates, presidential candidate evaluations exert roughly three times more influence on vote choice than those of the vice presidential candidates (see Devine and Kopko 2016, 157).

This chapter builds on previous studies to provide the most comprehensive analysis of direct running mate effects, to date. Specifically, we begin by using descriptive statistics and logistic regression analyses to replicate and extend previous studies of direct running mate effects. Then, for the first time in this literature, we use vector autoregression (VAR) to evaluate the dynamic relationship between vice presidential candidate evaluations, presidential candidate evaluations, and intended vote choice, over the course of a campaign. In each stage of this analysis, we identify the inferential limitations inherent in one methodology before advancing to another, more rigorous methodology designed to overcome those limitations. In doing so, we hope to clarify why it is so difficult to determine whether running mates influence presidential voting—and why our analysis is better equipped to do so than in previous studies.

DESCRIPTIVE STATISTICS

Perhaps the simplest way to determine whether running mates influence presidential voting is to examine descriptive statistics measuring the relationship between (vice) presidential candidate evaluations and vote choice. For instance, do voters ever prefer presidential versus vice presidential candidates from different tickets? And, if so, how often do they vote for the ticket that includes their preferred vice presidential candidate but a less-preferred presidential candidate? This, after all, would be the most obvious evidence of someone voting to elect a vice president.

To answer these questions, we adopt the methodology employed by Grofman and Kline (2010; see also Kenski, Hardy, and Jamieson 2010). These authors use feeling thermometer ratings to group respondents to the 1968–2008 ANES into nine categories, based on their presidential versus vice presidential candidate preferences. Then, they calculate the proportion of voters within each category who voted for the Republican presidential ticket in a given election, to determine how often voters prioritize their vice presidential over presidential candidate preferences. Specifically, Grofman and Kline (2010, 304) label respondents as follows: "DD, DN, DR, ND, NN, NR, RD, RN, RR, with the first letter indicating which party's presidential candidate is preferred, and the second letters indicating which party's vice presidential candidate is preferred (with N indicating no preference reported, or a tie)." Ultimately, they conclude that "the net impact of vice presidential selection is at most 1 percentage point" (308).

Here, we use the same approach but with two slight changes. First, we calculate the proportion of voters who voted for the Democratic presidential ticket in each election. We do so because in later analyses our dependent variable measures Democratic vote choice. This recoding allows us to maintain consistent measures of vote choice throughout our analysis. Second, we extend Grofman and Kline's analysis to include the 2012 and 2016 presidential elections—thereby making this a pooled analysis of data from the 1968–2016 ANES.[5] Table 3.1 presents the results of this analysis.

To be sure, the data presented in table 3.1 are limited with respect to causal inference; that is to say, this analysis does not account for other variables that might affect the relationship between candidate evaluations and vote choice, nor does it account for the effects of presidential candidate evaluations on vice presidential candidate evaluations (or vice versa). Indeed, this represents the most basic method of evaluating direct running mate effects. Nonetheless, this analysis is informative—at least in terms of establishing a baseline before proceeding to more advanced methods of analysis.

First, consider the proportion of same-party candidate preferences. It is

Table 3.1. Candidate Preferences and Vote Choice, 1968–2016 ANES

President/ VP Preference	No. of Respondents	Percent of Respondents	No. Voted for Democrat	Percent Voted for Democrat
DD	6,333	31.24%	6,166	97.36%
DN	1,030	5.08%	939	91.17%
DR	1,790	8.83%	1,612	90.06%
ND	434	2.14%	275	63.36%
NN	427	2.11%	208	48.71%
NR	533	2.63%	224	42.03%
RD	871	4.30%	165	18.94%
RN	1,173	5.79%	98	8.35%
RR	7,683	37.90%	531	6.91%

R = Republican candidate preference; D = Democratic candidate preference; N = No candidate preference.

Note: Responses and percentages are based on weighted data. According to the 1948–2016 ANES Cumulative File codebook, "[f]or study years where the same thermometer appeared in both the Pre and Post [election wave], the Pre data are used" (212).

noteworthy, but not surprising, that a strong majority of respondents (69.14 percent) prefer presidential and vice presidential candidates from the same party ticket (i.e., "DD" or "RR"). However, 13.13 percent of respondents favor one party's presidential candidate and the other party's vice presidential candidate (i.e., "DR" or "RD"). In addition, there are few respondents with an apparent favorite for the vice presidency, but not the presidency (4.77 percent). What do these data tell us? First and foremost, the majority of voters align their presidential versus vice presidential candidate evaluations by party, such that preferring one also means preferring the other. In these cases, we cannot say that the running mate has a separate, or distinguishable, effect on vote choice. However, approximately three out of ten voters do not align their candidate preferences by party, with one out of eight voters actually preferring presidential and vice presidential candidates from different parties. In these cases, running mates might have an independent effect on vote choice.

Second, consider the change in the percentage of respondents who voted for the Democratic ticket across candidate preference categories. Generally, the data seem to indicate a linear decline in support for the Democratic ticket as the categories shift from DD to RR. More important, in comparison to respondents who prefer both Democratic candidates (DD), we see a greater decrease in Democratic vote share when voters no longer prefer the party's *presidential* candidate (ND) than when they no longer prefer the party's *vice presidential* candidate (DN)—by 34.00 percentage points and 6.19 percentage points, respectively. Likewise, in comparison to respondents who prefer both Republican candidates (RR), we see a greater increase in Democratic vote share when voters no longer prefer the party's *presidential* candidate (NR) than when they no longer prefer the party's *vice presidential* candidate (RN)—by 35.12 percentage points versus 1.44 percentage points, respectively. These data indicate that vice presidential candidate evaluations *can* have an independent effect on vote choice. But presidential candidate evaluations have a much greater effect, and voters rarely have to choose between their preferred presidential versus vice presidential candidate, anyway.

This evidence provides a useful baseline for the analysis that follows, by indicating that vice presidential candidate evaluations have the potential to exert an independent influence on presidential vote choice—albeit to a lesser extent than presidential candidate evaluations. However, descriptive statistics are quite imprecise when it comes to estimating the relative weight of presidential versus vice presidential candidate evaluations on vote choice, and pooled data cannot clarify the influence of *individual* vice presidential candidacies. The preceding analysis also does not allow us to disentangle the effects of presidential versus vice presidential candidate evaluations on vote choice, independent of other potentially confounding variables. In order to more precisely estimate direct running mate effects, in the next section we turn to logistic regression analysis.

LOGISTIC REGRESSION

In comparison to the descriptive analysis presented in table 3.1, logistic regression allows us to more precisely estimate the effects of our independent variable (vice presidential candidate evaluations) on our dependent variable (vote choice), while controlling for the effects of presidential candidate evaluations and other relevant covariates. Specifically, this method allows us to determine whether the independent effects of vice presidential candidate evaluations on vote choice are statistically significant (based on the 95 percent confidence intervals) and, if so, to quantify the magnitude of those effects (based on the regression coefficients).

Table 3.2 presents the results from three logistic regression models, once more using pooled data from the 1968–2016 ANES.[6] Model 1 includes the

Table 3.2. Predictors of Presidential Vote Choice, 1968–2016 ANES

Variables	Model 1	Model 2	Model 3
Republican presidential candidate rating	−0.071***	−0.079***	−0.087***
0 = Most unfavorable, to 97 = most favorable	(0.004)	(0.005)	(0.004)
Republican vice presidential candidate rating	−0.019***	−0.024***	—
0 = Most unfavorable, to 97 = most favorable	(0.003)	(0.002)	—
Democratic presidential candidate rating	0.071***	0.083***	0.093***
0 = Most unfavorable, to 97 = most favorable	(0.005)	(0.006)	(0.005)
Democratic vice presidential candidate rating	0.023***	0.027***	—
0 = Most unfavorable, to 97 = most favorable	(0.002)	(0.002)	—
Republican	−0.742***	—	—
0 = No, 1 = yes	(0.190)	—	—
Democrat	0.749***	—	—
0 = No, 1 = yes	(0.210)	—	—
Conservative	−0.756***	—	—
0 = No, 1 = yes	(0.136)	—	—
Liberal	0.675***	—	—
0 = No, 1 = yes	(0.202)	—	—
Female	−0.104	—	—
0 = No, 1 = yes	(0.069)	—	—
Age	0.001	—	—
Continuous	(0.002)	—	—
Household income	−0.033	—	—
1 = Under 17th percentile, to 5 = over 95th percentile	(0.050)	—	—
Education	−0.012	—	—
1 = No HS degree, to 5 = advanced degree	(0.032)	—	—
White	−0.680***	—	—
0 = No, 1 = yes	(0.138)	—	—
South	−0.119	—	—
0 = No, 1 = yes	(0.1−07)	—	—
Incumbent president's party	−0.180*	—	—
0 = Republican, 1 = Democrat	(0.173)	—	—
Constant	0.489	−0.484*	−0.323*
	(0.311)	(0.199)	(0.211)
Reduction in error	88.74%	86.71%	84.85%
Percent correctly predicted	94.55%	93.58%	92.78%
Observations	15,218	17,025	19,616

Entries are logistic regression coefficients. Robust standard errors are in parentheses. Standard errors are clustered by year.

***$p < .001$, **$p < .01$, *$p < .05$, +$p < .10$.

presidential and vice presidential candidate feeling thermometers, along with a wide range of control variables that also could influence vote choice—namely, the respondent's party identification, ideological identification, and demographic characteristics, as well as the party affiliation of the incumbent president. Model 2 excludes the control variables from Model 1, so as to include only the presidential and vice presidential candidate feeling thermometers. Model 3 includes only the presidential candidate feeling thermometers. We present all three models in order to gauge the relative effects of presidential versus vice presidential candidate evaluations on vote choice and to evaluate the sensitivity of their effects to the inclusion of other relevant variables.

Sure enough, the candidate feeling thermometer ratings have a statistically significant ($p < .001$) effect on vote choice in each model, and in the expected direction. This means that as a respondent's evaluation of the Democratic (Republican) presidential or vice presidential candidate becomes more favorable, or positive, he or she becomes more (less) likely to vote for the Democratic ticket. Indeed, presidential *and* vice presidential candidate evaluations matter, according to these models. But *how much* do they matter, particularly in relation to one another? Logistic—unlike linear—regression model coefficients cannot be interpreted directly for the purposes of quantifying an independent variable's effects. Instead, we must calculate predicted probabilities in order to demonstrate how changes in (vice) presidential candidate feeling thermometers influence changes in a respondent's likelihood of voting for the Democratic ticket. We present these predicted probabilities in table 3.3, using the results from Model 1.[7]

The second column in table 3.3 estimates the baseline probability of a Democratic vote, for the "typical respondent"—meaning someone for whom *all* of the independent variables from Model 1 are set to their median values. The baseline probability of voting for the Democratic ticket is 62.55 percent. The third column then shows how a five-point increase in thermometer ratings for a given presidential or vice presidential candidate (listed by row in table 3.3) would change the respondent's probability of voting for the Democratic ticket, while holding all other variables constant at their median level. The fourth column calculates changes in the probability of a Democratic vote when comparing the baseline (second column) versus increased (third column) candidate ratings.

The results show that a five-point increase in *presidential* candidate thermometer ratings changes the probability of a Democratic vote by about eight

Table 3.3. Predicted Probabilities of Democratic Vote by Candidate Thermometer Rating, 1968–2016 ANES

Feeling Thermometer	Baseline Probability of Democratic Vote: "Typical Respondent" Values	Probability of Democratic Vote after 5-Point Increase in Candidate Thermometer Rating	Difference in Probability of Democratic Vote
Republican presidential	62.55	53.89	−8.66
	(56.45–68.65)	(47.47–60.31)	
Republican vice presidential	62.55	60.35	−2.20
	(56.45–68.65)	(54.11–66.59)	
Democratic presidential	62.55	70.46	+7.91
	(56.45–68.65)	(65.05–75.87)	
Democratic vice presidential	62.55	65.22	+2.67
	(56.45–68.65)	(59.04–71.40)	

Note: 95 percent confidence intervals are in parentheses.

To derive estimates for the "typical respondent," we set all variables in Model 1 from table 3.2 to their median values. Both presidential candidate thermometer ratings = 60, Republican vice presidential candidate thermometer rating = 50, Democratic vice presidential candidate thermometer rating = 55, Republican party identification = 0, Democratic party identification = 1, conservative self-identification = 0, liberal self-identification = 0, female = 1, age = 48, income = 3, education = 3, white = 1, South = 0, incumbent president = 1.

percentage points (−8.66 for Republican ratings, and +7.91 for Democratic ratings). A five-point increase in *vice presidential* candidate thermometer ratings also changes the probability of a Democratic vote, but only by about 2 to 3 percentage points (−2.20 for Republican ratings, and +2.67 for Democratic ratings). Thus, according to this analysis, vice presidential candidate evaluations *do* have an independent effect on vote choice. However, as in previous studies that use a similar method of analysis (e.g., Devine and Kopko 2016), the magnitude of the running mate's effect is only one-fourth (Republican) to one-third (Democrat) that of the corresponding presidential candidate.[8]

Nonetheless, this analysis is limited by the fact that it relies on pooled data from the 1968–2016 ANES. While pooled data may be helpful in estimating potentially causal relationships, in a general sense—by maximizing statistical power or allowing for more precise estimates due to the greater number of available cases—relying on such data exclusively obscures the effects of individual vice presidential candidacies on vote choice. That is to say, while running mate evaluations may influence vote choice generally, in some cases

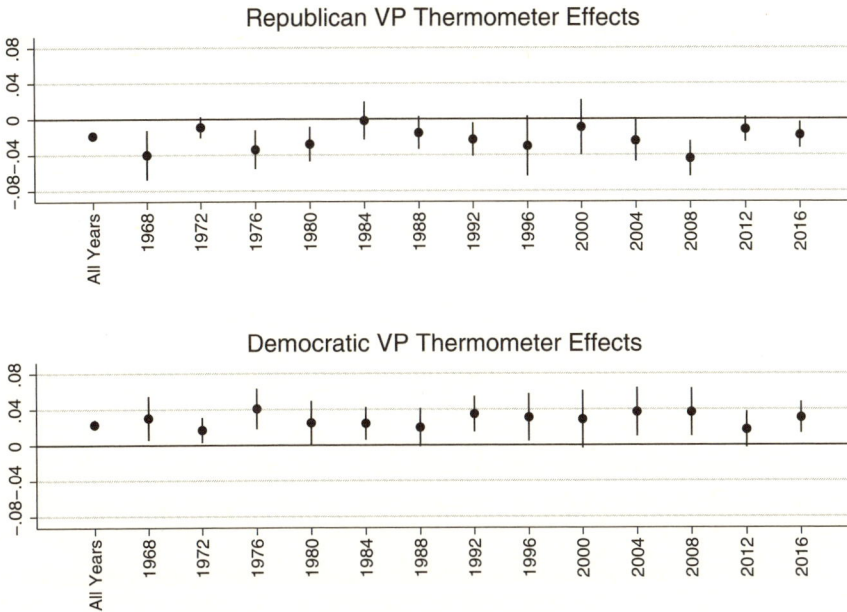

Figure 3.1. Vice presidential candidate feeling thermometer ratings' effect on Democratic vote choice (logit estimates), 1968–2016 ANES

they may have no effect and in other cases they may have a very sizable effect. Indeed, it is possible that a few outliers are responsible for the small but statistically significant effect of vice presidential candidate evaluations, in general, that we see in table 3.3. Also, it is possible that some running mates might have a negative effect on vote choice. Only by disaggregating these effects across individual candidacies can we provide an appropriately nuanced assessment of direct running mate effects.

Next, then, we estimate the effects of vice presidential candidate evaluations on vote choice using cross-sectional data from each of the 1968–2016 ANES.[9] Once more, we use a logistic regression model to derive our estimates—specifically, Model 1 from table 3.2, which controls for presidential candidate evaluations and a battery of relevant covariates. To make this analysis more intuitive, in figure 3.1 we graph the coefficient estimates for each vice presidential candidacy from 1968 to 2016.[10] Also, we include 95 percent confidence intervals, to indicate whether the effect is statistically significant (i.e., distinguishable from zero).

The estimates presented in figure 3.1 affirm that vice presidential candidate evaluations generally have a statistically significant, independent effect on presidential vote choice. However, this effect is much more consistent for Democrats than Republicans. Indeed, only three (Lloyd Bentsen, 1988; Joe Lieberman, 2000; Joe Biden, 2012) of the thirteen Democratic running mates included in our dataset did not have a statistically significant effect on vote choice, among ANES respondents in general. But only seven Republican running mates (Spiro Agnew, 1968; Bob Dole, 1976; George H. W. Bush, 1980; Dan Quayle, 1992; Dick Cheney, 2004; Sarah Palin, 2008; Mike Pence, 2016) had a statistically significant effect on vote choice—barely half! Of the significant effects on presidential voting, all were in the expected direction; in other words, more favorable evaluations of the Democratic (Republican) running mate were associated with an increased likelihood of voting for the Democratic (Republican) ticket.

As a general matter, then, *do* vice presidential candidate evaluations influence presidential vote choice? Based on our logistic regression analysis, the most succinct answer is: yes—but it's complicated. When pooling together all respondents to the 1968–2016 ANES, we identify a statistically significant, but relatively modest, effect for Democratic as well as Republican running mates. But, when disaggregating the data to analyze individual elections, we see that in many cases—nine out of twenty-six (or 35 percent), to be exact—they have no such effect. For Democrats, running mate effects almost always are evident. But for Republicans, almost half the time we find no such effects. In that case, it is fair to say that running mate evaluations generally influence presidential vote choice. But it is not fair to assume that this will be true in every election, particularly for Republicans.

Nonetheless, the preceding analysis has two major limitations, which also apply to previous studies using logistic regression models to estimate the relationship between vice presidential candidate evaluations and presidential vote choice. Specifically, these limitations include, first, the inability of cross-sectional survey data to account for the dynamic influence of running mates over the course of a campaign; and, second, the inability of such data to account for the potential interdependence, or endogeneity, of presidential versus vice presidential candidate evaluations (i.e., the fact that a respondent's evaluation of one candidate may influence his or her evaluation of the other).

This is not to say that scholars who rely on such data and methods are to blame for these shortcomings, since most election-related surveys are cross-sectional in nature. Also, the resulting datasets often do not include variables that can be used to account for the interdependence that we reference earlier.[11] But in recent years, new opportunities for more rigorous analysis of direct running mate effects have emerged—specifically, with the introduction of rolling cross-sectional surveys, as exemplified by the National Annenberg Election Survey (NAES), and an innovative research methodology capable of analyzing dynamic causal relationships over the course of a campaign, called vector autoregression. To this point, researchers have not capitalized on these new data sources and methods to study the dynamic effects of vice presidential candidate evaluations on presidential candidate evaluations and vote choice. In the next section, we do just that.

VECTOR AUTOREGRESSION

To date, only three studies have analyzed the running mate's effect on intended vote choice over the course of a campaign, namely, those by Elis, Hillygus, and Nie (2010), Kenski, Hardy, and Jamieson (2010), and Lenz (2012). Elis, Hillygus, and Nie (2010) use rolling cross-sectional data, collected via the Knowledge Networks (KN) KnowledgePanel, to analyze how changes in presidential and vice presidential candidate evaluations influenced respondents' intended vote choice throughout 2008. Their results, based on a series of multinomial logit and traditional logit models, indicate that Sarah Palin cost the Republican ticket 1.6 percentage points in that year's election. In other words, they estimate, Republicans' share of the presidential vote would have been higher, by 1.6 percentage points, if voters had viewed Palin as favorably at the time of the election, in November, as they had in September.[12] Kenski, Hardy, and Jamieson (2010) also use rolling cross-sectional data, from NAES, to estimate the effects of Palin's favorability on intended vote choice. Specifically, they show that Palin's favorability had the greatest effect on intended vote choice in mid-October and then in the last three days of the campaign. Finally, Lenz finds that respondents' likelihood of voting for McCain increased as their views of Palin became more favorable over the course of the campaign (i.e., from September to November). In this case, he uses panel data from the 2008 ANES (Lenz 2012, 99–104).

These studies, however, analyze only one election year, with a focus on Palin's candidacy, in particular. In this section, we use vector autoregression to analyze the effects of four vice presidential candidacies in the 2000 and 2004 elections. The objective of this analysis, for present purposes, is to estimate the dynamic effects of vice presidential candidate evaluations on intended vote choice over the course of the campaign. (In chapter 5, we return to this analysis in order to evaluate the interdependent relationship between same-party presidential and vice presidential candidate evaluations.) This approach has major advantages over what is possible when using cross-sectional data. Specifically, this is because same-party presidential and vice presidential candidate evaluations are likely to be endogenous (i.e., influencing each other simultaneously), and cross-sectional data measure them together, at a single point in time. Therefore, when using cross-sectional data, it is difficult to ascertain the independent effects of vice presidential candidate evaluations on vote choice. By using *rolling* cross-sectional data, instead, we can observe greater variation in the relationship between same-party candidate evaluations, and therefore better estimate whether, and to what extent, running mates exert an independent effect on voting behavior over time.[13]

For this analysis, we use data from the preelection telephone versions of the 2000 and 2004 NAES.[14] Each dataset comprises a nationally representative, rolling cross-sectional sample of respondents, surveyed daily over the course of the campaign—including 28,438 respondents in 2000 (interviewed between August 7 and November 6) and 8,664 respondents in 2004 (interviewed between July 15 and November 1). Moreover, the 2000 and 2004 NAES measure each of our variables of interest, including presidential and vice presidential candidate evaluations—using a scale of 0 to 100 in 2000 and a scale of 0 to 10 in 2004, each ranging from the least to the most favorable ratings—as well as intended presidential vote choice (coded 1 for Democrats, and 0 for Republicans or others).

To analyze the interrelationship between candidate evaluations and vote choice, in the 2000 and 2004 NAES, we use vector autoregression.[15] This innovative methodology is ideal for the purposes of analyzing dynamic and potentially causal relationships because VAR allows candidate evaluations to be endogenous and to influence each other over time. However, this method has been used sparingly in the political science literature and never to study running mate effects, in large part because it requires using rolling cross-sectional or panel data. Fortunately, for our purposes, the NAES data make such an analysis possible. Our application of VAR is guided by the example of Box-Steffensmeier, Darmofal, and Farrell (2009), who use this methodology to analyze the interdependent relationship between campaign expenditures, positive/negative media coverage, and intended vote choice in the 2000 presidential election. Indeed, they find that these variables, from the 2000 NAES, were interdependent, and that campaign expenditures and media coverage influenced intended vote choice over the course of the campaign. In the same way, we use this methodology to analyze the interdependent relationship between presidential versus vice presidential candidate evaluations and vote choice. For technical guidance regarding our VAR analysis, specifically in terms of model specifications and variable transformations, we invite readers to consult this chapter's appendix.

Specifically, we use VAR to (1) determine whether there is evidence of "Granger causality" in the candidate favorability and intended vote choice time series, and, (2) if so, to estimate the cumulative effect of changes or "shocks" in one series on another.[16] In other words, we ask: How does a positive change in one candidate's favorability ratings influence intended vote choice over several days? Does an increase in favorability lead to a long-lasting, increased probability of voting for that candidate's ticket? Or does this effect last for a short period of time and then dissipate quickly? Or, finally, is there no effect at all?

In the interest of brevity, we omit the table output of the VAR model and the Granger causality test and instead present a graphical representation of the model's cumulative effects. However, it is important to note that in both election years that we analyze, every series attains statistical significance at $p < .05$ when testing for Granger causality. Substantively, this means that candidate evaluations and vote choice are interdependent. In other words, changes in vice presidential candidate evaluations cause changes in presidential candidate evaluations, over time, and vice versa. And both cause changes in intended vote choice, over time. For example, based on these results, we would expect an increase in Dick Cheney's popularity to cause an increase in George W. Bush's popularity, and vice versa—and, then, for both to cause a decrease in support for the Democratic ticket. In this way, a running mate's (un)popularity may have a direct effect on a presidential candidate's (un)popularity, and on vote choice.

But that is not the end of the story. In fact, Granger causality tests and raw VAR output cannot tell us how strong these effects are or how long they last. Quite possibly, they are very weak and last only briefly. Or they may be strong and long-lasting. To find out, we must graph the cumulative impulse response function (CIRF) for each series. The CIRF allows us to estimate the effects of a one-unit positive shock to (vice) presidential candidate evaluations

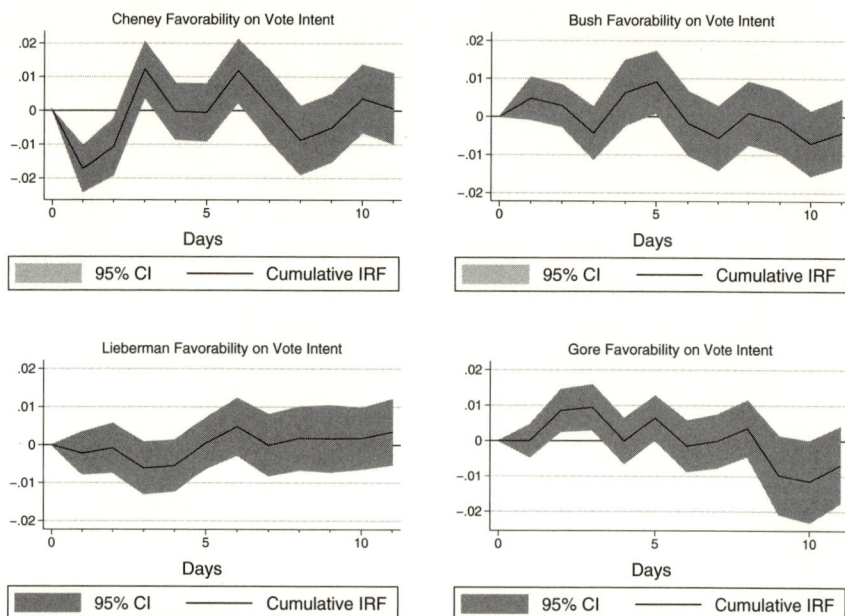

Figure 3.2. Cumulative impulse response function of candidate favorability and intended Democratic vote choice, 2000 NAES

on same-party candidate evaluations and intended vote choice.[17] A *cumulative* function is appropriate for this analysis because we seek to estimate the lasting effects of such shocks over time, rather than their daily values in isolation.[18] Figures 3.2 and 3.3 present the CIRF estimates—with gray bands representing 95 percent confidence intervals—for candidate favorability and intended vote choice in the 2000 and 2004 NAES, respectively.[19]

In 2000, we see that a positive shock to Dick Cheney's popularity (i.e., an increase in his favorability rating) has an immediate, and statistically significant, effect on presidential vote choice. Specifically, this makes voters less likely to support the Democratic ticket for two days afterward. But then the effect fades away; it is not statistically significant for the remainder of the time series, except for two blips actually favoring the Democratic ticket.[20] Interestingly, we see no effect—positive or negative—for Cheney's Democratic counterpart, Joe Lieberman, at any point in the time series. That is to say, his CIRF never reaches statistical significance. And the same is nearly true for George W. Bush, except for a blip in the Democratic ticket's favor on day five. Finally, for Al Gore, a positive shock to his favorability rating significantly increases

Cheney Favorability on Vote Intent

Bush Favorability on Vote Intent

Edwards Favorability on Vote Intent

Kerry Favorability on Vote Intent

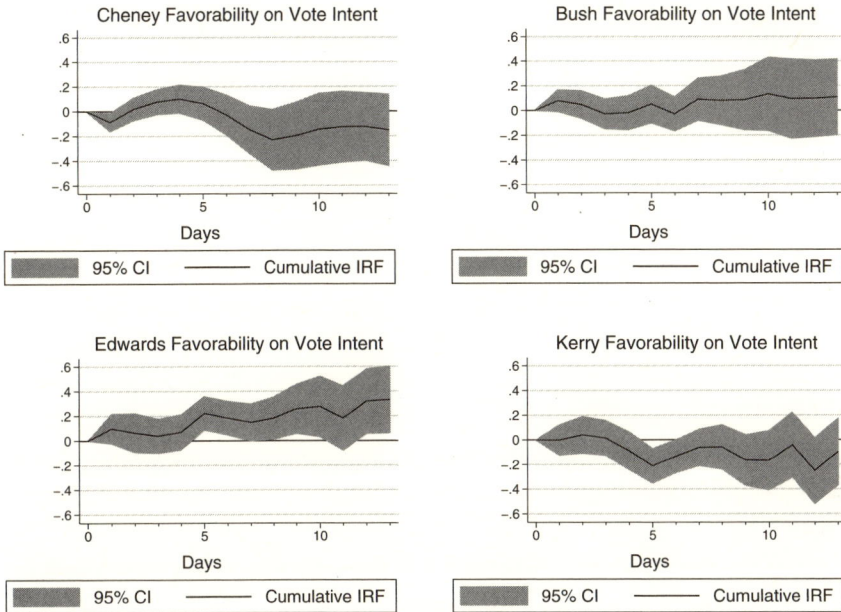

Figure 3.3. Cumulative impulse response function of candidate favorability and intended Democratic vote choice, 2004 NAES

intentions to vote for the Democratic ticket on days two and three. But, much as for Cheney, this effect then dissipates and is not distinguishable from zero for the remainder of the time series.

In 2004, once again, a positive shock to Cheney's favorability rating causes an immediate decrease in intentions to vote for the Democratic ticket. But this effect is weaker and less enduring than in 2000; it disappears by day two of the time series, never to return. Bush, for his part, exhibits no such effect at any point in the time series, and his Democratic opponent, John Kerry, matches this except for a brief, statistically significant loss of (intended) votes on day five. Then there is John Edwards—whose performance is not just impressive but exceptional. Indeed, a positive shock to Edwards's favorability ratings causes an increase in intended Democratic vote choice that starts at day five and persists, with two brief exceptions, through the final day of the time series (day thirteen).[21]

Should we be surprised not to find much evidence of a dynamic relationship between presidential candidate evaluations and vote choice? Probably not. After all, many voters decide for whom they will vote prior to the start of the fall campaign season, based on party identification and other relatively stable political attitudes. Then, during the campaign, either they see no reason to depart from their initial preferences, or they find reasons to correct any inclination to deviate from them (e.g., A. Campbell et al. 1960; Lazarsfeld, Berelson, and Baudet 1948; Sides and Vavreck 2013). Given these tendencies, it may be the case that presidential candidate evaluations have little effect on voters' preferences during the campaign because, for the most part, they already know enough about those candidates to have made up their minds.

But the same is not necessarily true for vice presidential candidates. For instance, in 2004, voters were less familiar with John Edwards than with the Democratic presidential candidate, John Kerry, or with the incumbent US president, George W. Bush, and vice president, Dick Cheney.[22] Yet, at the same time, NAES data indicate that Edwards had the highest approval ratings of any candidate through mid-September. It may be the case that Edwards's favorability ratings were especially high early in the campaign because, at that time, many voters who would eventually form a negative impression of him registered no opinion at all. A similar phenomenon is evident in 2008 with regard to Sarah Palin's vice presidential candidacy (see Kenski, Hardy, and Jamieson 2010; see also Elis, Hillygus, and Nie 2010).

By way of summary, the VAR analysis suggests two important conclusions. First, running mates *can* have a direct effect on presidential vote choice, over and above that of the presidential candidate. Indeed, three of the four running mates included in our analysis at some point had a statistically significant effect on intended vote choice, and in favor of their party ticket. Most notably, in 2004, John Edwards's relative popularity seems to have had a lasting effect on voters' preferences—and may have gained votes for the Democratic ticket on Election Day. But, to our second point, Edwards is the exception. In other cases, when these effects occur, they are short-lived—much like Box-Steffensmeier, Darmofal, and Farrell (2009) find with respect to the effect of campaign advertising in the 2000 election. This suggests that, in order for running mates to have a positive effect on actual vote choice: (a) they must be popular enough to maintain a series of positive shocks throughout the campaign; or, (b) what limited, positive shocks they produce must occur within close proximity to Election Day (or at least within the window for early voting, in those states that legally permit it). Again, though, we must be cautious in interpreting the significance of these results, since they are based on evidence from only two election years.

To better asssess the generalizability of our conclusions would require evidence from other, preferably more recent, election years.

CONCLUSION

Do running mates directly influence vote choice? Yes—*but* their effects are quite limited, as compared with presidential candidates, and usually short-lived. Moreover, only a small minority of voters have divergent preferences for presidential versus vice presidential candidates that would require them to prioritize one over the other when casting their vote in the first place.

We derive these conclusions from a multimethod analysis of direct effects. First, using descriptive statistics based on the 1968–2016 ANES, we determine that the preferences of approximately seven out of ten voters are aligned with respect to the presidential and vice presidential candidates. And when those preferences diverge, vote choice is far more sensitive to shifts in presidential than vice presidential candidate preferences.

Our logistic regression analysis indicates similar dynamics. Indeed, we find that the effect of presidential candidate evaluations on vote choice is approximately three to four times greater than that of vice presidential candidate evaluations. And while vice presidential candidate evaluations directly influence vote choice in elections, generally, this is not the case in every election; for example, this relationship is statistically significant for only about half of the Republican running mates since 1968.

Finally, to more precisely estimate the running mate's independent effect on voting behavior, over the course of a campaign, we use VAR to analyze rolling cross-sectional data from the 2000 and 2004 NAES. This analysis indicates that vice presidential candidate evaluations often have a statistically significant effect on vote choice, separate from the effect of presidential candidate evaluations. However, if these effects occur, they are likely to be short-lived and—depending on how close to Election Day they occur—they may have no direct consequences for vote choice. In exceptional cases, a relatively popular running mate—such as John Edwards in 2004—may have more lasting effects on voting behavior. But, given other evidence summarized in this chapter, the running mate's direct effect on vote choice is likely to pale in comparison to that of the presidential candidate who selected him or her.

In that case, one might conclude that running mates matter—*just not that much.* In our opinion, this is a reasonable—if overly simplistic—summary of the evidence for direct effects. But that hardly tells the full story. In fact, many people would argue that running mates are not chosen to win *just anyone's* vote. No, their job is to "deliver" those constituencies, or voting blocs, that the presidential candidate needs in order to win—be that a state in the Electoral College or a key demographic group such as women or Latinos. This may be the most popular conception of running mate effects; indeed, it is the one to which presidential candidates seem to give the most credence (see chapter 1). But is it credible, after all? Do voters rally to support a running mate who shares with them a particular group identity—in effect, delivering their votes in the election? Or do they resist such symbolic appeals and vote for the presidential candidate whose party or policies they prefer instead? And if these "targeted running mate effects" occur, then to which groups do they apply (most)? We turn to these questions next, in chapter 4.

CHAPTER 3 APPENDIX: VAR MODELS

To conduct our vector autoregression analysis of the 2000 and 2004 National Annenberg Election Studies (NAES), we begin by estimating the order of integration (d) for each time series (i.e., Democratic or Republican presidential candidate evaluations, Democratic or Republican vice presidential candidate evaluations, and intended Democratic vote choice). As Box-Steffensmeier, Darmofal, and Farrell (2009, 315) explain, the order of integration

> tells us how quickly the effects of shocks to a process die out over time. When $d =$ 0, the series has no long-term memory, and an increase or decrease in the process due to external shocks dies out completely and quickly as soon as the shocks are over. When $d = 1$, the series has permanent memory, which means the effect of the shocks lasts forever. A series is fractionally integrated when d is between 0 and 1. The persistence of the series increases as the value of d increases.

We employ Robinson's semiparametric estimator to estimate d for each of our time series (see Baum and Wiggins 2000).[23]

All five of the time series that we analyze in the 2000 NAES are fractionally integrated. However, only three of the time series from the 2004 NAES are fractionally integrated. These include favorability ratings for the Republican vice presidential candidate, Dick Cheney; the Democratic vice presidential candidate, John Edwards; and the Democratic presidential candidate, John Kerry. For those series that are fractionally integrated, Box-Steffensmeier, Darmofal, and Farrell (2009, 315) note that "fractional differencing is needed" to ensure accurate statistical inferences; that is, we must "pre-whiten" the fractionally integrated series to "purge autocorrelation and ensure stationarity before examining the multivariate interactions" (Box-Steffensmeier, Darmofal, and Farrell 2009, 316; see also Mills 1992; Pierce and Haugh 1977).[24] Failing to do so could produce spurious findings. Therefore, we fractionally difference all series from the 2000 NAES, and evaluations of Cheney, Edwards, and Kerry in the 2004 NAES.

Before estimating the VAR model, we determined the appropriate number of lags to include in the analysis and account for significant dummy variables that may cause "shocks" to the time series, in either the short or the long term. For each election, we control for the Democratic and Republican National Conventions, each of the three presidential debates, and the vice presidential debate. For the 2004 election analysis, we also control for the release of the Osama bin Laden tape in October.[25] Based on the Akaike Information Criterion, we employ eleven lags for our 2000 analysis, and thirteen lags for our 2004 analysis.

4. Targeted Effects

On a Sunday morning in mid-October 2016, nearly two weeks after the vice presidential debate, pastor Christian Garcia welcomed a guest speaker to the pulpit at Pneuma Church in West Kendall, Florida. "Buenos dias a todos," the speaker began, greeting the congregation. He went on to deliver a five-minute sermon, entirely in Spanish. This was hardly unusual at the bilingual Miami-area church; in fact, Garcia had delivered his introduction in Spanish, as well. What was unusual—actually, unprecedented—about this Spanish-only speech is that it came from a vice presidential candidate: Tim Kaine. And for those who had ears to hear, Kaine had a message: "Yo soy cristano, un catolico" (I am a Christian, a Catholic; Morin 2016).

Kaine's Catholicism and his fluency in Spanish were linked together, in fact: he learned the language while serving for nine months as a Jesuit missionary to Honduras, at the age of twenty-two. As many people saw it, these two aspects of Kaine's identity also were linked to his selection as Hillary Clinton's running mate—and her path to victory in 2016. Indeed, Kaine's perceived appeal to Latino voters, as a Spanish speaker, figured prominently in media coverage of his vice presidential candidacy. For example, a Univision article—titled "Why It Matters That Tim Kaine Speaks Spanish"—claimed: "Kaine's bilingualism could be a key factor in winning over . . . Latinos, especially in the three key swing states (Florida, Ohio and Pennsylvania) that could decide the election" (Felix and Shaik 2016). To support this argument, one profile in the *New Yorker* cited a Univision Noticias poll in which 26 percent of Latino voters overall, and 39 percent of those whose primary language was Spanish, said that they would be more likely to vote for a Spanish-speaking presidential—note, not *vice* presidential—candidate.[1] "The fact that Kaine is a practicing Catholic," the author added, "like sixty-two percent of Hispanics in the United States, probably won't hurt either" (Krauze 2016).

Media coverage of Kaine's vice presidential candidacy, as a whole, tended to highlight four identity-based aspects of his electoral appeal: ethnicity (i.e., Spanish-speaking ability), religion (i.e., Catholicism), ideology (i.e., moderation/centrism), and geography (i.e., being from Virginia/the South). For example, the aforementioned *New Yorker* profile cited "two assets that have now made him Hillary Clinton's choice for Vice-President: First . . . Kaine is known as a centrist bridge builder. . . . [Second,] his fluent, colloquial Spanish" (Krauze 2016). Another article, in the *Christian Science Monitor*, bore this headline: "Clinton Picks Tim Kaine, Devout Catholic and Bridge-Builder" (Kiefer 2016). Likewise, a profile in the *Guardian* described him as "a Catholic who holds a reputation of being a more centrist Democrat, which could help appeal to moderate constituencies but could also draw concerns from progressives" (Siddiqui 2016). And a CBS News profile of Clinton's potential running mates, prior to selection, summarized the case for picking Kaine this way: "In a word, Virginia." To elaborate: "For veepstakes, one thing a running mate might offer is help at the top of the ticket in a key swing state—and Kaine, a former Virginia governor and relatively popular first-term senator, would do just that" (Rahn and Schultheis 2016).

Demography, ideology, and geography also figured prominently in discussions of Mike Pence's vice presidential candidacy—specifically, in terms of his perceived appeal to fellow evangelical Christians, conservatives, and midwesterners. Reportedly, many of Donald Trump's closest advisers—including his then campaign manager Paul Manafort, pollster Kellyanne Conway, and sons Donald Jr. and Eric—urged Pence's selection because he would "unify the party and appeal to evangelical Christians who had not supported Trump in the primary" (Short 2016; see also Alberta 2016, 2019).[2] Sure enough, many conservative leaders believed that Pence—who proudly described himself on the campaign trail as "a Christian, a conservative, and a Republican, in that order"—would help Trump win over wary members of the party's base. Indiana representative Luke Messer, for one, said that Pence's "strong record as both a national security and social conservative . . . will help bring those coalitions home for the fall campaign." Iowa representative Steve King agreed: "He fills in a lot of blanks on the social conservative side of this and he gives a lot of confidence to the evangelical community in America, to the pro-life, to the pro-family people and to the constitutionalist" (McPherson 2016). Likewise, following Pence's selection, the *New York Times* reported, "Christian leaders say they feel reassured they will have access to the White House and a seat at the table" (Goodstein 2016).

Fellow vice presidential finalist Newt Gingrich explained Pence's selection primarily in geographic terms. "I think that Mike Pence would have a huge Midwestern appeal," he reasoned, "so if you're trying to compete for western Pennsylvania, Ohio, Michigan, Wisconsin, Missouri, Illinois, there's a certain value to an Indiana candidate" ("Newt Gingrich" 2016). Indeed, some analysts saw Pence's geographic identity as essential to understanding his campaign persona and his travel schedule. One reporter, for example, described Pence as being "set on using Midwestern reserve to win over small-town and rural conservatives in battleground states" (Beaumont 2016).[3]

This analysis illustrates a second process by which running mates might influence voting in presidential elections, which is the focus of this chapter: "targeted effects." Specifically, this term refers to a running mate's ability to win over voters with whom he or she shares a salient political or social identity. As in the previous chapter, here we analyze whether—and to what extent—running mates *directly* influence vote choice. However, in contrast to the previous chapter, we analyze these effects only among particular electoral subgroups—not the electorate as a whole. To be clear, "direct effects" (chapter 3) and "targeted effects" (this chapter) are not mutually exclusive; running mates might be successful at increasing their ticket's vote share among voters, in general, while also boosting its performance by that much more among targeted subgroups. For that matter, a running mate's effect on the electorate, in general, might be primarily or exclusively driven by his or her effect on a given subgroup (particularly if it is one that represents a large proportion of the electorate, such as women).

In this chapter, we analyze targeted running mate effects among electoral subgroups defined by their geographic (i.e., home state, home region), demographic (i.e., gender, religious, ethnic), or ideological (i.e., liberal, conservative) identity.[4] Focusing on these three identity categories is consistent with the existing literature on vice presidential selection (see chapter 2),[5] and the existing literature on running mate effects (see later in this chapter). Also, these categories correspond to the most common targets of ticket-balancing strategies, as identified by presidential candidates (chapter 1) and pollsters (chapter 2). Finally, recent vice presidential candidates have been sufficiently diverse, with respect to these three categories, to test their effect on vote choice among relevant subgroups. For example, in terms of demographic identity, our data encompass elections in which the vice presidential candidate was a woman (1984, 2008), Catholic (1964, 1968, 1972, 1984, 2008, 2012, 2016), evangelical Christian (2008, 2016), or Jewish (2000).

This chapter puts to the test the most salient and enduring perception of running mate effects: that vice presidential candidates are able to win over key segments of the electorate with whom they share a salient in-group identity, even if they have little to no direct influence on vote choice in the general electorate. In other words, as the conventional wisdom goes, running mates are effective at targeting the particular voting blocs that a presidential campaign needs in order to win an election. But is that the case? Do voters, in fact, rally behind a running mate that they see as "one of us"—and vote for his or her presidential ticket on that basis? Or do they dismiss such considerations as irrelevant and simply vote for their preferred presidential candidate? Perhaps these effects vary depending on the target group in question. For instance, do evangelical Christians support a running mate who shares their religious identity in a way that, say, Catholics do not? How about women, who represent a majority of the electorate? Simply put, does targeting voters through vice presidential selection even *work*? And, if so, under what conditions? These questions guide the analysis that follows.

WHY TARGETED EFFECTS?

Before proceeding to our empirical analysis, first we must ask a fundamental question: Why *would* anyone expect running mates to have targeted effects on vote choice? Actually, this must be broken into two questions. First, why would anyone expect voters to prefer candidates, *in general*, who share with them a salient geographic, demographic, or ideological identity? Second, do targeted effects necessarily apply to vice presidential candidates?

To the first question, social identity theory explains that individuals define themselves, in part, by the social groups to which they (subjectively) belong (Tajfel and Turner 1979; Turner et al. 1987). In essence, self-categorization within a social group causes individuals to incorporate that group's identity into their self-identity. Social identity therefore motivates individuals to positively evaluate in-groups and act in ways that advance group interests, in order to maintain a positive self-image and advance self-interest (but see Brewer 1991; Mullin and Hogg 1998). This provides a psychological incentive to think and act in ways that favor one's in-group (and, by extension, oneself). Social identity theory applies to even the most arbitrary groups (Tafjel et al. 1971), and to the social categories that we examine in this chapter.[6] Thus, when it comes to elections, it is reasonable to expect that voters will be more likely to vote for a candidate whom they perceive to be a member of their geographic, demographic, or ideological in-group.[7]

But, to the second question, can we assume that these effects apply to vice presidential candidates? If voters were to cast a separate vote for vice president, then the answer would be simple: yes. But, as we discuss in chapter 3, voters cast their vote for a presidential *ticket*, consisting of a presidential candidate and a vice presidential candidate. Also, as we discuss in this book's introduction, vice presidents have very little formal power—indeed, far less than presidents have. Thus, it is unclear whether—and to what extent—voters see their presidential vote as an opportunity to advance in-group interests by electing a vice president who also belongs to that group (especially if the presidential candidate does not).

Moreover, if targeted running mate effects occur, we should not expect them to be uniform across every social group or election year. Social identities must be salient in order to influence behavior, for example (see Bettencourt, Miller, and Hume 2010; Lalonde and Silverman 1994; Mullen, Brown, and Smith 1992). If the running mate belongs to a social group that is not particularly salient in the context of a given election (e.g., athlete, academic), then he or she probably will not have a targeted effect on in-group voters. Likewise, if the running mate belongs to a social group that has become significantly less salient, in an electoral context, over time (e.g., Catholic), he or she probably will have less of a targeted effect than other such running mates in past elections, or none at all. Also, some social groups (e.g., women) may be too large and amorphous to provide many in-group members with a coherent sense of identity and a consistent set of behavioral cues for acting in the group's interest. Other groups (e.g., African Americans) may elicit a strong sense of social identity and group loyalty because they satisfy many in-group members' opposing needs for "assimilation" and "differentiation" (Brewer 1991) or because the in-group's historical and contemporary experiences cause many members to perceive that they share in a "linked fate" (Dawson 1995; Simien 2005).

In summary, running mates may not attract in-group support in the same way, or to the same degree, as other candidates who run for office on their own or at the head of a ticket. Indeed, it may be unclear to voters how electing "one of our own" to the vice presidency would meaningfully advance the in-group's interests—especially to such an extent that this consideration would override a voter's preference for another presidential candidate. If targeted running mate effects occur, they should be limited to instances in which the electoral subgroup in question is salient in a given election and, in terms of size, is big enough to provide its members with a clear sense of belonging within society yet also small enough to maintain a distinctive sense of identity in comparison to other social groups.

Of course, many previous studies have examined targeted running mate effects. But this literature is limited in several important respects. First, most studies of targeted running mate effects focus on geography, specifically in terms of the vice presidential home state advantage. The vast majority of these studies find that running mates generally do not deliver a statistically significant home state advantage, or that such effects are conditional and rare (J. Campbell 1992; J. Campbell, Ali, and Jalalzai 2006; Devine and Kopko 2011, 2013, 2016, 2019; Dudley and Rapoport 1989; Garand 1988; Holbrook 1991; Kahane 2009; Mixon and Tyrone 2004; Morini 2015; Rosenstone 1983; Schultz 2016; Tubbesing 1973; but see Heersink and Peterson 2016). Only a small number of studies examine targeted running mate effects in terms of demography, specifically with respect to gender (Brox and Cassels 2009; Keeter 1985; Miller 1988; Ulbig 2010), religion (Jelen 2018), and ideology (Brox and Cassels 2009; Court 2012; Court and Lynch 2015; Krumel and Enami 2017). These studies indicate that Catholic and conservative running mates influence voting behavior among fellow in-group members, but women running mates do not.

Second, many of these studies analyze data from only one election, which limits the generalizability of their findings. Conversely, other studies (e.g., Dudley and Rapoport 1989; Jelen 2018) analyze pooled data from many elections, which limits their ability to detect the targeted effects of individual candidacies.

Third, most—if not all—previous studies of targeted running mate effects use only aggregate or cross-sectional survey data.[8] As a result, these studies cannot tell us whether voters' preferences actually *change* in response to the selection of an in-group running mate. The only way to directly measure such changes is to use panel data, whereby survey respondents report their intended vote choice before and after a running mate's selection.

Our analysis is designed to address all three of the existing literature's most significant limitations. First, we analyze targeted effects in terms of geography, demography, *and* ideology. Second, we use data from numerous elections years, beginning in 1952. In one case, we pool the data in order to draw general conclusions about the relationship between geographic identities and presidential vote choice. In all other cases, we disaggregate the data in order to evaluate targeted effects across individual election years.[9] Third, when possible, we use panel data to determine whether, and to what extent, individuals' voting preferences change in response to the selection of a running mate who shares their in-group identity. Altogether, this chapter represents the most comprehensive analysis of targeted running mate effects to date.

METHODOLOGY

In this chapter, we analyze cross-sectional data from the 1952–2016 American National Election Studies (ANES) Cumulative File, as well as panel data from the Knowledge Networks (KN) Associated Press–Yahoo! News Panel, in 2008, and The American Panel Survey (TAPS), in 2012 and 2016. As noted earlier in the chapter, previous studies of targeted running mate effects exclusively have relied on aggregate or cross-sectional data. Using aggregate data for such analyses is problematic because targeted running mate effects necessarily involve an individual-level relationship between social or political characteristics and vote choice; that is to say, *individuals*—not states or other aggregate populations—cast presidential votes, and so they are the proper units of analysis for any study of the determinants of vote choice. While aggregate data (e.g., state-level election results) are most readily available, and for some elections they represent the only viable option for analysis, using them to study an individual relationship, such as targeted running mate effects, risks errors in causal inference known as ecological fallacies (see Devine and Kopko 2019). Therefore, in this chapter we only use individual-level data. Moreover, for reasons already discussed, we prefer to use panel data whenever possible. Due to their more complex and resource-intensive design, however, panel surveys (especially ones that include three or more waves, as our methodology requires; see later discussion) are less readily available than cross-sectional data, particularly for elections occurring in the twentieth century. These practical realities compel us to use cross-sectional and panel data in the analysis that follows.

Cross-Sectional Data

For the first part of this analysis, we use cross-sectional data, from ANES, to estimate the relationship between a respondent's identification with a particular geographic, demographic, or ideological group (independent variable) and his or her presidential vote choice (dependent variable), in the 1952–2016 presidential elections. We present these estimates for each election year, so as to make comparisons in relation to whether an in-group running mate was or was not on the ballot in that election. For some groups, we may find a statistically significant relationship across most election years, or no such relationship. Our expectation is that, if targeted running mate effects occur, this relationship should change, and in the expected direction, in those election years that featured a running mate who belonged to the group in question. In other words, this relationship should be statistically significant, and positively related to voting for the presidential ticket that included the in-group running mate.

By way of example, consider the relationship between gender and vote choice. If women running mates "deliver" votes among women, we should find that in 1984 (Geraldine Ferraro, Democrat) and in 2008 (Sarah Palin, Republican), the effect of gender on vote choice (a) was statistically significant, whereas it had not been so in most or all other election years, and signed so as to indicate an increased likelihood of voting for the Democratic and Republican tickets, respectively; or, (b) was statistically significant, as in most or all other election years, but with a coefficient that was greater than in other election years and signed so as to indicate an increased likelihood of voting for the Democratic and Republican tickets, respectively.

Our cross-sectional data analysis uses logistic regression to estimate the relationship between identification with a particular group (1 = identifies with the group, 0 = does not identify with the group) and presidential vote choice (1 = Democratic vote, 0 = Republican vote), while controlling for those factors included in our direct effect models from chapter 3. For ease of interpretation, we use graphs to plot the independent variable's coefficient estimate, with 95 percent confidence intervals, in each election. This is the same approach used by Knuckey (2012, 285) and Burmila and Ryan (2013, 955) to depict the relationship between vice presidential candidate evaluations and presidential vote choice in the 2008 election.

Panel Data

For the second part of this analysis, we use panel data, from KN and TAPS, to estimate *changes* in the relationship between the respondent's identification with a particular geographic, demographic, or ideological group (independent variable) and his or her intended presidential vote choice (dependent variable), following the selection of an in-group running mate. Our analysis is modeled on Lenz's (2012) three-wave test for panel data.[10] This methodology estimates the extent to which an intervening event causes changes in the hypothesized relationship between a given independent variable and a given dependent variable, by comparing the dynamics of that relationship in the periods prior to versus subsequent to the event in question. For example, Kinder and Kalmoe (2017, 108) use this approach to analyze ideological priming in the 1980 election, citing Ronald Reagan's nomination for president by the Republican Party as a potential intervening event. They conclude that Reagan did not prime ideological voting because the effect of ideological identification on intended vote choice was no greater after his nomination than it had been beforehand.

Using this methodology requires that we estimate at least two models, the first of which uses data from two waves of panel respondents surveyed *prior* to the intervening event, and the second of which uses data from the wave immediately preceding that event *and* one subsequent to it. For each model, we regress the dependent variable on the independent variable, controlling for the dependent variable's value in the previous wave. This allows us to determine whether the independent variable (i.e., identification with a particular geographic, demographic, or ideological group) has a statistically significant effect on the dependent variable (i.e., vote choice), subsequent to the intervening event (i.e., vice presidential selection), *that is independent of preexisting preferences.* In other words, it tells us whether, and to what extent, the relationship between group identification and intended vote choice *changed* following the selection of an in-group running mate. Evidence of targeted running mate effects could take two forms when one uses this methodology. First, the relationship described earlier might be statistically significant, and correctly signed, subsequent to but not prior to vice presidential selection. Second, the relationship might be statistically significant, and correctly signed, both prior to and subsequent to vice presidential selection, but clearly to a greater degree in the postselection period.

For example, in 2008, we would conclude that Sarah Palin had a targeted effect on women voters if (a) gender's effect on intended vote choice, controlling for previous intentions, was statistically significant and correctly signed in the wave immediately following Palin's selection on August 29 (i.e., September), whereas this had not been the case in the wave that most closely preceded it (i.e., June); or, (b) gender's effect on intended vote choice, controlling for previous intentions, was statistically significant and correctly signed in the waves prior to *and* subsequent to her selection but greater in magnitude, with respect to coefficient estimates, in the latter period.

Our panel data analysis uses logistic regression to estimate the relationship between identification with a particular group and intended presidential vote choice, while controlling for intended vote choice in the previous, preselection wave, and those other factors included in our direct effects models from chapter 3.[11] The independent variables are coded 1 for respondents who identify with the group in question and 0 for those who do not. The dependent variable is coded in two different ways, depending on the party of the running mate in question. When analyzing targeted effects for Democratic running mates (i.e., Joe Biden, 2008; Tim Kaine, 2016), the vote choice variables are coded 1 for a Democratic vote and 0 for a Republican vote. When analyzing targeted effects for Republican running mates (i.e., Sarah Palin, 2008; Paul Ryan, 2012; Mike Pence, 2016), the vote choice variables are coded 1 for a Republican vote and 0 for a Democratic vote.

Finally, it is important to note that KN and TAPS provide panel data from multiple waves following vice presidential selection in each of the years that we analyze. This allows us to estimate targeted effects not only in the immediate aftermath of those selections but also over the course of the campaign and in terms of actual vote choice, as reported by respondents after Election Day.[12]

CROSS-SECTIONAL (ANES) ANALYSIS

Our analysis of targeted running mate effects begins with cross-sectional data from the 1952–2016 ANES. First, we analyze these effects in terms of geographic identity (i.e., home state, division, or region); second, demographic identity (i.e., female, Catholic, evangelical Christian, Jewish); and third, ideological identity (i.e., liberal, conservative).

Geographic Effects

In this section, we examine targeted geographic effects—that is, the running mate's effect on voters in his or her home state, division, or region. It is only appropriate to begin our analysis here, since geography dominates considerations of targeted running mate effects. Indeed, as we note earlier, scholars have devoted far more attention to studying running mates' geographic effects than their demographic or ideological effects. Also, geography clearly has been the most salient strategic consideration with respect to vice presidential selection, throughout US history (see Devine and Kopko 2016, chaps. 1–2). Even in recent years, more than half of all media profiles of potential running mates have referenced their (in)ability to "deliver" a home state or region in the presidential election (22–23).

Yet, as we note earlier in this chapter, nearly all previous studies of this topic find that running mates generally do not have a statistically significant effect on voting in their home state or region, or that these effects occur only under conditions that most vice presidential candidacies do not meet. Our analysis expands on previous studies in three important ways: first, by using individual- rather than aggregate-level data to analyze the individual-level relationship between where one lives and for whom one votes (see also Devine and Kopko 2016, 2019); second, by adding data from recent presidential elections that were not available for inclusion in many previous studies; and, third, by assessing geographic running mate effects at three levels—home state, region, and division—in order to capture the full scope of their effects in a way that previous studies do not.[13]

Data for this analysis come from the ANES Cumulative File, which includes 38,558 survey respondents from the 1952–2016 presidential election years, in total. Of these respondents, 930 lived in the same state as the Democratic running mate in a given election year (2.41 percent); 4,975 lived in the same census division (12.90 percent); and 12,674 lived in the same census region (32.87 percent). Additionally, 1,241 respondents lived in the same state as the Republican running mate in a given election year (3.22 percent); 5,107 lived in the same census division (13.24 percent); and 9,457 lived in the same census region (24.53 percent). We pool across election years to construct six independent variables, capturing whether respondents were subject to targeted geographic effects in the 1952–2016 elections. Specifically, these variables correspond to the party of the running mate in question (Democratic or Republican) and the geographic level of measurement (home state, home division, or home region). Each independent variable is coded 1 for living in the same state/division/region as the Democratic or Republican Party's running mate, and 0 otherwise. In addition, we construct a parallel set of variables indicating whether respondents lived in the same state, division, or region, as a given *presidential* candidate.

Table 4.1 presents the results from our pooled data analysis, including Model 1 (home state effects), Model 2 (home division effects), and Model 3 (home region effects).[14] It is necessary to test each type of geographic effect separately, given their interdependence. That is to say, every respondent who lives in the running mate's home state by definition also lives in his or her home division and region. Including each of these variables in a single model therefore would violate a key assumption of logistic regression—that all observations are independently distributed.

None of the geographic variables in table 4.1 are statistically significant, at $p < .05$. Thus, we *cannot* say, with 95 percent confidence, that those respondents who lived in the running mate's home state, division, or region, in a given election year, were any more likely than other respondents to vote for his or her presidential ticket. However, as is the case in previous studies (e.g., Devine and Kopko 2013, 2016; Holbrook 1991; Lewis-Beck and Rice 1983), we do find that presidential candidates enjoy a statistically significant home state advantage (Model 1). Also, for the first time in the literature, we identify a similar advantage within the home division (Model 2)—but this is only for Republican presidential candidates, and, judging by its coefficient, it is weaker than the presidential home *state* advantage. However, we find no evidence of an electoral advantage at the regional level (Model 3).

But geographic regions generally do not provide the coherent sense of identity or the consistent set of behavioral cues that, as we explain earlier in this chapter, should be a prerequisite for achieving targeted effects. That is, with one exception: the US South. Indeed, the South always has been the most culturally distinctive and politically cohesive region in the United States (e.g., Key 1949), and it continues to command scholarly attention to this day (e.g., Aldrich and Griffin 2018; McKee 2018). Furthermore, southern voters often have been the target of ticket-balancing strategies, most notably when John F. Kennedy selected Lyndon Johnson, of Texas, as his running mate in 1960. While the conventional wisdom has it that Johnson "delivered" Texas and the South for Kennedy in that election, the most comprehensive analysis of available survey data, to date, indicates that he provided no such advantage (Devine and Kopko 2016, chap. 6; but see Court 2012, 45–52, for a survey-based analysis of southern versus nonsouthern Democrats). Whatever effect Johnson might have had in that year's election, certainly the perception that southern running mates are effective at winning over southern voters influenced his selection and the Democratic ticket's campaign strategy, as has been the case

Table 4.1. Geographic Effects on Democratic Vote Choice, 1952–2016 ANES

Variables	Model 1	Model 2	Model 3
Republican presidential home state	−0.339*	—	—
0 = No, 1 = yes	(0.150)	—	—
Republican vice presidential home state	0.091	—	—
0 = No, 1 = yes	(0.280)	—	—
Democratic presidential home state	0.426*	—	—
0 = No, 1 = yes	(0.207)	—	—
Democratic vice presidential home state	−0.132	—	—
0 = No, 1 = yes	(0.168)	—	—
Republican presidential home division	—	−0.190*	—
0 = No, 1 = yes	—	(0.089)	—
Republican vice presidential home division	—	0.069	—
0 = No, 1 = yes	—	(0.122)	—
Democratic presidential home division	—	0.102	—
0 = No, 1 = yes	—	(0.107)	—
Democratic vice presidential home division	—	0.166	—
0 = No, 1 = yes	—	(0.101)	—
Republican presidential home region	—	—	−0.080
0 = No, 1 = yes	—	—	(0.069)
Republican vice presidential home region	—	—	0.009
0 = No, 1 = yes	—	—	(0.111)
Democratic presidential home region	—	—	0.034
0 = No, 1 = yes	—	—	(0.059)
Democratic vice presidential home region	—	—	0.047
0 = No, 1 = yes	—	—	(0.102)
Republican	−1.985***	−1.982***	1.981***
0 = No, 1 = yes	(0.170)	(0.168)	(0.167)
Democrat	1.932***	1.936***	1.934***
0 = No, 1 = yes	(0.120)	(0.121)	(0.122)
Female	0.065+	0.063	0.065+
0 = No, 1 = yes	(0.038)	(0.039)	(0.039)
Age	−0.002	−0.002	−0.002
Continuous	(0.002)	(0.002)	(0.002)
Income	−0.124***	−0.123***	−0.112**
1 = Under 17th percentile, to			
5 = over 95th percentile	(0.037)	(0.037)	(0.038)
Education	0.151*	0.148*	0.149*
1 = No HS degree, to 5 = advanced degree	(0.066)	(0.068)	(0.068)
White	−1.502***	−1.496***	−1.492***
0 = No, 1 = yes	(0.107)	(0.106)	(0.105)
South	−0.535***	−0.581***	−0.571***
0 = No, 1 = yes	(0.084)	(0.084)	(0.086)
Constant	1.153***	1.140***	1.139***
	(0.305)	(0.311)	(0.306)
Reduction in error	70.10%	70.01%	70.06%
Percent correctly predicted	85.62%	85.58%	85.61%
Observations	22,668	22,668	22,668

Robust standard errors are in parentheses. Standard errors are clustered by years.

   ***p < .001, **p < .01, *p < .05, +p < .10.

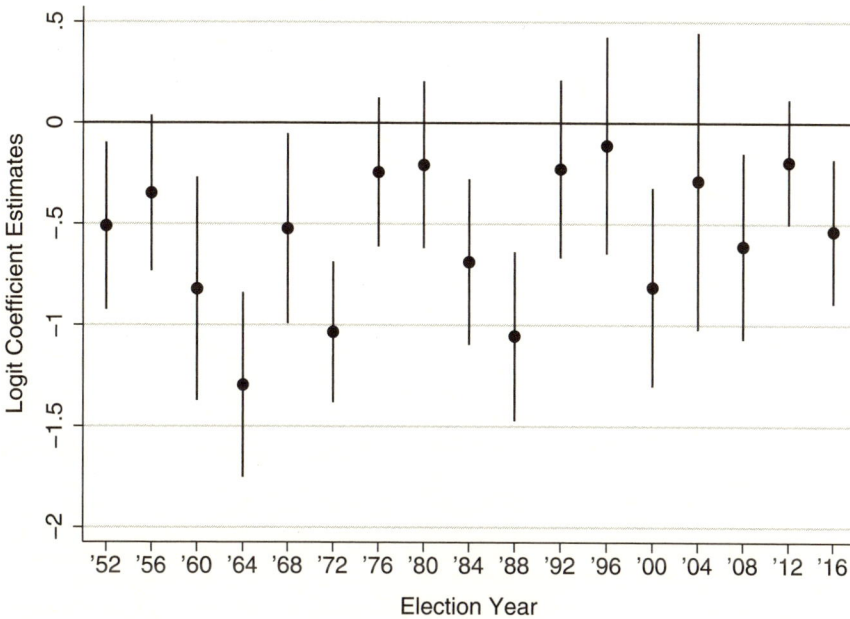

Figure 4.1. Effect of region (southerner) on Democratic vote choice, 1952–2016 ANES

in other elections since that time (e.g., Lloyd Bentsen in 1988, John Edwards in 2004; see chapter 1).

But is this assumption correct? Are southerners, in fact, more likely to vote for a presidential ticket that includes one of their own as the running mate? The ANES data are ideal for testing this relationship because they include large samples of southern respondents in each election year since 1952, including many years in which the Democratic (1952, 1956, 1960, 1988, 1992, 1996, 2004, 2016) or Republican (1980, 1984) running mate also was a southerner.[15] We use these data to estimate the effect of southern identification (1 = southerner, 0 = nonsoutherner)[16] on presidential vote choice (1 = Democratic vote, 0 = Republican vote) in each of the 1952–2016 elections, controlling for party identification and other relevant covariates.[17] For ease of interpretation, figure 4.1 plots the coefficient estimates for the southern variable, with 95 percent confidence intervals, for each election year.[18]

Of course, in many of these elections, more than one presidential or vice presidential candidate came from the South. Therefore, to determine whether southern running mates had a targeted effect on vote choice, we must focus on those elections in which the *only* southerner on either ticket was the

Democratic (Lyndon Johnson, 1960; Tim Kaine, 2016) or Republican (George H. W. Bush, 1984) running mate. Specifically, we should find that southern respondents were significantly more likely than in other elections to vote for the Democratic ticket in 1960 and 2016, and the Republican ticket in 1984, after controlling for the effects of party identification and other relevant covariates.

That is not what we see in figure 4.1. Southern identification was a statistically significant predictor of *Republican* voting in 1960 and 2016—this, despite the Democratic running mate being the only southerner on the ballot in those elections.[19] While we see the same result in 1984, it is hardly clear that the Republican running mate, George H. W. Bush, deserves credit for delivering the South. After all, southerners were significantly more likely to vote for the Republican ticket in most of the 1952–2016 elections—ten out of seventeen, to be exact. For that matter, this relationship is not particularly strong in 1984, and its confidence intervals overlap with those of every other estimate.

Simply put: there is no reason to believe, on the basis of this evidence, that southern running mates deliver southern votes.[20] Nor do we find any evidence that running mates, in general, win votes for their ticket based on home state or regional appeal. When it comes to vice presidential selection, our analysis suggests, geography is overrated.

Demographic Effects

One advantage when analyzing geographic effects is that there are plenty of cases to study; after all, every running mate has a home state. But when it comes to demographics, not every running mate can appeal to a salient, distinctive in-group. Indeed, the vast majority of running mates—even in recent years—have been white, male, and/or (mainline) Protestant. In other words, very few of them have belonged to the demographic groups that presidential campaigns typically target for particular strategic appeals. At the time of this writing, for instance, there has never been an African American, Latino, or Asian American running mate on a major party ticket. And only two women have run for vice president on a major party ticket: Geraldine Ferraro, in 1984, and Sarah Palin, in 2008. In terms of religion, there has been only one Jewish running mate: Joe Lieberman, in 2000. And several running mates have identified with religious groups that, while not underrepresented minorities in modern politics, arguably fit our criteria for targeted effects (i.e., salience,

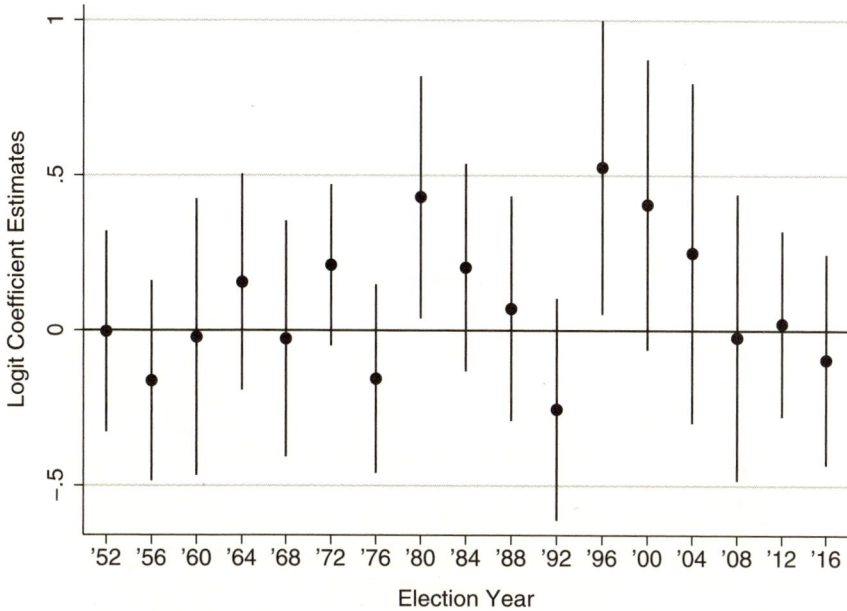

Figure 4.2. Effect of gender (woman) on Democratic vote choice, 1952–2016 ANES

a coherent sense of identity, sizable but not constituting a majority group): Catholics and evangelical Christians. Catholic running mates since 1952 include Republicans William Miller (1964) and Paul Ryan (2012), as well as Democrats Edmund Muskie (1968), Sargent Shriver (1972), Geraldine Ferraro (1984), Joe Biden (2008, 2012), and Tim Kaine (2016). Evangelical Christian running mates include Republicans Sarah Palin (2008) and Mike Pence (2016).[21] In this section, we use the same methodolocial approach as in figure 4.1 to estimate these running mates' effects on voters who shared their gender or religious identity.

Figure 4.2 plots the effect of gender on presidential vote choice in the 1952–2016 elections. If—as even presidential candidates, including Walter Mondale and John McCain, have believed (see chapter 1)—selecting a woman running mate increases a ticket's vote share among women, gender (1 = woman, 0 = man) should be clearly and positively associated with voting for the Democratic ticket (Mondale-Ferraro) in 1984, and the Republican ticket (McCain-Palin) in 2008. Plainly, this is not the case. In fact, we cannot reject the null hypothesis that gender—when controlling for other relevant covariates, including party identification—has *no* effect on vote choice in either election.

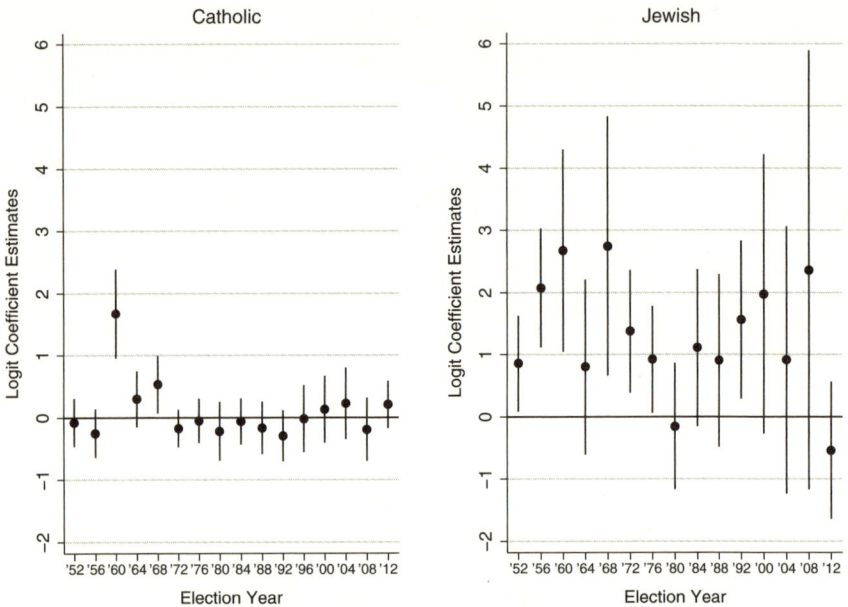

Figure 4.3. Effect of religion (Catholic or Jewish) on Democratic vote choice, 1952–2012 ANES

This result is the same as in most other elections; gender had a statistically significant, independent effect on vote choice only in 1980 and 1996, with women favoring the Democratic ticket in both elections.

What about religion? Figure 4.3 plots the effects of identification with two major religious groups, Catholics and Jews, in the 1952–2012 elections.[22] Figure 4.4 does the same for evangelical Christians, in the 1964–1968 and 1980–2016 elections.[23] Unfortunately, the ANES did not use a consistent measure of evangelical identification throughout much of its time series, including in several recent elections. However, in the 1960s and then again for every election since 1980, it has included a measure of biblical literalism that scholars commonly use as a proxy for Christian evangelicalism or fundamentalism (see Hoffman and Bartkowski 2008, 1245). Specifically, respondents who agree with a statement endorsing literal interpretation of the Bible as the Word of God are coded as 1 (i.e., evangelical), while those who do not agree with this statement are coded as 0 (i.e., not evangelical).[24]

First, with respect to Catholics, we find very little evidence of targeted effects in figure 4.3. In fact, this variable is statistically significant in only two

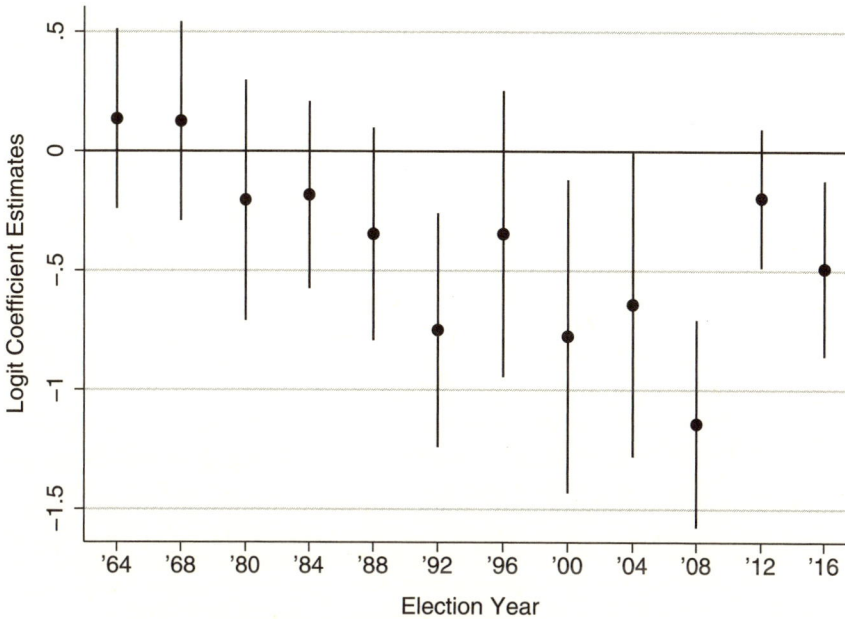

Figure 4.4. Effect of religion (evangelical Christian) on Democratic vote choice, 1964–1968 and 1980–2016 ANES

election years. The first was in 1960, when John Kennedy became only the second Catholic to win a major party's presidential nomination, and the first to win a presidential election. Catholic identification clearly had a strong effect on vote choice in that election, and in Kennedy's favor. The second, and last, instance in which Catholic identification significantly influenced vote choice was in 1968. That year, Edmund Muskie became the Democratic Party's first Catholic vice presidential nominee. And, sure enough, Catholics were significantly more likely to cast a vote for the Democratic ticket that year. But four years earlier, when William Miller became the first Catholic running mate on any major party ticket, Catholic identification had no discernible effect on vote choice.[25] In that case, it cannot be taken for granted that Catholic running mates will win over Catholic voters, or that they have done so consistently in past elections. In fact, according to our data, Catholic identification has not had a statistically significant effect on vote choice in any election since 1968—including several in which the Democratic (1972, 1984, 2008, 2012) or Republican (2012) running mate has been Catholic.

Our analysis of Jewish voters is quite different from that of Catholics. First, there has been only one Jewish running mate: Joe Lieberman, in 2000. Second, as figure 4.3 indicates, Jewish identification often has had a statistically significant effect on presidential vote choice—in seven of the fifteen elections that we analyze, to be exact, and always in favor of the Democratic Party.[26] But in 2000, as in all but one election since 1980, this effect is not statistically significant. What do we make of this result? Did the first Jewish vice presidential candidate in US history really fail to have *any* effect on Jewish voters?

Actually, one must interpret these results with great caution. The problem is that Jews represent only about 2 percent of the US population (Lipka 2013), and therefore a comparable percentage of respondents in nationally representative surveys. Because the ANES typically surveys about two thousand respondents, many of whom did not cast a vote for president, this means that our estimates from figure 4.3 are based on a very limited sample of Jewish voters. In fact, the 2000 ANES included only thirty-two Jewish voters! Surely, this is why the 95 percent confidence intervals for that year's estimate, as in other years, are so wide. Given the relative imprecision of these estimates, it might be the case that Jewish identification significantly influenced vote choice in 2000, and in favor of the Democratic ticket, after all. But even if so, this would not constitute clear evidence of running mate effects. If, for instance, Jewish identification had a similar effect on voting behavior in other elections right before and after 2000, one might conclude that Lieberman's candidacy did not have any discernible, targeted effect; in other words, this relationship might have been what one would expect, with or without Lieberman on the ticket.[27]

Finally, figure 4.4 illustrates the effect of Christian evangelicalism on presidential vote choice in the 1964–1968 and 1980–2016 elections. While all but one running mate during these periods identified as Christian (Lieberman being the exception), most were mainline Protestants or Catholics, and only two stand out as being closely identified with evangelical Christianity: Sarah Palin, in 2008, and Mike Pence, in 2016. Indeed, evangelicalism had a statistically significant effect on vote choice in both of these elections, and in favor of Republicans. But it is difficult to say whether this in itself constitutes evidence of targeted running mate effects, since evangelical Christians, broadly speaking, have become increasingly associated with the Republican Party since the 1980s and 1990s (e.g., Levendusky 2009). In fact, we see similar effects in other recent elections, including 1992, 2000, and 2004.[28] And we cannot say, with 95 percent confidence, that evangelicalism had a greater effect on vote choice in 2008 and 2016 than in other years, since the confidence intervals on those estimates overlap with most (2008) or all (2016) of those from other election years.

Ideological Effects

In comparison to the geographic and demographic categories that we analyze earlier, it might seem odd to study ideology in terms of group identity and targeted effects. However, recent research shows that ideological groups (i.e., liberals and conservatives) often function as important sources of social identity and influence political attitudes and behaviors in ways that social identity theory would predict (e.g., Devine 2015; Malka and Lelkes 2010). Indeed, given low levels of ideological sophistication and constraint in the mass public (Converse 1964; Kinder and Kalmoe 2017), some scholars argue that it makes more sense to think of ideology in social identity, or symbolic, terms than as an abstract belief system (see Devine 2015).

Sure enough, discussions of vice presidential selection often invoke the running mate's ideological identity and his or her likely effect on voting behavior within certain ideological groups. For example, some of the journalists and politicians cited at the beginning of this chapter speculated that Tim Kaine's vice presidential candidacy "could appeal to moderate constituencies but could also draw concerns from progressives" (Siddiqui 2016), or that Mike Pence's "strong record as both a national security and social conservative . . . will help bring those coalitions home for the fall campaign" (McPherson 2016).

In this section, we analyze the effects of ideological identification on vote choice in the 1964–2016 presidential elections.[29] To maximize the scope of this analysis, we use two measures of ideological identification from the ANES. First, for 1964 and 1968, we use respondents' feeling thermometer ratings of "liberals" and "conservatives." Second, for elections since 1972, we use the traditional ideological self-placement scale introduced in that year's ANES. Specifically, we classify respondents as liberals (conservatives) if they placed themselves at one of the following positions: "slightly liberal (conservative)," "liberal (conservative)," or "very liberal (conservative)."[30] Then, as in the previous analyses, we regress presidential vote choice on ideological identity in each election year and plot the regression coefficients (with 95 percent confidence intervals).

But what are we looking for, exactly, in terms of targeted effects? After all, conservatives, in general, always should be expected to vote for Republicans, and liberals for Democrats. Moreover, it seems fair to assume that every Republican running mate since 1964 has been conservative, at least more so than moderate or liberal, and vice versa for Democratic running mates. In that case, certainly our expectation is not that conservative (liberal) identification will have a statistically significant effect on vote choice *only* in those elections that featured a conservative (liberal) as the Republican (Democratic) running mate; quite simply, this should be the case in every election. Rather, our expectation is that, if these targeted effects occur, ideological identification should have a *greater* effect on vote choice whenever the running mate most clearly qualifies as a member of, and perhaps a leader within, the ideological in-group in question.

And when has that been the case? To identify such candidacies, we use the ideological classifications developed by Sigelman and Wahlbeck (1997, 858) and Hiller and Kriner (2008, 411) and extend them to encompass the 2008–2016 elections. This procedure identifies ten particularly conservative Republican running mates (in the context of their time): William Miller, 1964; Bob Dole, 1976; Dan Quayle, 1988 and 1992; Jack Kemp, 1996; Dick Cheney, 2000 and 2004; Sarah Palin, 2008; Paul Ryan, 2012; and Mike Pence, 2016. Also, it identifies five particularly liberal Democratic running mates: Hubert Humphrey, 1964; Sargent Shriver, 1972; Walter Mondale, 1976 and 1980; and Geraldine Ferraro, 1984.

Figure 4.5 depicts the effects of conservative or liberal identification on vote choice, in the 1964–2016 presidential elections. As expected, conservatives have been significantly more likely to vote for the Republican ticket, and liberals for the Democratic ticket, in nearly every election since 1964 (and every one since 1980). But there is no clear evidence of targeted effects. For conservatives, we do find that the coefficient estimates generally are greater in later elections, when Republicans consistently chose more conservative running mates. However, the confidence intervals on these coefficients overlap with several earlier elections that did not feature such running mates. Also, in earlier years, the estimates differ minimally across elections that featured a particularly conservative running mate (1964, 1976) and many of those that did not (1972, 1980, 1984). Finally, it is worth noting that in 2008 and 2016—despite the Republican running mates' conservative bona fides, and the presidential candidates' relative lack thereof—conservative identification had virtually the same effect on vote choice as in 2004, when Dick Cheney ran for reelection as George W. Bush's vice president.

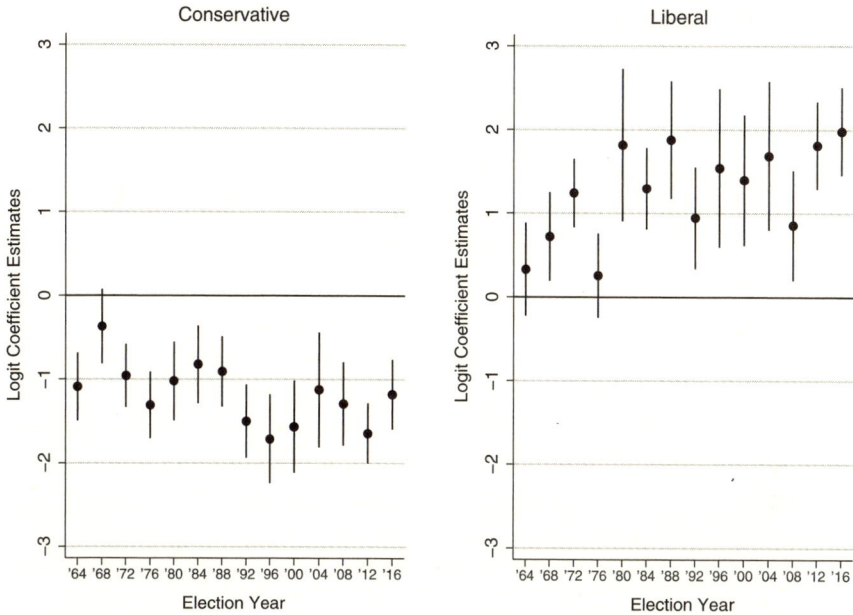

Figure 4.5. Effect of ideology (conservative or liberal) on Democratic vote choice, 1964–2016 ANES

We find no clear evidence of targeted ideological effects among liberals, either. In fact, liberal identification has the weakest effect on vote choice in those earlier elections that featured a particularly liberal running mate, and in two of those elections (1964 and 1976) the effect is indistinguishable from zero. Moreover, the coefficient estimate for this variable was highest in 2016, when many wondered whether Tim Kaine's centrism would alienate progressive voters, and second highest in 1988, when Lloyd Bentsen—whom Sigelman and Wahlbeck (1997) actually rate as "conservative"—was Michael Dukakis's running mate. Quite simply, this pattern of results provides no reason to believe that the effect of liberal—or, for that matter, conservative—identification on vote choice is systematically related to vice presidential selection.

Discussion

Thus far, our analysis provides little evidence that running mates have targeted effects on vote choice—whether in terms of geography, demography, or ideology. However, this may be attributable to the methodological limitations of using cross-sectional data. Consider that in this section, we make inferences about targeted running mate effects only based on the relationship between a given independent variable (e.g., Catholic or conservative identification) and our dependent variable, presidential vote choice. But, in each case, it is quite likely—if not certain—that factors other than vice presidential selection caused these relationships to vary across elections. For instance, Catholics' shift toward the Democratic Party in 1968 might have been attributable not to Edmund Muskie's vice presidential candidacy but to faith-based opposition to the Vietnam War, allegiance to the Kennedy legacy following then presidential candidate Robert Kennedy's assassination in June of that year, or any number of other factors. Likewise, the somewhat increased effect of conservative identification on vote choice since the 1990s probably is not attributable to a series of conservative Republican running mates but to much broader trends in ideological and partisan polarization (see L. Mason 2018)—particularly given that liberal identification had a parallel effect during this period, while Democratic running mates became (relatively) *less* liberal.

In short, we need better data in order to evaluate targeted running mate effects. Indeed, we need data that tell us whether voters actually *change their minds* about the presidential race following the selection of an in-group running mate. Panel surveys provide an obvious solution—particularly when respondents report their intended presidential vote over successive panel "waves," including those that take place before *and* after the vice presidential candidate's selection. We examine two such data sources in the next section to determine—across a limited number of recent elections, but with greatly enhanced methodological precision—whether running mates are effective at targeting voters who share their geographic, demographic, or ideological identities.

PANEL DATA

In this section, we analyze panel data from the 2008, 2012, and 2016 presidential elections. The 2008 data come from the KN Associated Press–Yahoo! News Panel—specifically, its June, September, early October, late October, and November waves.[31] The 2012 and 2016 data come from TAPS—specifically, the monthly waves conducted between May (2016) or June (2012) and November of those years.

Our purpose, in analyzing panel data, is to estimate *changes* in the relationship between a particular group identity and intended presidential vote choice, following the selection of an in-group running mate. In other words, *after controlling for a respondent's preexisting preferences*, does identification with the group in question significantly predict intended vote choice in the postselection period? And is this effect clearly stronger after the selection of an in-group running mate than it was beforehand?

Our panel data encompass five vice presidential selections: Sarah Palin (August 29) and Joe Biden (August 23), in 2008; Paul Ryan (August 11), in 2012; and Mike Pence (July 16) and Tim Kaine (July 22), in 2016. When estimating each running mate's targeted effects, we only focus on the most salient aspects of his or her identity. Specifically, we analyze the following groups: midwesterners (Ryan, Pence); southerners (Kaine); women (Palin); Catholics (Biden, Ryan, Kaine); evangelical Christians (Palin, Pence); and conservatives (Palin, Ryan, Pence). Also, we analyze Tim Kaine's potential appeal to Latino voters.

Sarah Palin and Joe Biden (2008)

Figure 4.6 illustrates the effects of three identities on presidential vote choice, before and after Sarah Palin's selection as John McCain's running mate: gender (1 = female, 0 = male), evangelicalism (1 = evangelical Christian, 0 = not evangelical Christian), and conservatism (1 = conservative, 0 = not conservative).[32] As in subsequent analyses, we present these effects for the preselection wave (June) and each of the postselection waves (September, early October, late October, November). This allows us to determine whether any potential effects persisted throughout the campaign and ultimately manifested in vote choice.

Our analysis indicates that Palin's selection did not deliver votes among women, evangelicals, or conservatives. That is to say, none of these identities had a statistically significant effect on reported vote choice (November wave), independent of—or, when controlling for—respondents' electoral preferences from the period just *prior* to Palin's selection (June wave). With respect to gender, Palin's selection did not cause women to become more willing to vote for the Republican ticket at any point during the campaign; indeed, gender's effect is indistinguishable from zero in each postselection wave, when controlling for intended vote choice in the preselection wave. Evangelicals and conservatives, however, were significantly more likely to prefer the Republican

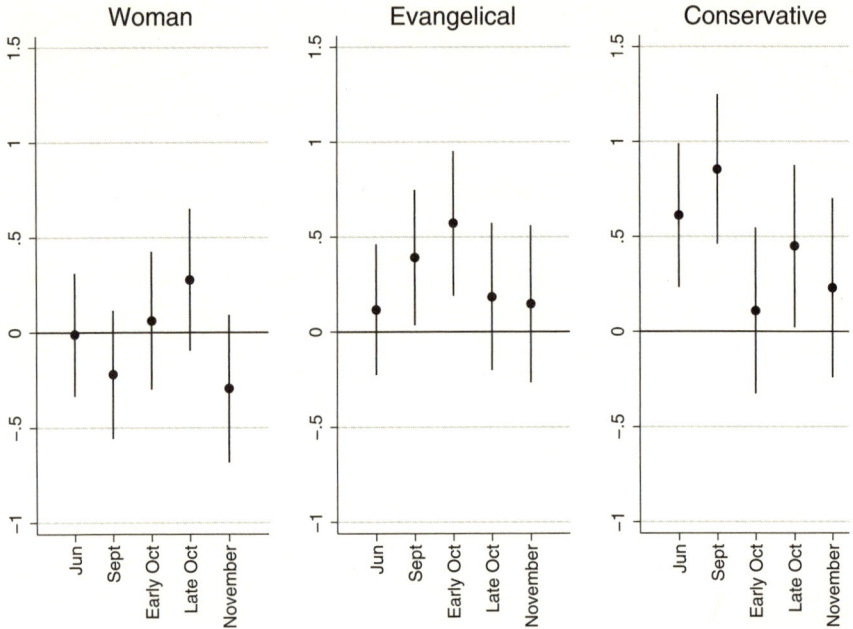

Figure 4.6. Dynamic effects of gender (woman), religion (evangelical Christian), and ideology (conservative) on intended Republican vote choice, 2008 KN

ticket following Palin's selection—at least for a while. These effects apparently lasted until early October, for evangelicals, and late October, for conservatives. But they disappeared by Election Day.

Figure 4.7 suggests the same conclusion with respect to Joe Biden's effect on fellow Catholics in 2008, but in the opposite direction.[33] Following Biden's selection as Barack Obama's running mate on August 23 of that year, Catholics actually became significantly *less* likely to support the Democratic ticket in September. And this was the case, again, in late October. By November, though, this effect had disappeared; in other words, being Catholic did not make respondents any more or less likely to vote for Biden's Democratic ticket, after accounting for their preselection preferences.[34]

Paul Ryan (2012)

To estimate Paul Ryan's targeted effect on voters in 2012, we use panel data from TAPS. Specifically, we analyze the two waves conducted just prior to

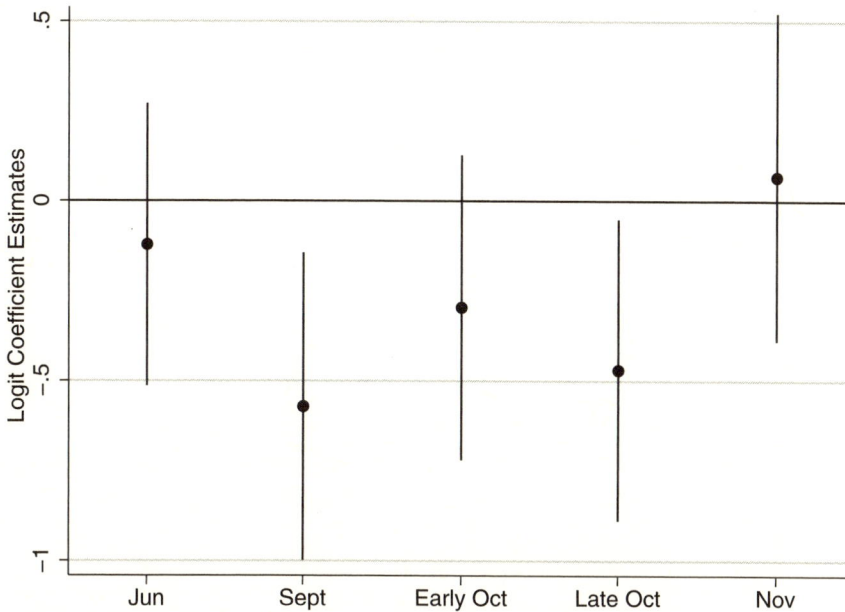

Figure 4.7. Dynamic effect of religion (Catholic) on intended Democratic vote choice, 2008 KN

Ryan's selection on August 11 of that year (June and July), one wave conducted during the same month (August), two waves conducted afterward but before the election (September and October), and one wave conducted after the election (November).[35] In each wave, we regress (intended) presidential vote choice on one of three group identities that Paul Ryan shared: midwesterner (1 = lives in the Midwest, 0 = does not live in the Midwest), Catholic (1 = Catholic, 0 = not Catholic), and conservative (1 = conservative, 0 = not conservative).[36] We provide no such analysis for Joe Biden in 2012 because he was the incumbent vice president that year and so most voters probably assumed that he was going to be the Democratic running mate again; thus, Biden's renomination does not constitute an intervening event, for the purposes of our analysis.

Figure 4.8 indicates that Paul Ryan's selection did not win over midwesterner and Catholic voters to the Republican ticket. We do see a spike in midwesterners' preferences for that ticket in August, when Ryan was announced as Mitt Romney's running mate. But this effect faded one month later and did not return by Election Day. For Catholics, we observe no change in intended

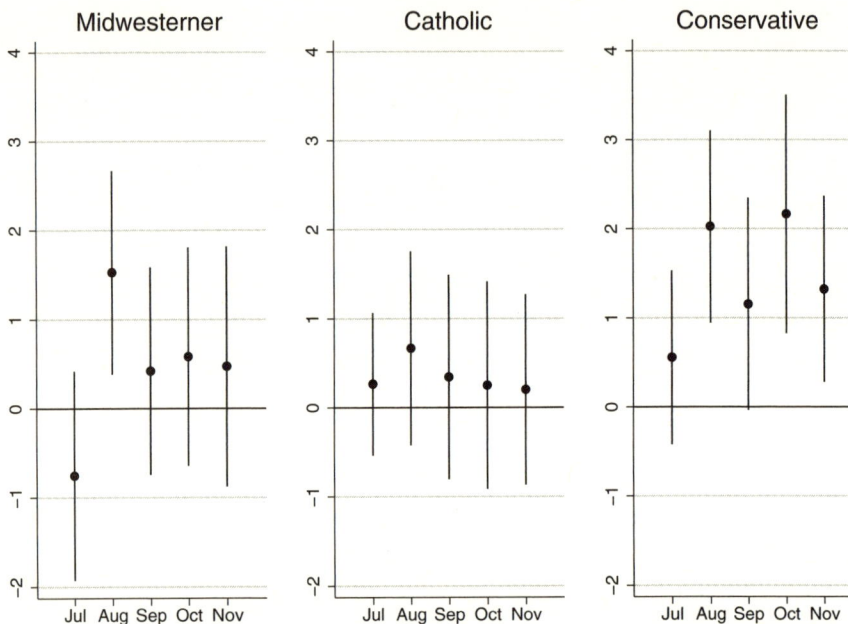

Figure 4.8. Dynamic effects of region (midwesterner), religion (Catholic), and ideology (conservative) on intended Republican vote choice, 2012 TAPS

vote choice at any point during the campaign. One might attribute this to Biden and Ryan simply canceling out each other's influence on fellow Catholics. However, as noted previously, Biden was an incumbent, and our methodology controls for preexisting electoral preferences. This tell us that the addition of a Catholic running mate to the Republican ticket did nothing to shift Catholic voters in that party's direction.

There is good reason to believe, however, that Paul Ryan's vice presidential candidacy won votes from one critical target group: conservatives. Indeed, Ryan had the reputation of being a conservative leader within the Republican Party—a visionary, to his admirers, and an extremist, to his critics. It was this reputation that later helped him win election as the Republican Speaker of the House, in 2015. And, quite clearly, this reputation also contributed to his selection as Mitt Romney's running mate. Romney, whose mixed ideological record raised doubts among many conservatives during the 2012 Republican presidential primaries, and even into the general election, seemed to believe that Ryan's ideological orthodoxy would help bring disaffected conservatives back into the Republican coalition. Judging by the available evidence, this just might have worked. Prior to Ryan's selection (July), we see no change in the relationship between conservative identification and intended vote choice, when controlling for earlier preferences (June). But in the immediate wake of Ryan's selection, in August, conservative support for the Republican ticket spiked. This effect seemed to dissipate by the next month, just barely, but it was statistically significant again in October and, most important, at the time of the election. This is the first clear evidence of a targeted running mate effect, in terms of influencing actual (reported) vote choice in the election, to emerge from our panel data analysis.

Mike Pence and Tim Kaine (2016)

Finally, we examine targeted running mate effects in the 2016 presidential election, using TAPS data from the May–November (monthly) waves. Specifically, this includes two waves (May and June) conducted prior to Pence's selection as Donald Trump's running mate, on July 16, and Kaine's selection as Hillary Clinton's running mate, on July 22; one wave conducted during the same month (July); three waves conducted after their selections (August, September, and October); and one wave conducted after the election (November). Our analysis focuses on three group identities shared by Mike Pence: midwesterner (1 = lives in the Midwest, 0 = does not live in the Midwest), evangelical Christian (1 = evangelical, 0 = not evangelical), and conservative (1 = conservative, 0 = not conservative).[37] Also, we focus on two group identities shared by Tim Kaine: southerner (1 = lives in the South, 0 = does not live in the South) and Catholic (1 = Catholic, 0 = not Catholic). Finally, to evaluate widespread perceptions that Kaine's fluency in Spanish would help him win over Latino voters to the Democratic ticket (see earlier in this chapter), our analysis focuses on Latinos (1 = Latino, 0 = not Latino), as well.[38]

Given Donald Trump's unorthodox Republican candidacy, one might suspect that Mike Pence, of all running mates, really did help to bring midwesterners, evangelical Christians, and conservatives (back) into the party's electoral coalition. But, judging by the evidence in Figure 4.9, he did not. Midwesterners and conservatives did not shift in favor of the Republican ticket at any point during the campaign, nor in their ultimate vote choice, following

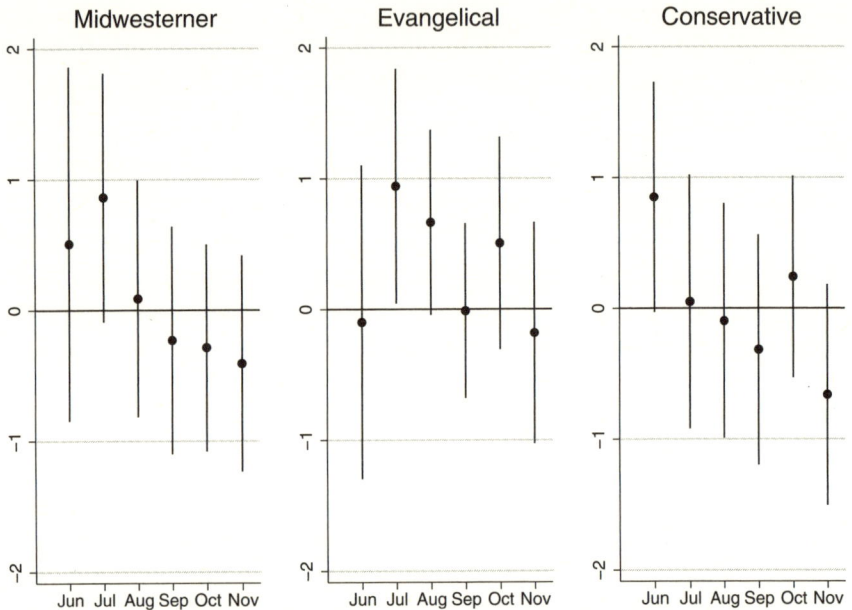

Figure 4.9. Dynamic effects of region (midwesterner), religion (evangelical Christian), and ideology (conservative) on intended Republican vote choice, 2016 TAPS

Pence's selection. Among evangelicals, we see only a slight shift toward Republicans in July, when Trump selected Pence. By the next month, this effect fell just short of conventional significance levels. There would be no lasting change in evangelical support for the Republican ticket; throughout the remainder of the campaign, and in terms of eventual vote choice, we find no evidence that evangelicals were significantly more likely to vote for Trump than they had been in June, just prior to Pence's selection.

Nor does figure 4.10 indicate that Tim Kaine delivered votes among southerners, Catholics, or Latinos in 2016. Indeed, we see no statistically significant increase in these respondents' support for the Democratic ticket at any point during the campaign or in their eventual vote choice, following Kaine's selection. Only southerners showed some indication of a change in support, after controlling for their preselection preferences, with the November estimate falling just short of conventional significance levels. But this effect is in the wrong direction; if anything, after Kaine's selection, southerners became *less* likely to support the Democratic ticket.

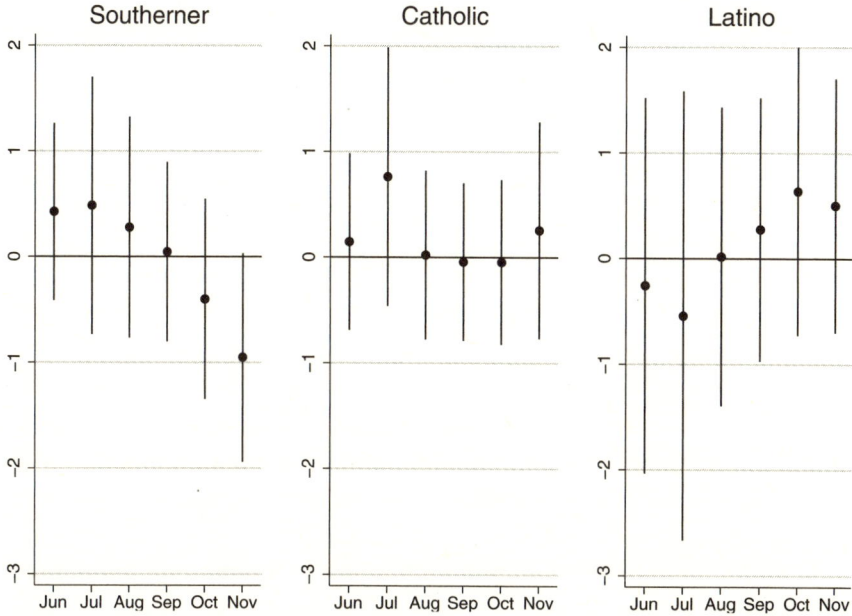

Figure 4.10. Dynamic effects of region (southerner), religion (Catholic), and ethnicity (Latino) on intended Democratic vote choice, 2016 TAPS

Discussion

Our analysis of panel data, from KN in 2008 and TAPS in 2012 and 2016, provides almost no evidence of targeted running mate effects. In most cases (Palin: women; Ryan: Catholics; Pence: midwesterners, conservatives; Kaine: southerners, Catholics, Latinos), we do not see any statistically significant changes in respondents' electoral preferences following the selection of a running mate from their geographic, demographic, or ideological in-group. In four cases (Palin: evangelicals, conservatives; Ryan: midwesterners; Pence: evangelicals), we see only temporary increases in support for the Republican ticket following the running mate's selection, all of which disappear by the time of the election. And we see a temporary *decrease* in support for the Democratic ticket among Catholics, following Joe Biden's selection, but no such change in terms of eventual vote choice. Only in terms of conservatives in 2012 do we see an enduring, statistically significant increase in intended and eventual vote choice, independent of respondents' preexisting preferences, which may be attributable to Paul Ryan's vice presidential candidacy.

CONCLUSION

This chapter represents the most comprehensive analysis of targeted running mate effects to date. First, this is because we estimate targeted effects across three major categories—geographic, demographic, and ideological—whereas previous studies typically analyze only one category. Second, we estimate and compare these effects across a wide range of elections, from as early as 1952 to as recently as 2016. Third, and most important, we use panel, as well as cross-sectional, data to estimate these effects. As noted earlier, while cross-sectional surveys represent the most accessible data sources for conducting such analyses, they have significant limitations with respect to making causal inferences. Panel data, although less readily available, are much better equipped to identify *changes* in electoral support due to vice presidential selection. Specifically, our analysis draws on Lenz's (2012) three-wave test to determine whether identification with a particular group had a greater effect on (intended) vote choice following the selection of an in-group running mate, independent of the respondent's preexisting electoral preferences.

In short, we find very little evidence of targeted running mate effects. First, in terms of geography, our analysis of pooled data from the 1952–2016 ANES indicates that vice presidential candidates, in general, do not deliver an electoral advantage in their home state, division, or region. Nor do running mates from the United States' most culturally distinctive and politically cohesive region, the South, clearly perform better among southerners than running mates from other regions, according to our cross-sectional analysis. Panel data largely confirm these null results. In 2016, we find no statistically significant changes in electoral support among southerners or midwesterners after Tim Kaine, of Virginia, and Mike Pence, of Indiana, were selected as the Democratic and Republican running mates, respectively. Only in 2012 do we see a temporary increase in midwesterners' support for the Republican ticket at the time of Paul Ryan's vice presidential selection, but this effect disappeared immediately afterward, and it was not evident at the time of the election.

Second, in terms of demography, we examine targeted effects among women, Catholics, evangelical Christians, Jews, and Latinos. We find no evidence that women running mates "deliver" votes among women; in fact, gender did not have a statistically significant effect on vote choice in 1984 and 2008—when Geraldine Ferraro and Sarah Palin, respectively, ran for vice president—and women's support for the Republican ticket did not significantly increase, at any point, following Palin's selection in August 2008. Catholics' support for the relevant party ticket also did not increase, at conventional significance levels, following the selections of Joe Biden in 2008, Paul Ryan in 2012, or Tim Kaine in 2016, according to our panel data analysis. Catholics were significantly more likely to vote for the Democratic ticket in 1968, when Edmund Muskie ran for vice president, but our cross-sectional analysis indicates that no similar effect has occurred in any subsequent elections that featured a Catholic running mate (1972, 1984, 2008, 2012). Nor does the cross-sectional analysis indicate that Jews were significantly more likely to vote for Joe Lieberman's Democratic ticket in 2000, although we must interpret this result with great caution given how few Jewish respondents were included in that year's ANES sample. We do find limited evidence of targeted effects among evangelical Christians in the 2008 and 2016 ANES; this variable's effect is statistically significant and is signed so as to indicate increased support for the Republican tickets that featured Sarah Palin and Mike Pence, respectively. But in both cases the coefficient is comparable in size to other elections that did not feature an evangelical running mate. Our panel data provide a more precise estimate of this effect, over time. Here, we find evidence of a temporary increase in evangelical support for the Republican ticket following Palin's and Pence's selections, but in both cases that effect did not last until Election Day. Finally, in 2016, Latinos' support for the Democratic ticket did not increase at any point after Hillary Clinton selected the Spanish-speaking Tim Kaine as her running mate.

Third, in terms of ideology, it is here that we find the clearest evidence of targeted effects. This was in 2012, when conservatives' support for the Republican ticket significantly increased following Paul Ryan's selection as Mitt Romney's running mate—not just during the campaign but through to Election Day. Also, in 2008, we see an initial spike in conservative support for the Republican ticket following John McCain's selection of Sarah Palin, but this did not last throughout the campaign, and we see no such effect in terms of respondents' eventual vote choice. Finally, in 2016, the panel data indicate no significant increase in conservative support for the Republican ticket, at any point, following Donald Trump's selection of Mike Pence as his running mate. Our cross-sectional data, from the 1964–2016 ANES, also provide no clear evidence of targeted ideological effects, among liberals or conservatives. However, for reasons that we elaborated on earlier, it is especially difficult to make causal inferences about these effects based on the available cross-sectional data.

It is important to note that, while our analysis is designed to isolate the

independent effects of vice presidential selection, we cannot make any definitive claims about causality. After all, our methodology does not allow us to
determine, in a direct sense, whether it was the *running mate* that caused any
potential changes in respondents' preferences. Instead, following Lenz (2012)
and Kinder and Kalmoe (2017), our panel data analysis treats vice presidential
selection as an intervening event, to which subsequent changes in vote choice
may be attributed. But, of course, other factors might have caused changes in
voting behavior during the same time frame; for example, perhaps it was the
party conventions or other aspects of Mitt Romney's and Barack Obama's
candidacies that caused conservative support for the Republican ticket to increase starting in August 2012, rather than Paul Ryan's selection as the Republican running mate.

Our approach would be more problematic if we were to claim widespread
targeted effects, based on the panel or cross-sectional data. But in the vast
majority of cases, we find no such effects—or, at most, temporary effects. If
these effects *had* occurred in many or all of the cases that we analyze, our
methodology would allow us to identify statistically significant changes in the
target groups' voting behavior—even if we could not be certain whether those
changes had been caused by the running mate or some other factor. In other
words, if targeted effects occur with any regularity, surely we would have been
able to reject the null hypothesis (i.e., no change in voting behavior among the
respondents in question) more often than we do so here.

So, is the "targeted running mate effect" a myth? We think that conclusion
would be going much too far, for two reasons. First, while our analysis covers
a wide range of candidacies, we face significant limitations with respect to data
availability and real-world examples. In terms of data availability, panel data are
hard to come by, and even more so when using a methodology that requires at
least three waves of respondent interviews. Thus, our panel data analysis comprises only the three most recent presidential elections. In terms of real-world
examples, many social groups that might be ripe for targeted effects—such as
African Americans, Latinos, Asian Americans, Muslims, or gays and lesbians—
have not had the opportunity to vote for an in-group running mate because, at
the time of this writing, no major party ever has nominated such a candidate
for the vice presidency. Thus, we cannot say whether a running mate from one
of these groups would have a targeted effect on voters, and there is good reason
to believe that they might be particularly capable of doing so.

Second, one could argue that running mates often *do* have targeted effects, but that these effects "wear off" quickly—and probably well before Election Day. Indeed, this appears to be the case for other dynamic forces in presidential campaigns, such as campaign advertisements (Sides and Vavreck 2013, 128–131) and the postconvention "bump" (Holbrook 1996, 79–97). Sure enough, our panel data analysis indicates that several running mates had a temporary effect on intended vote choice among in-group respondents. Specifically, we see this among midwesterners in 2012 (Ryan), evangelicals in 2008 (Palin) and 2016 (Pence), and conservatives in 2008 (Palin). These temporary effects may be attributable to the same logic that Holbrook (1996) uses to explain postconvention bumps: the initial event (i.e., the vice presidential rollout) causes a surge in media coverage, most of which is positive, which results in very favorable ratings for the object of that coverage (i.e., the running mate) and a subsequent increase in electoral support. Such an effect might be particularly pronounced among voters who share with the running mate an in-group identity made salient by media coverage of the vice presidential announcement. Indeed, target group voters thus might be primed to weight the running mate more heavily when considering their presidential vote—at least at first. However, as the running mate inevitably begins to attract less, or more negative, media coverage, his or her direct effect on targeted voters—and voters as a whole—likely will decrease, and perhaps disappear altogether, by the end of the campaign.

Future research can, and should, address the methodological and interpretive considerations that we raise here. For present purposes, it is sufficient to conclude that we find minimal evidence of targeted running mate effects, across a wide range of geographic, demographic, and ideological groups, in this chapter. Given that we also find weak evidence of direct running mate effects, among voters as a whole, in chapter 3, still we must ask: How, if at all, do running mates substantially influence voting behavior? It is a distinct possibility that voters focus their attention on the presidential candidate and rarely think of themselves as voting for the vice presidential candidate, in any meaningful sense. If so, this does not foreclose the possibility of substantial running mate effects altogether. Rather, it leaves us with one major pathway left to explore in our next, and final, empirical chapter: indirect effects—or, the effects of vice presidential candidate evaluations on vote choice via their influence on presidential candidate evaluations. In essence, we ask: Do voters judge presidential candidates based on their choice of a running mate? And, if so, does reevaluating the presidential candidate on this basis lead to a change in vote choice?

5. Indirect Effects

Whatever Tim Kaine's vice presidential candidacy might have done to help Hillary Clinton win over Virginians, Catholics, or Latinos in 2016 (and, judging by the evidence from chapter 4, that wasn't much), it only seemed to alienate the Democratic Party's progressive base. At worst, to these voters, picking Kaine was an act of betrayal. At best, it simply confirmed their doubts about Hillary Clinton.

Clinton, of course, had won her party's presidential nomination only after beating back a strong, and rather unexpected, challenge by the self-described democratic socialist US senator from Vermont, Bernie Sanders. Given Sanders's impressive performance, together with his frequent criticism of Clinton as a pro-business centrist and an unapologetic creature of the political establishment, many progressives expected that Clinton would extend to them an olive branch by selecting Sanders or an ideological ally, such as Massachusetts senator Elizabeth Warren or Ohio senator Sherrod Brown, as her running mate. By choosing a relative centrist, in Kaine, Clinton seemed to be telling disaffected progressives that she could take their votes for granted; in a general election against Donald Trump, surely they would "come home" to her by November. At least, that is how many progressives interpreted Clinton's message. And it infuriated them.

As rumors of Kaine's selection picked up, in late June, many pro-Sanders activists reacted with disdain. Radio host Katie Halper, for one, warned: "Picking Kaine, a DLC [Democratic Leadership Council] Democrat . . . would just confirm that Clinton is the triangulating, centrist, DLC Democrat who many Sanders supporters have claimed her to be. It would send a message that she's not even pretending to pander to us, which"—she added sardonically—"is both refreshingly honest and alarming." Jordan Chariton, of the Young Turks, echoed this sentiment: "An establishment Wall Street Democrat like Tim Kaine . . . will do nothing but confirm to progressives she's learned nothing from this primary." The Republican National Committee even picked up on the theme, in a press release headlined: "Tapping the Virginia Senator Would Be a Slap in the Face to Bernie Backers" (Scher 2016).

What is so telling about these reactions, for our purposes, is not that progressives objected to Clinton's running mate on ideological grounds but that they interpreted this selection *as a statement about Hillary Clinton*—about who she was, how she would conduct herself as a candidate, and, if elected, how she would conduct herself as president. In their words, the selection "confirmed" what they already knew and did not like about Clinton. Presumably, selecting Sanders or another bona fide progressive would have signaled that—whatever her past record or political predispositions—Clinton was resolved to campaign and govern in a way that duly recognized and responded to progressives' concerns. Because she did no such thing, even in the immediate aftermath of a divisive and ideologically driven party primary, many progressives inferred that what they had seen from Clinton already—and did not like—would be what they would get, going forward.

This framework for interpreting vice presidential selection—as a statement about the presidential candidate's identity, values, and likely performance as president—actually is quite familiar. Take, for example, the focus group participant that we cited in chapter 3, who thought that Tim Kaine came across as a a "total jerk" at the 2016 vice presidential debate.[1] Why did this matter? Because, he said, "I think he reinforced the *worst* of Hillary"—presumably, referring to negative perceptions of her character and conduct.[2] Prior to the debate, another participant summarized this inferential logic, precisely, in response to pollster Frank Luntz's question: "Does it surprise you that you feel, as a group, so disappointed with the presidential candidates and so hopeful for the VP?" She responded: "Yeah. So, I feel like the vice presidential candidates give us a window into the presidential candidate's *judgment*."[3]

Actually, George W. Bush used nearly the same words to describe the significance of choosing a running mate. In his 2010 memoirs, *Decision Points*, Bush stated: "The vice presidential selection provides voters with a window into a candidate's decision-making style. It reveals how careful and thorough he or she will be. And it signals a potential president's priorities for the country" (66–67). Other presidential candidates have endorsed much the same view. Indeed, Barack Obama used one of the same terms as Bush, in 2008, to describe how he would go about choosing a running mate: "This is one of the most important decisions I can make and I think it will signal how I want to operate my presidency."[4] Obama's opponent in that election, John McCain, indicated a similar approach to vice presidential selection when he recalled, "My biggest predicament was my difficulty convincing voters that I was an agent of change. That was our principal concern as we assembled a list of potential vice presidents that summer" (McCain and Salter 2018, 49). This insight helps to explain McCain's preference for selecting Joe Lieberman, the former Democratic vice presidential candidate and then an Independent U.S. senator from Connecticut. "Were Joe to join the ticket it would send a clear message of change," McCain reasoned. "It would be an emphatic statement that I intended to govern collaboratively with an emphasis on problem solving not politics, which in 2008 would have been very good politics" (51).

Thus, like many other salient campaign activities or events, vice presidential selection affords an opportunity to (re)shape the presidential candidate's message or image. It is, in the candidates' own words, a "window," a "signal," a "message." In political science terms, one might call it a "cue" or a "heuristic" that provides voters with symbolic information to reinforce the campaign's strategy.

Presidential campaign advisers frequently cite this theme, as well. For example, in 2008, McCain adviser Steve Schmidt argued that Sarah Palin was the only vice presidential finalist capable of helping to reinforce McCain's image as a "maverick" (Heilemann and Halperin 2010, 360). Other leading campaign advisers have emphasized the running mate's (perceived) ability to remake the presidential candidate's public image. Paul Brountas, for one, described Michael Dukakis's selection of Lloyd Bentsen, in 1988, as an opportunity to recast the presidential candidate ideologically. He recalled: "That was the key, is when, you know, how to balance the ticket, because Dukakis was perceived to be so liberal that maybe, well this is a guy that picks somebody who isn't that liberal, and so he's comfortable with Bentsen."[5] In other words, voters might conclude: well, I guess Dukakis can't be *that* liberal, if he'd pick Bentsen as his running mate. In other cases, the "makeover" argument seems almost literal, as when George H. W. Bush's campaign adviser Roger Ailes said that "a youthful-looking [Dan] Quayle would make Bush seem the fatherly, senior figure." The veteran television producer, true to form, even referred to this as the "casting dimension" of the case for picking Quayle (Meacham 2015, 336).

The preceding analysis illustrates the third, and final, pathway to running mate effects that we analyze in this book: indirect effects. By this, we mean the running mate's ability to shape perceptions of the presidential candidate who selected him or her—perceptions that, in turn, may influence vote choice. For example, we ask: Does the selection of a relatively conservative running mate cause voters to view a relatively moderate presidential candidate as more conservative (or vice versa)? Likewise, does the selection of a relatively inexperienced running mate cause voters to doubt the presidential candidate's judgment or experience (or vice versa)? In short, does vice presidential selection cause voters to *reevaluate* a presidential candidate with whom they are already familiar—in essence, giving that candidate the opportunity to neutralize his or her weaknesses and accentuate his or her strengths? And, most important for the purposes of this book, do the resulting changes in presidential candidate evaluations directly influence voting behavior? That is to say, as perceptions of the presidential candidate's attributes change, on account of the running mate, do the voters' electoral preferences change with them?

Our analysis indicates that running mates do, in fact, have indirect effects on voting behavior. Specifically, we demonstrate, first, that changes in vice presidential candidate evaluations cause changes in presidential candidate evaluations, on a variety of relevant dimensions; and, second, these changes in presidential candidate evaluations can directly influence presidential vote choice. In fact, we argue that the indirect effects framework represents the most nuanced and realistic means of understanding running mate effects— acknowledging, on the one hand, that *running mates matter* and, on the other hand, that voters cast their ballot primarily with the *presidential*, rather than vice presidential, candidates in mind.

METHODOLOGY

Our inferential approach in this chapter is straightforward: if running mates influence perceptions of the presidential candidate who selected him or her (i.e., same-party perceptions), then changes in the former should cause changes in the latter. Furthermore, these changes in candidate evaluations should cause changes in voting behavior; that is to say, as perceptions of the running mate and, in turn, the presidential candidate become more positive (negative), an individual's likelihood of voting for that ticket should increase (decrease).

While our inferential approach may be straightforward, quite frankly the methodology required to test for indirect effects across a diverse range of data sources (e.g., using vector autoregression, three-wave tests of panel data, structural equation models) is not. Indeed, it is fair to say that, in comparison to the previous chapters, this chapter is especially "data intensive." We derive our empirical results from more than two hundred statistical models based on cross-sectional, rolling cross-sectional, and panel data from five nationally representative surveys. To analyze these data, we use a diverse range of research methods, including linear and logistic regression, vector autoregression (VAR), and an adaptation of Lenz's (2012) three-wave (panel data) test. Substantively, we examine the running mate's effect on a same-party presidential candidate's favorability rating, as well as perceptions of the latter's political experience, ideology, and various professional and personal attributes including judgment, honesty, and decisiveness. As such, this chapter constitutes the first broad, systematic analysis of indirect running mate effects ever conducted, and the most sophisticated with respect to methodology and data sources.[6]

To make this analysis as comprehensible as possible, then, we make every attempt to present the results in a concise and intuitive manner. For example, when discussing the results from our empirical models, we focus on the effects of vice presidential candidate evaluations and provide little, if any, discussion of the control variables. Even when presenting the output from our regression models, we truncate the tables to focus only on the key independent variables. Also, where appropriate, we use graphs, rather than tables, to visually illustrate our main empirical findings.

Additional points of clarification are in order regarding the breadth, and not just the depth, of this chapter's analysis. First, most of our data—excepting the 1968–2016 American National Election Studies (ANES)—come from recent presidential elections, only. Why? Because most election-related surveys use a cross-sectional—rather than rolling cross-sectional or panel—design that is problematic for the purposes of estimating indirect effects (given the potentially endogenous relationship between same-party candidate evaluations and vote choice; see chapter 3). Moreover, most datasets that are amenable to such analysis were conducted in recent election years. Second, much of our analysis focuses on the 2008 presidential election. The principal reason for this is a practical one, as well: two high-quality, nationally representative surveys were conducted during 2008, both of which allow us to analyze an exceptionally diverse range of vice presidential and/or presidential attributes and their dynamic effects over time. Specifically, we analyze rolling cross-sectional data from the 2008 National Annenberg Election Survey (NAES) and panel data from the 2008 Associated Press–Yahoo! News Panel conducted by Knowledge Networks (KN).

As it happens, the 2008 election represents an ideal test case for identifying indirect running mate effects.[7] That year, John McCain chose Sarah Palin as his running mate, on the Republican ticket, in hopes that she would prove to be an electoral "game changer" (see chapter 1), and she was only the second woman running mate on a major party ticket. Indeed, Palin's candidacy attracted an extraordinary amount of media coverage (see Ulbig 2013) and public interest (Baumgartner with Crumblin 2015, table 6.6, 112), much of which focused on controversies regarding her qualifications for the vice presidency and her ideological conservatism. In that case, there is good reason to believe that Palin's selection, and her subsequent performance on the campaign trail, might have influenced voters' evaluations of McCain, in terms of his perceived ideology, judgment, and many other attributes represented in our data. Moreover, previous studies indicate that Palin might have influenced the election by alienating independent voters (Elis, Hillygus, and Nie 2010), while also rallying ideological conservatives behind McCain's candidacy (Court and Lynch 2015; but see chapter 4). As for the Democratic ticket, selecting Joe Biden—a longtime US senator with extensive foreign policy experience—might have caused voters to reevaluate Barack Obama's experience, his judgment, and other relevant attributes. Perhaps with Biden by his side, Obama—a relatively young, first-term US senator—came across to voters as more capable of serving as commander in chief, or governing in general, than he had beforehand.

By way of overview, our empirical analysis proceeds in two parts. First, we analyze the relationship between presidential and vice presidential candidate evaluations, specifically in terms of overall favorability ratings. In essence: Does choosing a popular running mate increase the presidential candidate's popularity (and vice versa)? Second, we analyze the relationship between presidential and vice presidential candidate evaluations, in terms of specific attributes. In essence: Does choosing a running mate with a particular attribute reinforce voters' perceptions of the presidential candidate as possessing that attribute, or counteract their perception that he or she does not? In addition to answering these two research questions, we also analyze the relationship between same-party candidate evaluations and intended presidential vote choice. In essence: Do vice presidential candidate evaluations influence vote choice, *via their influence on presidential candidate evaluations?*

INDIRECT EFFECTS: FAVORABILITY RATINGS

Let's start by playing devil's advocate: *of course* an unpopular running mate is a drag on the presidential candidate's popularity (and vice versa). Isn't that obvious? Logic, alone, may be sufficient to justify this argument: presidential candidates get to choose their running mate; surely, then, voters will blame the former if they are unimpressed, even disgusted, by the latter (and vice versa). But, if evidence is needed to prove the point, perhaps we can just cite our findings from chapter 3. There, we see that most voters prefer presidential and vice presidential candidates from the same party ticket. And we introduce the VAR analysis, which establishes the interdependence of same-party candidate evaluations, together with intended presidential vote choice, in the 2000 and 2004 presidential elections. Why go any further?

Well, for two reasons. First, one might be skeptical of the logical argument just presented. After all, presidential candidates are much more salient than their running mates during the campaign, and the latter clearly are expected to be subservient to the former—advocating for, rather than challenging, the presidential candidate's policies; echoing, rather than crafting, the presidential campaign's message; and so forth. Indeed, as we see in chapter 1, presidential candidates often cite loyalty as an important selection criterion. In that case, running mates may have little opportunity or incentive to exert an independent effect on voters' perceptions of the presidential candidate. In essence, voters may not distinguish their evaluation of the running mate from that of the presidential candidate in whose shadow he or she stands.

Second, the evidence from chapter 3 has significant limitations, with respect to our present research question. For one thing, our substantive focus in chapter 3 is on direct effects—that is, the effects of vice presidential candidate evaluations on vote choice. Thus, when presenting the VAR analysis, we only reference—but do not discuss in detail—the interdependent relationship between presidential versus vice presidential candidate evaluations. We present those findings more fully in the present chapter, instead, because they are most relevant to demonstrating indirect effects. Similarly, our analysis of 1968–2016 ANES data, from chapter 3, does not directly establish the causal relationship between presidential and vice presidential candidates' feeling thermometer ratings. It is important that we do so in this chapter in order to provide a comprehensive analysis of that relationship. In particular, we use this evidence to indicate the generalizability of our substantive conclusions from the VAR analysis, which encompasses data from only two presidential elections (2000 and 2004).

In this first empirical section of the present chapter, our overarching objective is to establish that running mates directly influence presidential candidates' popularity, and that this has an indirect effect on vote choice. To that end, we conduct two separate analyses. First, we use linear regression analysis to estimate the effects of vice presidential candidates' favorability ratings on presidential candidates' favorability ratings, in the 1968–2016 ANES (pooled, cross-sectional data). Second, we use VAR to estimate the dynamic effects of vice presidential candidate evaluations on presidential candidate evaluations, over the course of the campaign, in the 2000 and 2004 NAES (rolling cross-sectional data). For the ANES analysis, we also use structural equation models (SEMs) to estimate *indirect* running mate effects—that is, the extent to which (changes in) vice presidential candidate evaluations influence (changes in) intended presidential vote choice, via their influence on (changes in) presidential candidate evaluations.

American National Election Studies, 1968–2016
(Pooled, Cross-Sectional Data)

We begin by analyzing pooled, cross-sectional data from the 1968–2016 ANES. Admittedly, cross-sectional data are not ideal for the purposes of establishing a causal relationship between presidential and vice presidential candidate evaluations. This is because cross-sectional surveys require measuring presidential and vice presidential candidate evaluations *at the same time*, and the relationship between those evaluations may be endogenous (thus, making it difficult to tell whether, and to what extent, changes in one variable are causing changes in the other). As we explain in chapter 3, rolling cross-sectional or panel data are much more appropriate for making causal inferences about such relationships because they allow us to estimate the dynamic effects of one set of evaluations on the other, over time. But such data can be rather difficult to come by; indeed, their availability is limited to a select number of election years, most of which are fairly recent. Cross-sectional data, however, are available for every presidential election over the last several decades. In particular, the ANES Cumulative File includes presidential and vice presidential candidate feeling thermometers for every election year since 1968.

By pooling together respondents from the 1968–2016 ANES, we seek to maximize the generalizability of our conclusions regarding the relationship between same-party candidate evaluations. In essence, this analysis provides a baseline against which to evaluate the results from our VAR analysis (see later discussion), which maximizes causal inference but relies on data from only two election years. To the extent that each analysis yields consistent results, this will allow us to have greater confidence in our substantive conclusions.

For the present analysis, we estimate four linear regression models. The dependent variable in each model is the Republican or Democratic presidential candidate's feeling thermometer rating, pooled across election years. The main independent variable in each model is the same-party vice presidential candidate feeling thermometer rating. In Models 1 and 3, we estimate the independent variable's effect on the dependent variable without controlling for opposite-party candidate evaluations. In Models 2 and 4, we add opposite-party presidential and vice presidential candidate thermometer ratings, as control variables. In each model, we cluster standard errors by year.

The results from table 5.1 indicate that vice presidential candidate evaluations influence same-party presidential candidate evaluations. Indeed, the independent variable is statistically significant and correctly signed in each model, with a coefficient of nearly 0.6. This means that for every 1-point increase in a respondent's rating of the running mate, on the 0–100 feeling thermometer scale, his or her rating of the presidential candidate from the same party increases by nearly six-tenths of a point. This finding is remarkably consistent across models; it applies to Republicans and Democrats, whether including or excluding opposite-party candidate evaluations. Model 4 also suggests that running mates may influence evaluations of the opposite party's presidential candidate; specifically, a 1-point increase in the Republican running mate's thermometer rating causes the Democratic presidential candidate's thermometer rating to decrease by nearly one-tenth of a point. However, we see no such effect in Model 2, for Democratic running mates.

In short, it appears that when the popularity of the running mate increases, so does the popularity of the presidential candidate who selected him or her. But, we must ask, how much of a difference can the running mate really make? Take the results from Model 2.[8] If the Republican candidate for president had an average thermometer rating of just 50 (i.e., neutral), what would it take for the Republican running mate to make him or her "popular"—say, to boost that rating to 60? The coefficient tells us that, holding all other variables constant, this would require an 18-point increase in the running mate's thermometer rating! It is difficult, indeed, to imagine a running mate experiencing such a boost—or, for that matter, a drop—in popularity, particularly given the strength of partisan identities in modern

Table 5.1. Predictors of Presidential Candidates' Feeling Thermometer Ratings, 1968–2016 ANES

Variables	Republican Candidates		Democratic Candidates	
	Model 1	Model 2	Model 3	Model 4
Republican presidential candidate rating	—	—	—	−0.092***
0 = Most unfavorable, to 97 = most favorable				(0.021)
Republican vice presidential candidate rating	0.585***	0.569***	—	−0.088***
0 = Most unfavorable, to 97 = most favorable	(0.030)	(0.027)		(0.014)
Democratic presidential candidate rating	—	−0.101***	—	—
0 = Most unfavorable, to 97 = most favorable		(0.021)		
Democratic vice presidential candidate rating	—	0.017	0.593***	0.569***
0 = Most unfavorable, to 97 = most favorable		(0.019)	(0.023)	(0.017)
Republican	11.030***	10.012***	−9.270***	−5.996***
0 = No, 1 = yes	(1.700)	(1.856)	(0.541)	(0.494)
Democrat	−6.792***	−5.108***	11.673***	10.201***
0 = No, 1 = yes	(0.708)	(0.699)	(1.979)	(2.104)
Female	0.367	0.178	1.219***	1.355***
0 = No, 1 = yes	(0.402)	(0.386)	(0.325)	(0.296)
Age	−0.027	−0.024	−0.015	−0.002
Continuous	(0.036)	(0.037)	(0.014)	(0.012)
Household income	0.928*	0.890	−1.072***	−0.809**
1 = Under 17th percentile, to 5 = over 95th percentile	(0.357)	(0.388)	(0.247)	(0.206)
Education	−2.530**	−2.503**	−0.306	−0.064
1 = No HS degree, to 5 = advanced degree	(0.827)	(0.819)	(0.522)	(0.448)
White	6.725*	6.052*	−7.698***	−6.409***
0 = No, 1 = yes	(2.313)	(2.341)	(1.086)	(0.852)
South	2.282***	2.065***	−1.686***	−1.028
0 = No, 1 = yes	(0.493)	(0.504)	(0.632)	(0.609)

(continued on the next page)

Table 5.1. *Continued*

Variables	Republican Candidates		Democratic Candidates	
	Model 1	Model 2	Model 3	Model 4
Constant	22.454***	27.732***	31.529***	39.682***
	(4.212)	(4.752)	(2.330)	(2.504)
Adjusted R-squared	0.533	0.549	0.570	0.592
Observations	25,247	23,254	24,479	23,254

Entries are linear regression coefficients. Robust standard errors are in parentheses. Standard errors are clustered by year.

***p < .001, **p < .01, *p < .05, +p < .10.

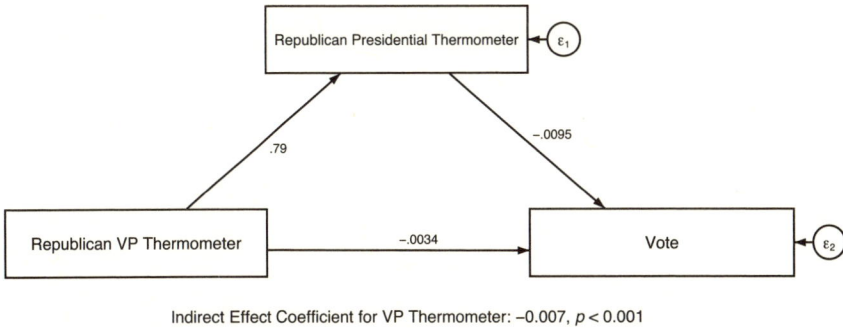

Figure 5.1. SEM of Republican ticket thermometer ratings and Democratic vote choice, 1968–2016 ANES

American politics, and the extent to which those identities tend to bias political judgments (e.g., L. Mason 2018).

But, more to the point, does this relationship subsequently influence vote choice? To test for indirect effects, based on the ANES data, next we estimate two SEMs.[9] An SEM allows us to test an independent variable's *direct* effect on a dependent variable, as well as its *indirect* effect via a mediator variable. More intuitively, for present purposes, an SEM tells us whether, and to what extent, the running mate's influence on vote choice is attributable to his or her effects on the presidential candidate's popularity. In each model—the first of which pertains to the Republican ticket, and the second to the Democratic ticket—we estimate the relationship between three variables: the vice presidential candidate's feeling thermometer rating (independent variable), presidential vote choice (dependent variable), and the presidential candidate's feeling thermometer rating (mediator variable). In the interest of parsimony, we do not include any control variables in these models.[10] We present the SEM results, graphically, in figure 5.1 (Republicans) and figure 5.2 (Democrats).

The SEMs provide clear evidence of indirect running mate effects. In both models, the independent variable's indirect—as well as direct—effect on the dependent variable is statistically significant, at $p < .001$, and its coefficient is correctly signed.[11] In other words, running mates have a direct effect on the popularity of same-party presidential candidates, and this effect, in turn, leads to changes in vote choice. So, for example, if the Democratic nominee for president in 2020 were to choose a particularly well-liked running mate, probably he or she also would become more popular and would gain votes as a result. At the same time, in keeping with our results from chapter 3, the

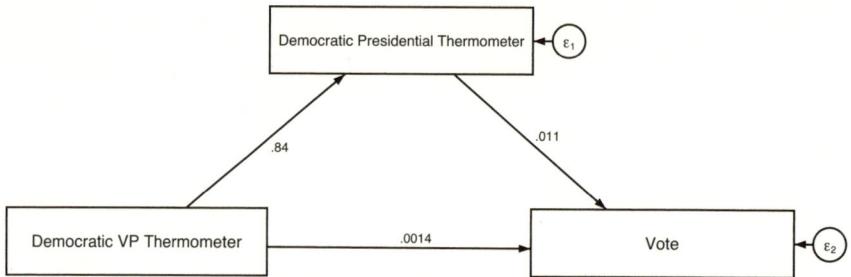

Figure 5.2. SEM of Democratic ticket thermometer ratings and Democratic vote choice, 1968–2016 ANES

running mate's popularity, in and of itself, would gain votes for the Democratic ticket. This provides the clearest illustration yet as to how, exactly, running mates matter.

But what do these results mean, in substantive terms? That is to say, *how much* of an indirect, versus direct, effect on vote choice do running mates have? To find out, we use the results from figures 5.1 and 5.2 to compute the predicted outcome of same-party presidential candidate evaluations and the predicted probability of party vote choice, in response to changes in vice presidential candidate evaluations. For example, if the Republican running mate's favorability rating were 60 rather than 50, to what extent would the Republican presidential candidate's favorability rating improve? And how much would the Republican ticket gain, in terms of votes? Such an analysis is particularly appropriate when analyzing thermometer ratings, as we do in this section, because—more so than the specific candidate attributes that we examine later in this chapter—these provide a summary measure of vice presidential candidate evaluations. Also, because these are the only such measures included in the 1968–2016 ANES, here we can provide the most generalizable, substantive estimates of indirect effects.

Table 5.2 presents the results of this analysis. The first column specifies the values of the independent variable (vice presidential candidate thermometer rating) or the mediating variable (presidential candidate thermometer rating), which we manipulate in order to calculate changes in the dependent variable. The second and third columns present predicted outcomes (same-party presidential candidate thermometer rating) or predicted probabilities

Table 5.2. Predicted Outcomes from Structural Equation Models, 1968–2016 ANES

Independent Variable Values	Republican Ticket Predicted Outcome/Probability	Democratic Ticket Predicted Outcome/Probability
VP thermometer rating = 40	Presidential thermometer rating = 46.04 (45.70–46.38)	Presidential thermometer rating = 43.81 (43.45–44.16)
VP thermometer rating = 50	Presidential thermometer rating = 53.90 (53.59–54.22)	Presidential thermometer rating = 52.12 (51.80–52.45)
VP thermometer rating = 60	Presidential thermometer rating = 61.77 (61.44–62.09)	Presidential thermometer rating = 60.44 (60.11–60.77)
VP thermometer rating = 40	Vote choice = 53.11% (52.53%–53.69%)	Vote choice = 48.44% (47.83%–49.05%)
VP thermometer rating = 50	Vote choice = 49.75% (49.24%–50.25%)	Vote choice = 49.97% (49.46%–50.47%)
VP thermometer rating = 60	Vote choice = 46.39% (45.83%–46.94%)	Vote choice = 51.49% (50.96%–52.03%)
Presidential thermometer rating = 40	Vote choice = 63.49% (62.88%–64.11%)	Vote choice = 34.46% (33.86%–35.07%)
Presidential thermometer rating = 50	Vote choice = 55.86% (55.33%–56.39%)	Vote choice = 43.20% (42.68%–43.72%)
Presidential thermometer rating = 60	Vote choice = 48.24% (47.73%–48.74%)	Vote choice = 51.94% (51.44%–52.44%)

Thermometer ratings range from 0 = most unfavorable to 97 = most favorable. Vote choice is coded 0 = Republican presidential vote, 1 = Democratic presidential vote. Predicted probabilities for vote choice represent the respondent's likelihood of voting for the Democratic ticket, when rating the vice presidential or presidential candidate at a given point on the ANES feeling thermometer. Ninety-five percent confidence intervals for each predicted outcome (thermometer rating) or predicted probability (vote choice) are in parentheses.

(of Democratic vote), at each of the specified independent or mediating variable values, with 95 percent confidence intervals in parentheses. We present these estimates for the Republican ticket in column two, and the Democratic ticket in column three.

In the first three rows of table 5.2, we see that a 10-point increase in the vice presidential candidate's thermometer rating (from 40 to 50, or 50 to 60) is predicted to cause a 7.87-point increase in the Republican presidential candidate's thermometer ratings, and a 8.32-point increase for Democrats. In the second three rows, we see that the same 10-point increase in vice presidential candidate thermometer ratings causes a 3.36 percentage-point decrease in the predicted probability of a Democratic vote, for Republican running mates, but only a 1.52 percentage-point increase in the predicted probability of a Democratic vote, for Democratic running mates.

Finally, to evaluate the running mate's indirect effect on voting behavior, in the last three rows we estimate the effects of an 8-point increase in the *presidential candidate's* favorability rating on vote choice. This simulates the effect of a 10-point increase in the *vice presidential candidate's* favorability rating, as demonstrated in the first three rows of table 5.2 and indicated earlier in the text. For Republicans, each 8-point increase in the presidential candidate's favorability rating—again, simulating the effects of a 10-point increase in the running mate's favorability rating—decreases a respondent's probability of voting for the Democratic ticket by 7.62 percentage points. For Democrats, an equivalent change in favorability ratings increases a respondent's probability of voting for the Democratic ticket by 8.74 percentage points.[12]

Let's put these results in perspective. First, suppose that a Republican running mate's thermometer rating were to increase by 10 percentage points (i.e., 10 points on a 100-point scale). According to our estimates, the *direct* effect on vote choice (i.e., predicted probability of casting a Democratic vote) would be 3.36 percentage points, versus an *indirect* effect of 7.62 percentage points. In that case, for Republicans, the ratio of indirect to direct running mate effects would be 2.3 to 1. Now, suppose that a Democratic running mate's thermometer rating were to increase by the same percentage. According to our estimates, the direct effect on vote choice would be 1.52 percentage points, versus an indirect effect of 8.74 percentage points. In this case, the ratio of indirect to direct effects would be much greater, at 5.7 to 1. In short, this analysis indicates that, while running mates have a direct *and* an indirect effect on vote choice, the latter is much more powerful than the former. That is to say, running mates influence presidential vote choice primarily—but not solely—via indirect effects.

National Annenberg Election Survey, 2000–2004
(Rolling Cross-Sectional Data)

The ANES data provide clear evidence of indirect effects. However, as noted previously, cross-sectional data are not ideal for the purpose of analyzing the causal relationship between same-party candidate evaluations and vote choice because they cannot account for potential endogeneity between these variables. Time series data, from rolling cross-sectional or panel surveys, are much better equipped for that purpose because they allow us to treat these variables as interdependent and model indirect effects dynamically—specifically, over the course of a campaign. Thus, we can determine whether changes in vice presidential candidate evaluations cause changes in presidential candidate evaluations—and whether those, in turn, "Granger-cause" changes in intended vote choice. That is why, in this section, we return to the VAR analysis introduced in chapter 3.[13]

Once more, we use data from the 2000 and 2004 NAES, which include favorability measures for each presidential and vice presidential candidate. In both cases, these measures range from the least to the most favorable evaluations, but the 2000 NAES uses a 0–100 scale while the 2004 NAES uses a 0–10 scale. Also, these datasets include measures of intended presidential vote choice. We code this variable as 1 for Democratic vote choice and 0 for Republican or other vote choice. Our method of analysis is the same as in chapter 3: we use VAR, following the example of Box-Steffensmeier, Darmofal, and Farrell (2009). Chapter 3 provides a detailed description of this methodology and its application to the 2000 and 2004 NAES.

We use the cumulative impulse response function (CIRF) to estimate the interdependent relationship between our variables of interest. Specifically, the CIRF allows us to estimate the effects of a one-unit positive shock to (vice) presidential candidate evaluations on same-party candidate evaluations and intended vote choice. A *cumulative* function is appropriate for this analysis because we seek to estimate the lasting effects of such shocks over time, rather than their daily values in isolation.[14] Figures 5.3 and 5.4 present the CIRF estimates—with gray bands representing 95 percent confidence intervals—for

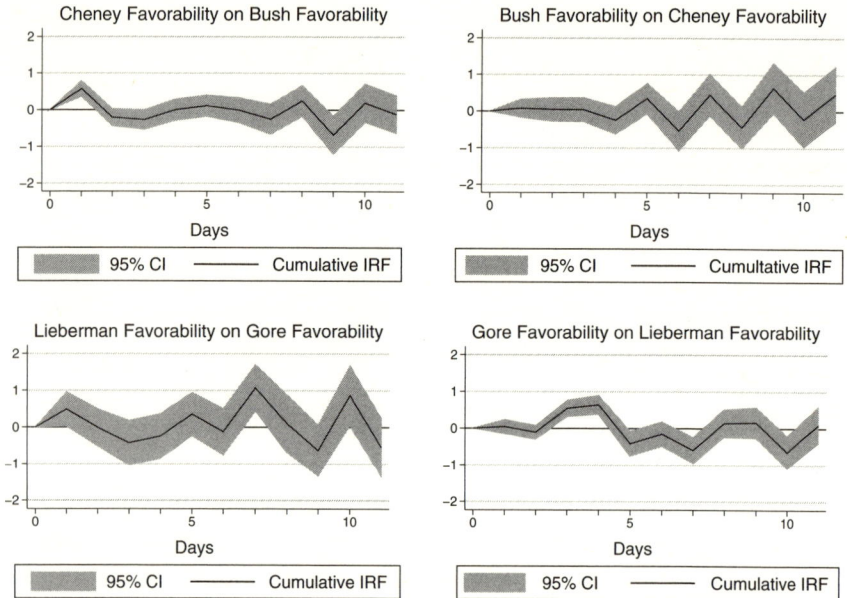

Figure 5.3. Cumulative impulse response function of candidate favorability ratings, 2000 NAES

presidential and vice presidential candidate favorability in the 2000 and 2004 NAES, respectively.

Do running mates influence the presidential candidate's favorability over the course of a campaign? Yes—*but* these effects tend to be short-lived. For instance, in figure 5.3, we see that a one-unit positive shock to Dick Cheney's favorability causes an immediate, statistically significant increase in favorability ratings for the Republican presidential candidate, George W. Bush. But those effects last for only one day; after that, they are indistinguishable from zero or, for one day (day nine), negative. Figure 5.4 shows a similar effect for Cheney in 2004; a positive shock to his favorability increases Bush's favorability on day one, then again on days seven and eight, but otherwise its effect is indistinguishable from zero. Also in 2000, Joe Lieberman has a positive effect on favorability ratings for the Democratic presidential candidate, Al Gore, on days one and seven, only. As in chapter 3, however, John Edwards's performance in 2004 is exceptional. A positive shock to Edwards's favorability rating initially has no effect on Democratic presidential candidate John Kerry's favorability. But starting on day five, we see a statistically

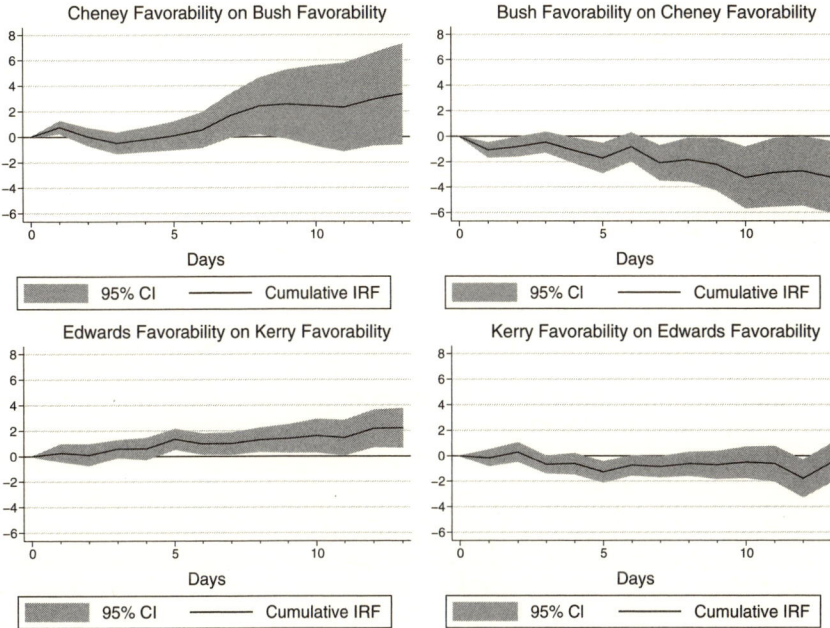

Figure 5.4. Cumulative impulse response function of candidate favorability ratings, 2004 NAES

significant and positive effect that lasts throughout the remainder of the time series. In other words, Edwards's popularity has a positive, enduring effect on Kerry's favorability.[15]

What do these results tell us? First, to the extent that we can generalize from the available evidence, it appears that running mates really do affect presidential candidates' popularity. Indeed, we see this in all four cases from figures 5.3 and 5.4. However, in three of the four cases, this effect disappears almost immediately, and, if it returns, it does not endure past the first week of the time series. In other words, any effect that the running mate may have soon fades away—well, usually. The only exception is John Edwards, whose effect on John Kerry's favorability materializes only after several days but then endures through the end of the time series. Edwards, as we note in chapter 3, was the most popular of these four candidates for much of the campaign. Therefore, it may be the case that exceptionally (un)popular running mates have a lasting effect on the presidential candidate's favorability, while most running mates have temporary effects, at best.

Of course, we must caution that these results come from only two election years. This limits the generalizability of any conclusions that we may draw from the VAR analysis. But recall that our analysis of the 1968–2016 ANES also indicates a statistically significant and positive relationship between vice presidential and presidential candidate evaluations. Thus, running mates *do* seem to influence presidential candidates' popularity. It is just that, judging by our VAR analysis, their influence tends to be short-lived.

INDIRECT EFFECTS: CANDIDATE ATTRIBUTES

Given the apparent relationship between vice presidential and presidential candidates' favorability ratings, it stands to reason that this relationship also might extend to other, more specific aspects of candidate evaluation. After all, a feeling thermometer or favorability rating is nothing more than a summary evaluation of a given candidate—and the components of that evaluation are likely to reflect judgments about the candidate as a person, a politician, and a potential executive. Is it the case, then, that running mates influence not just whether voters *like* a given presidential candidate but also their perception of who that presidential candidate *is* and what he or she stands for? To put a finer point on it, do running mates shape not just affective judgments about the presidential candidate but also cognitive judgments with direct bearing on their likely performance as president? For instance, does the running mate's selection or subsequent performance cause voters to reevaluate whether a presidential candidate is qualified to serve as president, will govern as an ideologue or a moderate, can be trusted to act ethically and keep promises, and so forth?

Evidence to this effect would help to explain *why* running mates matter. Essentially, it would indicate that voters use what is commonly referred to as the "first presidential act" to make inferences about just that—how the candidate would conduct him- or herself as president. In the words of the presidential candidates quoted at the beginning of this chapter, our analysis may show that voters, indeed, use vice presidential selection as a "window," a "message," or a "signal" when evaluating the presidential candidates and deciding for whom to vote. The evidence that we present in this section supports just such an interpretation of running mate effects.

The scope of this evidence, in comparison to the existing literature on running mate effects, is hard to overstate. This is because we use a multi-method approach—including logistic regression and an adaptation of Lenz's three-wave test—to analyze data from three election years and four nationally representative rolling cross-sectional or panel surveys: the 2000–2008 NAES and the 2008 Knowledge Panel. Most important, our data include survey items measuring a diverse range of presidential *and* vice presidential candidate attributes. We use these data to determine whether, and to what extent, perceptions of the running mate shape perceptions of the presidential candidate's *specific* political or personal attributes (e.g., judgment, experience, honesty, being too old/young to be president, ideology). In some cases, the data allow us to estimate these effects only in terms of the running mate's overall favorability. In other cases, we can estimate these effects in terms of the running mate's perceived ideology or readiness to be president. Where appropriate, we maximize causal inference by modeling these relationships dynamically—that is, by estimating the running mate's effect on *changes* in perceptions of the presidential candidate, over the course of a campaign. Finally, we use SEMs to demonstrate the running mate's indirect effects on vote choice, via his or her influence on the presidential candidate's perceived attributes.

We present three distinct sets of analyses in this section. First, we use pooled, rolling cross-sectional data from the 2008 NAES to estimate the relationship between perceptions of that year's vice presidential candidates (Sarah Palin and Joe Biden) and perceptions of their respective same-party presidential candidates (John McCain and Barack Obama), specifically in terms of the former's ideology and readiness to be vice president, and the latter's ideology, judgment, and fitness for the presidency given his age. Also, it is at this point that we use SEMs to determine whether these perceptions of the running mate indirectly influence vote choice. This is appropriate given the diverse range of running mate attributes measured in the 2008 NAES, as compared with the 2000 and 2004 NAES, which include favorability measures for those candidates, only. In fact, this is why we start with the 2008 NAES—and, for that matter, why we analyze this dataset at all, after excluding it from previous VAR analyses because it included too few daily observations subsequent to that year's vice presidential selection, for the purposes of that methodology (see note 14 of chapter 3). To overcome this problem, we treat the data as cross-sectional by pooling together all respondents, and conduct logistic regression analyses rather than VAR.

Second, we use pooled, rolling cross-sectional data from the 2000 and 2004 NAES to estimate the relationship between perceptions of the vice presidential candidate's favorability and perceptions of the presidential candidate on each of nineteen different attributes (e.g., inspiring, trustworthy, reckless, out of touch). To maximize comparability with the 2008 NAES results, in this instance we treat the 2000 and 2004 NAES data as cross-sectional, by pooling together respondents, and our empirical estimates are derived from ordinary least squares (OLS) and ordered logistic regression analyses.

Finally, we use panel data from the 2008 Associated Press–Yahoo! News Panel conducted by KN to estimate the *dynamic* relationship between perceptions of that year's running mates (Palin and Biden) and perceptions of their respective same-party presidential candidates (McCain and Obama). As in chapter 4, we use an adaptation of Lenz's (2012) three-wave test for this analysis of panel data. But why return to the 2008 election? And why conclude with this analysis? For two reasons. First, the 2008 KN panel data include two survey items measuring perceptions of the running mate's attributes (favorability and having the "right experience" to be president), as well as ten for the presidential candidate (likable, decisive, strong, experienced, compassionate, refreshing, attractive, inspiring, honest, and ethical). The 2008 KN dataset therefore represents the "best of both worlds" in comparison to the 2008 versus 2000–2004 NAES. That is to say, the 2008 KN dataset measures perceptions of a wide range of presidential candidate attributes (like the 2000–2004, but not the 2008, NAES) *and* one attribute associated with the running mate (like the 2008, but not the 2000–2004, NAES). Second, as we explain in chapter 4, using panel—rather than cross-sectional—data enhances our ability to make causal inferences. In that sense, this analysis serves as a check on our conclusions from the 2000–2008 NAES data.

National Annenberg Election Survey, 2008
(Pooled, Cross-Sectional Data)

For this first set of analyses, we use the 2008 NAES to estimate each running mate's effect on perceptions of the same-party presidential candidate's judgment, age (i.e., whether McCain is "too old" to be president, or Obama "too young"), or ideology. Also, we use the first two items to estimate SEMs of the running mate's indirect effect on vote choice, this time with respect to the presidential candidate's specific attributes rather than his overall favorability.[16]

There are compelling theoretical reasons to focus on these dependent variables in the context of the 2008 presidential election. First, the selections of

Sarah Palin and Joe Biden may have caused voters to reevaluate whether John McCain and Barack Obama, respectively, had the judgment required to serve effectively as president. In McCain's case, this is because he selected a relatively young and inexperienced, first-term governor whose frequent gaffes on the campaign trail caused many voters to question whether she was up to the job of being vice president, and whether McCain truly had chosen her for that role or just to help him win the election. In Biden's case, his wealth of political experience, particularly in the area of foreign policy, might have reassured voters who wondered whether Obama—as a relatively young, first-term US senator—was ready to serve as commander in chief.

Second, McCain (seventy-six) and Obama (forty-seven) were unusually old and young presidential candidates, respectively. And voters noticed. Consider a September 2008 poll asking respondents to identify one word that would describe each of the candidates. For McCain, the plurality of respondents said "old." For Obama, "inexperienced" came first, while "young/youthful" tied for third (Rosentiel 2008). Perhaps, then, balancing each ticket by age and experience helped to reassure voters that McCain was not "too old to be president," or Obama "too young." If voters had a positive view of the running mates, they might have become less concerned about the presidential candidates' age because McCain had lined up a qualified successor and Obama had enlisted a capable adviser.

Third, as Court and Lynch (2015, 902–903) note, McCain had difficulty appealing to many Republicans and conservatives who perceived him to be a relative moderate or even a liberal, within the party. Selecting Palin might have helped to win over these voters—not just because they wanted to elect a conservative as vice president but perhaps because it reassured them about McCain's ideology, as well. In other words, much as Paul Brountas interpreted the ideological implications of Michael Dukakis selecting Lloyd Bentsen in 1988 (see earlier in the chapter), in 2008 voters may have inferred that McCain was a conservative, after all, or at least would govern as such, if he was willing to pick Sarah Palin as his running mate.

Perceptions of the Presidential Candidates' Judgment
Table 5.3 presents the results from OLS models regressing perceptions of whether each presidential candidate has the judgment to be president (0 = does not apply at all, through 10 = applies extremely well) on perceptions of the running mates' readiness to be president (0 = does not apply at all, through 10

Table 5.3. Predictors of the Presidential Candidates' Judgment, 2008 NAES

Variables	McCain Judgment		Obama Judgment	
	Model 1	*Model 2*	*Model 3*	*Model 4*
Palin ready to be president	0.276***	0.200***	—	—
0 = Does not at all apply, to				
10 = applies extremely well	(0.011)	(0.010)	—	—
Biden ready to be president	—	—	0.213***	0.213***
0 = Does not at all apply, to				
10 = applies extremely well	—	—	(0.008)	(0.008)
Palin favorability	0.258***	0.041***	−0.085***	−0.067***
0 = Most unfavorable, to				
10 = most favorable	(0.011)	(0.010)	(0.007)	(0.008)
Biden favorability	0.032**	0.003	0.006	0.008
0 = Most unfavorable, to				
10 = most favorable	(0.011)	(0.009)	(0.010)	(0.010)
McCain Favorability	—	0.516***	—	−0.035***
0 = Most unfavorable, to				
10 = most favorable	—	(0.009)	—	(0.008)
Obama favorability	−0.085***	−0.036***	0.636***	0.632***
0 = Most unfavorable, to				
10 = most favorable	(0.010)	(0.009)	(0.008)	(0.008)
Adjusted R-squared	0.535	0.641	0.779	0.779
Observations	10,688	10,688	10,582	10,572

Entries are linear regression coefficients. Standard errors are in parentheses.

$***p < .001, **p < .01, *p < .05, +p < .10.$

Control variables have been omitted for brevity. They include Republican (0 = no, 1 = yes); Democrat (0 = no, 1 = yes); conservative (0 = no, 1 = yes); liberal (0 = no, 1 = yes); female (1 = no, 2 = yes); age (continuous); household income (1 = less than $10,000, to 9 = more than $150,000); education (1 = no high school degree, to 5 = advanced degree); white (0 = no, 1 = yes); southerner (0 = no, 1 = yes).

= applies extremely well) and his or her favorability rating (0 = least favorable rating, through 10 = most favorable rating), as well as our standard battery of controls.[17] Indeed, we find that respondents rate McCain's judgment more highly if they have a favorable view of Palin, and if they think she is ready to be president. In substantive terms, the estimates from Model 2 indicate that viewing Palin as "extremely" ready to be president, versus "not at all" improves perceptions of McCain's judgment by 2.2 points, on a 0–10 point scale. Biden's readiness to be president—although not his favorability rating—has the same effect on perceptions of Obama's judgment. In substantive terms, Model 4 indicates that viewing Biden as "extremely" versus "not at all" ready to be president improves perceptions of Obama's judgment by 2.3 points.

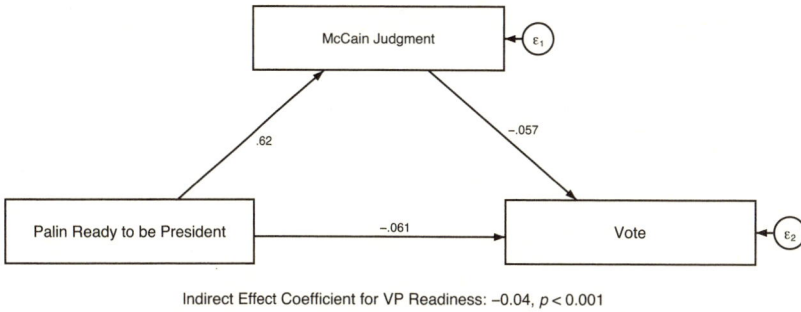

Indirect Effect Coefficient for VP Readiness: –0.04, $p < 0.001$

Figure 5.5. SEM of Republican ticket readiness, judgment, and Democratic vote choice, 2008 NAES

And what effect, if any, does this have on vote choice? To evaluate indirect effects, we estimate an SEM for each presidential ticket, in which the independent variable is the running mate's perceived readiness to be president, the dependent variable is intended presidential vote choice, and the mediating variable is the same-party presidential candidate's perceived judgment. In both models, the dependent variable is coded 1 for Democratic vote choice and 0 for Republican vote choice.

Figures 5.5 and 5.6 present the results from the Republican and Democratic SEM, respectively. Once more, we find clear evidence of indirect effects. That is to say, each of the estimated relationships is statistically significant, at $p < .001$, and correctly signed, including the indirect effect for Palin's and Biden's perceived readiness to be president. Thus, choosing a credible and well-qualified running mate seems to be an effective way to gain votes, in large

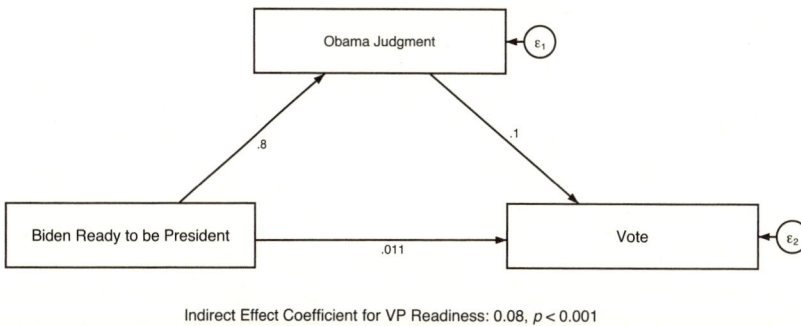

Indirect Effect Coefficient for VP Readiness: 0.08, $p < 0.001$

Figure 5.6. SEM of Democratic ticket readiness, judgment, and Democratic vote choice, 2008 NAES

part because it helps to convince voters that the presidential candidate who selected him or her has good judgment. This, at least, is the substantive implication of the results from figures 5.5 and 5.6.

But how much of an effect on vote choice are we talking about? To find out, we estimate the predicted outcomes associated with an increase in the running mate's perceived readiness to be president from just below (4) to just above (6) that scale's neutral point—in other words, from a slightly negative to a slightly positive view of his or her readiness.[18] Such a change in perceptions of Palin's readiness to be president causes perceptions of McCain's judgment to improve by 1.2 points, on the 11-point scale. And this, in turn, causes the predicted probability of voting for the Democratic ticket to decrease by approximately 7 percentage points. For Democrats, an equivalent shift in Biden's perceived readiness to be president causes perceptions of Obama's judgment to improve by 1.6 points, out of 11, and the predicted probability of voting for the Democratic ticket to increase by approximately 17 percentage points.

This analysis demonstrates—more directly than in any previous study— that it matters to voters whether a presidential candidate selects a credible and well-qualified running mate (as they claim in polls; see chapter 2). Voters do, in fact, reward presidential candidates who make such a responsible choice; conversely, voters can be expected to punish an irresponsible choice. This is not just conjecture or a strained inference; here, we have direct evidence of it. Granted, due to data limitations, that evidence comes from one election. But what better test case could there be than the 2008 election—when each candidate's experience was a salient feature of the campaign, and both tickets were balanced in terms of experience (one for better, and one for worse)?

Perceptions of the Presidential Candidates' Age
Next, in table 5.4, we present the results from logit models regressing perceptions of whether McCain and Obama, respectively, were "too old" or "too young" to be president (1 = yes, 0 = no) on perceptions of the vice presidential candidates' readiness to be president (0 = does not apply at all, through 10 = applies extremely well), as well as their favorability ratings (0 = least favorable, through 10 = most favorable). Here, too, we find that evaluations of a running mate's readiness to be president significantly, and positively, predict judgments about the same-party presidential candidate's attributes. Specifically, in Model 2, we see that positive perceptions of Palin's readiness to be president do more to reduce concerns about McCain's age than any other

Table 5.4. Predictors of the Presidential Candidates' Age (Too Old/Young to Be President), 2008 NAES

Variables	McCain Too Old		Obama Too Young	
	Model 1	*Model 2*	*Model 3*	*Model 4*
Palin ready to be president	−0.156***	−0.127***	—	—
0 = Does not at all apply, to				
10 = applies extremely well	(0.013)	(0.014)	—	—
Biden ready to be president	—	—	−0.107***	−0.082***
0 = Does not at all apply, to				
10 = applies extremely well	—	—	(0.016)	(0.016)
Palin favorability	−0.172***	−0.065***	—	−0.042*
0 = Most unfavorable, to				
10 = most favorable	(0.013)	(0.015)	—	(0.017)
Biden favorability	—	0.029*	−0.078***	0.026
0 = Most unfavorable, to				
10 = most favorable	—	(0.014)	(0.017)	(0.019)
McCain favorability	—	0.124***	—	−0.176***
0 = Most unfavorable, to				
10 = most favorable	—	(0.014)	—	(0.016)
Obama favorability	—	−0.159***	—	0.140***
0 = Most unfavorable, to				
10 = most favorable	—	(0.013)	—	(0.019)
Reduction in error	23.84%	27.92%	0.25%	0.00%
Percent correctly predicted	76.32%	77.35%	88.95%	88.90%
Observations	10,688	10,688	10,582	10,572

Entries are logistic regression coefficients. Standard errors are in parentheses.

***$p < .001$, **$p < .01$, *$p < .05$, +$p < .10$.

Control variables have been omitted for brevity. They include Republican (0 = no, 1 = yes); Democrat (0 = no, 1 = yes); conservative (0 = no, 1 = yes); liberal (0 = no, 1 = yes); female (1 = no, 2 = yes); age (continuous); household income (1 = less than \$10,000, to 9 = more than \$150,000); education (1 = no high school degree, to 5 = advanced degree); white (0 = no, 1 = yes); southerner (0 = no, 1 = yes).

variable except for McCain's favorability rating. In Model 4, we see that positive perceptions of Biden's readiness to be president also reduce concerns about Obama's youth, but Obama's and McCain's favorability ratings have a stronger effect. Palin's favorability ratings also significantly reduce concerns about McCain's age, but Biden's favorability has no such effect.

To provide context for these results, once more we compute predicted probabilities based on respondents' evaluations of Palin's and Biden's readiness to be president, in relation to their judgments about whether McCain is too old, or Obama too young, to be president, respectively.[19] For McCain,

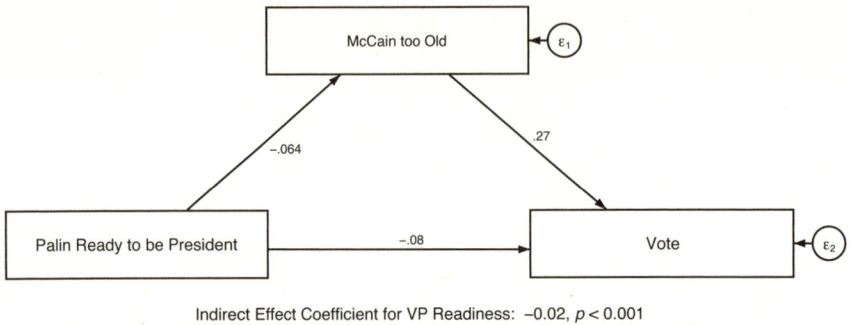

Indirect Effect Coefficient for VP Readiness: −0.02, $p < 0.001$

Figure 5.7. SEM of Republican ticket readiness, age, and Democratic vote choice, 2008 NAES

there is a 38.3 percent probability that a respondent who thinks Sarah Palin is "not at all" ready to be president would judge him as too old to be president. But that probability falls to only 14.9 percent if the respondent thinks that Palin is "extremely" ready to be president. For Obama, there is only a 17.6 percent probability of being judged too young to be president by a respondent who thinks that Joe Biden is "not at all" ready to be president. But that falls to 6.7 percent if the respondent thinks that Biden is "extremely" ready to be president.[20] In both cases, a shift from no confidence in the running mate's abilities to total confidence reduces concerns about the presidential candidate's age by approximately three-fifths (61 percent).

Figures 5.7 and 5.8 provide further confirmation of indirect effects. As in our previous SEMs, all coefficient estimates, including the indirect effect coefficient for perceptions of the running mate's readiness to be president, are statistically significant, at $p < .001$, and correctly signed. The implications of these findings are straightforward. Respondents who believe that Sarah Palin is ready to be president are less likely to believe that John McCain is too old to be president, and, in turn, they are more likely to vote for the Republican ticket. Likewise, respondents who believe that Joe Biden is ready to be president are less likely to think that Barack Obama is too young to be president, and, in turn, they are more likely to vote for the Democratic ticket.

As in the preceding analysis, we can clarify the substantive meaning of these results by estimating the predicted outcomes associated with an increase in the running mate's perceived readiness to be president from just below (4) to just above (6) that scale's neutral point—in other words, from a slightly negative to a slightly positive view of his or her readiness. For Palin, such an

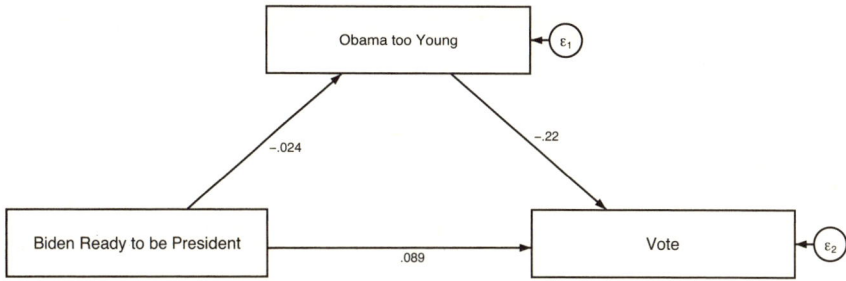

Indirect Effect Coefficient for VP Readiness: 0.005, $p < 0.001$

Figure 5.8. SEM of Democratic ticket readiness, age, and Democratic vote choice, 2008 NAES

improvement reduces the probability of a respondent saying that McCain is too old to be president by approximately 13 percentage points. And this, in turn, reduces his or her probability of voting for the Democratic ticket by nearly 27 percentage points. For Biden, an equivalent improvement in perceived readiness reduces the probability of a respondent saying that Obama is too young to be president by approximately 5 percentage points. And this, in turn, increases his or her probability of voting for the Democratic ticket by nearly 22 percentage points. Yet again, we find strong evidence of indirect running mate effects.

Perceptions of Presidential Candidates' Ideology
Finally, with respect to the 2008 NAES, we analyze the running mate's influence on perceptions of the same-party presidential candidate's ideology. Table 5.5 presents the results from ordered logit models regressing John McCain's and Barack Obama's perceived ideology (1 = very conservative, through 5 = very liberal) on Sarah Palin's and Joe Biden's perceived ideology (1 = very conservative, through 5 = very liberal) and their favorability ratings (0 = least favorable, through 10 = most favorable). Also, we control for the opposing presidential and vice presidential candidates' perceived ideology and favorability ratings, and include these variables in the table for purposes of comparison. The standard control variables are included in both models but are omitted from the table for the sake of brevity.

 The results from both models indicate that perceptions of the running mate's ideology significantly influence perceptions of the same-party

Table 5.5. Predictors of the Presidential Candidates' Ideology, 2008 NAES

Variables	McCain Ideology	Obama Ideology
McCain ideology	—	−0.129***
1 = Very conservative, to 5 = very liberal	—	(0.036)
Palin ideology	0.806***	−0.242***
1 = Very conservative, to 5 = very liberal	(0.033)	(0.034)
Obama ideology	−0.162***	—
1 = Very conservative, to 5 = very liberal	(0.037)	—
Biden ideology	0.107**	1.075***
1 = Very conservative, to 5 = very liberal	(0.036)	(0.040)
McCain favorability rating	0.006	0.014
0 = Most unfavorable, to 10 = most favorable	(0.016)	(0.017)
Palin favorability rating	−0.004	0.088***
0 = Most unfavorable, to 10 = most favorable	(0.015)	(0.016)
Obama favorability rating	−0.043**	−0.207***
0 = Most unfavorable, to 10 = most favorable	(0.016)	(0.018)
Biden favorability rating	−0.037*	0.021
0 = Most unfavorable, to 10 = most favorable	(0.017)	(0.018)
Reduction in error	5.46%	38.13%
Observations	4,389	4,389

Entries are ordered logistic regression coefficients. Standard errors are in parentheses.

    ***$p < .001$, **$p < .01$, *$p < .05$, +$p < .10$.

    Control variables have been omitted for brevity. They include Republican (0 = no, 1 = yes); Democrat (0 = no, 1 = yes); conservative (0 = no, 1 = yes); liberal (0 = no, 1 = yes); female (1 = no, 2 = yes); age (continuous); household income (1 = less than $10,000, to 9 = more than $150,000); education (1 = no high school degree, to 5 = advanced degree); white (0 = no, 1 = yes); southerner (0 = no, 1 = yes).

presidential candidate's ideology. In other words, as respondents perceive Sarah Palin to be more conservative, they also perceive John McCain to be more conservative. Similarly, as respondents perceive Joe Biden to be more liberal, they also perceive Barack Obama to be more liberal.

Consider the substantive implications of these findings. First, based on the estimates from Model 1, the predicted probability of perceiving McCain to be "very conservative" (1 on the 1–5 ideology scale) is 30.6 percent when a respondent also perceives Sarah Palin to be "very conservative." But, if the same respondent were to view Palin as "moderate" (3), his or her probability of perceiving McCain as "very conservative" drops by 22.5 percentage points, to 8.1 percent. Second, with respect to Model 2, the predicted probability of perceiving Obama to be "very liberal" (5, on the 1–5 ideology scale) is 60.5 percent when a respondent also perceives Biden to be "very liberal." But, if the same respondent were to view Biden as "moderate" (3), his or her probability of perceiving Obama as "very liberal" drops by nearly 45 percentage points, to 15.05 percent.[21]

These findings are particularly noteworthy for two reasons. First, by the time McCain ran for president in 2008, he had developed a reputation as a relatively moderate Republican—even a liberal one, according to some conservative critics. Thus, one reason for choosing Sarah Palin was to help shore up the party's conservative base (see chapter 1). The results from chapter 4 indicate that conservatives' support for the Republican ticket did not significantly increase following Palin's selection in August 2008. However, given Palin's strong conservative credentials and her increasingly conservative rhetoric toward the end of the campaign, she may have helped to convince conservatives over time that McCain was pretty conservative—or, at least, not so liberal— after all. And this, in turn, might have kept some conservatives from jumping ship, to vote for a minor party candidate or not at all. As discussed in note 16 of this chapter, it is not practical for us to test for such indirect effects in terms of ideology, given the available data. However, these results suggest that, while Palin's selection did not increase conservatives' support for the Republican ticket in 2008, it may have prevented an erosion of support over the course of the campaign, such as McCain might have experienced if he had gone with his gut and chosen Joe Lieberman instead.

Second, McCain is not the only presidential candidate to have chosen a running mate, in part, for ideological reasons. Indeed, Mitt Romney in 2012 and Donald Trump in 2016 faced similar resistance from conservatives within the Republican Party, and it may have been to reassure these voters that they chose Paul Ryan and Mike Pence, respectively, as their running mates. Indeed, we see in chapter 4 that conservatives' support for the Republican ticket increased following Ryan's selection in 2012, although this was not the case for Pence in 2016. While we cannot test for indirect effects on vote choice, in terms of ideology, in those elections,[22] these results suggest that the selection of Ryan and Pence may have helped to persuade conservatives that Romney and Trump, respectively, were "one of us"—or, at least, not "one of them." And that may have caused the increase in conservative support for the Republican ticket that we see in 2012, while perhaps preventing an erosion of support in 2016.

National Annenberg Election Survey, 2000 and 2004
(Pooled, Rolling Cross-Sectional Data)

A significant limitation of the preceding analysis is that it relies on data from just one election year—and, for that matter, one in which the running mates, particularly Sarah Palin, were exceptionally salient. That is why, in the present analysis, we use pooled, rolling cross-sectional data from the 2000 and 2004 NAES to validate our findings regarding the relationship between presidential and vice presidential candidate evaluations. As noted previously, these data provide an extraordinary range of variables measuring perceptions of the presidential candidates' attributes—nineteen in 2004, and seven in 2000. However, they include no variables measuring perceptions of the vice presidential candidate's attributes—only one summary measure, this being the running mate's favorability ratings. While less than ideal, this measure does provide a plausible basis for confirming the running mate's effect on perceptions of the presidential candidate. In short, it allows us to evaluate whether a positive assessment of the running mate, in general, leads to more positive assessments of the presidential candidate across various evaluative dimensions.

Tables 5.6 and 5.7 present the results of our ordered logit models from 2004, as do tables 5.8 and 5.9 for 2000. For each model, we regress perceptions of the Republican or Democratic presidential candidates' attributes on favorability ratings for the Republican and Democratic running mates, as well as both presidential candidates. Additionally, we include the standard battery of control variables in each model (not shown).

For the 2004 NAES, respondents were asked to rate how well a particular attribute applied to Bush or Kerry, on a 0–10 scale (0 = does not apply at all, through 10 = applies extremely well). We expect that increases in the running mate's favorability ratings will be positively associated with positively valenced same-party presidential candidate attributes (e.g., "inspiring," "strong leader," "trustworthy") and negatively associated with negatively valenced same-party presidential candidate attributes (e.g., "out of touch," "reckless," "arrogant").

The results from 2004 are overwhelmingly consistent with our expectations, and with our conclusions from the preceding analyses. First, in table 5.6, we see that Cheney's favorability ratings are statistically significant predictors of Bush's attributes, and in the expected direction, in seventeen of nineteen models. Generally speaking, a 1-point increase in Cheney's favorability rating results in approximately a 0.1-point change in the dependent variable (either

Table 5.6. Predictors of George W. Bush's Perceived Attributes, 2004 NAES

Variables	Inspiring	Strong Leader	Trustworthy	Shares My Values	Knowledgeable	Reckless	Steady
Bush favorability	0.557***	0.540***	0.546***	0.534***	0.465***	−0.288***	0.366***
	(0.016)	(0.016)	(0.016)	(0.016)	(0.016)	(0.022)	(0.025)
0 = Most unfavorable, to 97 = most favorable							
Cheney favorability	0.148***	0.107***	0.170***	0.118***	0.171***	−0.159***	0.103***
	(0.016)	(0.017)	(0.016)	(0.016)	(0.017)	(0.023)	(0.026)
0 = Most unfavorable, to 97 = most favorable							
Kerry favorability	−0.085***	−0.099***	−0.085***	−0.127***	−0.086***	0.146***	−0.082***
	(0.016)	(0.017)	(0.016)	(0.016)	(0.017)	(0.023)	(0.026)
0 = Most unfavorable, to 97 = most favorable							
Edwards favorability	0.003	−0.015	−0.030+	0.002	−0.021	0.063**	−0.031
	(0.016)	(0.017)	(0.016)	(0.016)	(0.017)	(0.023)	(0.026)
0 = Most unfavorable, to 97 = most favorable							
Adjusted R-squared	0.723	0.685	0.740	0.752	0.667	0.452	0.497
Observations	4,922	4,920	4,911	4,908	4,918	4,900	2,508

Variables	Says One Thing . . .	Right Experience	Easy to Like	Out of Touch	Stubborn	Arrogant
Bush favorability	−0.212***	0.530***	0.532***	−0.177***	−0.029	−0.279***
	(0.024)	(0.017)	(0.018)	(0.026)	(0.032)	(0.024)
0 = Most unfavorable, to 97 = most favorable						
Cheney favorability	−0.128***	0.153***	0.067***	−0.142***	−0.139***	−0.133***
	(0.024)	(0.017)	(0.019)	(0.026)	(0.034)	(0.025)
0 = Most unfavorable, to 97 = most favorable						
Kerry favorability	0.164***	−0.106***	−0.073***	−0.171***	0.026	0.121***
	(0.024)	(0.018)	(0.019)	(0.026)	(0.034)	(0.025)
0 = Most unfavorable, to 97 = most favorable						
Edwards favorability	0.039	−0.004	−0.020	0.061*	0.039	0.098***
	(0.025)	(0.018)	(0.019)	(0.027)	(0.034)	(0.026)
0 = Most unfavorable, to 97 = most favorable						
Adjusted R-squared	0.365	0.691	0.600	0.329	0.081	0.445
Observations	4,883	4,915	4,833	4,910	2,485	4,505

(continued on the next page)

Table 5.6. Continued

Variables	Optimistic	Effective	Decisive	Flip-Flops	Honest	Won't Admit Mistakes
Bush favorability	0.318***	0.408***	0.306***	-0.122***	0.664***	-0.164**
	(0.019)	(0.017)	(0.032)	(0.035)	(0.049)	(0.052)
0 = Most unfavorable, to 97 = most favorable						
Cheney favorability	0.063**	0.121***	0.078*	-0.118***	0.084+	-0.073
	(0.020)	(0.017)	(0.032)	(0.035)	(0.051)	(0.052)
0 = Most unfavorable, to 97 = most favorable						
Kerry favorability	-0.097***	-0.141***	-0.083**	0.213***	-0.030	0.099+
	(0.020)	(0.018)	(0.032)	(0.035)	(0.051)	(0.054)
0 = Most unfavorable, to 97 = most favorable						
Edwards favorability	-0.017	0.008	-0.021	0.073*	-0.101*	0.093+
	(0.020)	(0.018)	(0.032)	(0.036)	(0.050)	(0.056)
0 = Most unfavorable, to 97 = most favorable						
Adjusted R-squared	0.386	0.581	0.356	0.354	0.810	0.224
Observations	4,867	4,905	2,371	2,381	390	1,434

Entries are linear regression coefficients. Standard errors are in parentheses.

***$p < .001$, **$p < .01$, *$p < .05$, +$p < .10$.

Control variables have been omitted for brevity. They include Republican (0 = no, 1 = yes); Democrat (0 = no, 1 = yes); conservative (0 = no, 1 = yes); liberal (0 = no, 1 = yes); female (1 = no, 2 = yes); age (continuous); household income (1 = less than $10,000, to 9 = more than $150,000); education (1 = no high school degree, to 5 = advanced degree); white (0 = no, 1 = yes); southerner (0 = no, 1 = yes).

Table 5.7. Predictors of John Kerry's Perceived Attributes, 2004 NAES

Variables	Inspiring	Strong Leader	Trustworthy	Shares My Values	Knowledgeable	Reckless	Steady
Bush favorability	−0.063***	−0.085***	−0.048***	−0.115***	−0.036*	0.094***	−0.049*
	(0.017)	(0.015)	(0.105)	(0.016)	(0.017)	(0.022)	(0.023)
0 = Most unfavorable, to 97 = most favorable							
Cheney favorability	−0.045*	−0.083*	−0.065***	−0.042*	−0.073***	0.114***	−0.087***
	(0.018)	(0.015)	(0.016)	(0.016)	(0.017)	(0.023)	(0.024)
0 = Most unfavorable, to 97 = most favorable							
Kerry favorability	0.515***	0.526***	0.564***	0.514***	0.375***	−0.235***	0.453***
	(0.018)	(0.015)	(0.016)	(0.016)	(0.017)	(0.023)	(0.024)
0 = Most unfavorable, to 97 = most favorable							
Edwards favorability	0.130***	0.145***	0.143***	0.107***	0.123***	−0.040+	0.130***
	(0.018)	(0.015)	(0.016)	(0.016)	(0.017)	(0.023)	(0.024)
0 = Most unfavorable, to 97 = most favorable							
Adjusted R-squared	0.634	0.713	0.713	0.714	0.502	0.313	0.586
Observations	4,812	4,805	4,795	4,810	4,839	4,700	2,438

Variables	Says One Thing . . .	Right Experience	Easy to Like	Out of Touch	Stubborn	Arrogant
Bush favorability	0.139***	−0.099***	−0.070***	0.096***	0.028	0.154***
	(0.024)	(0.017)	(0.018)	(0.026)	(0.032)	(0.024)
0 = Most unfavorable, to 97 = most favorable						
Cheney favorability	0.080**	−0.075***	−0.023	0.066*	0.025	0.047+
	(0.025)	(0.017)	(0.018)	(0.027)	(0.034)	(0.025)
0 = Most unfavorable, to 97 = most favorable						
Kerry favorability	−0.292***	0.533***	0.535***	−0.217***	−0.090**	−0.287***
	(0.025)	(0.017)	(0.018)	(0.027)	(0.033)	(0.025)
0 = Most unfavorable, to 97 = most favorable						
Edwards favorability	−0.022	0.111***	0.095***	−0.051+	0.016	−0.061*
	(0.025)	(0.017)	(0.018)	(0.027)	(0.034)	(0.025)
0 = Most unfavorable, to 97 = most favorable						
Adjusted R-squared	0.326	0.668	0.578	0.204	0.038	0.345
Observations	4,692	4,824	4,731	4,817	2,295	4,414

(continued on the next page)

Table 5.7. Continued

Variables	Optimistic	Effective	Decisive	Flip-Flops	Honest	Won't Admit Mistakes
Bush favorability	−0.065***	−0.092***	−0.072**	0.167***	−0.077	0.116*
0 = Most unfavorable, to 97 = most favorable	(0.019)	(0.016)	(0.026)	(0.035)	(0.053)	(0.052)
Cheney favorability	−0.079***	−0.052**	−0.114***	0.126***	−0.061	0.048
0 = Most unfavorable, to 97 = most favorable	(0.019)	(0.016)	(0.027)	(0.035)	(0.055)	(0.052)
Kerry favorability	0.348***	0.445***	0.402***	−0.258***	0.538***	−0.197***
0 = Most unfavorable, to 97 = most favorable	(0.019)	(0.016)	(0.027)	(0.036)	(0.056)	(0.054)
Edwards favorability	0.152***	0.163***	0.152***	−0.002	0.129*	0.026
0 = Most unfavorable, to 97 = most favorable	(0.020)	(0.016)	(0.027)	(0.036)	(0.055)	(0.055)
Adjusted R-squared	0.457	0.647	0.603	0.389	0.714	0.160
Observations	4,797	4,611	2,326	2,352	381	1,384

Entries are ordered logistic regression coefficients. Standard errors are in parentheses.

***$p < .001$, **$p < .01$, *$p < .05$, +$p < .10$.

Control variables have been omitted for brevity. They include Republican (0 = no, 1 = yes); Democrat (0 = no, 1 = yes); conservative (0 = no, 1 = yes); liberal (0 = no, 1 = yes); female (1 = no, 2 = yes); age (continuous); household income (1 = less than $10,000, to 9 = more than $150,000); education (1 = no high school degree, to 5 = advanced degree); white (0 = no, 1 = yes); southerner (0 = no, 1 = yes).

positive or negative, depending on whether the attribute is or is not desirable). Similarly, in table 5.7, we see that Edwards's favorability ratings are statistically significant predictors of Kerry's attributes, and in the expected direction, in thirteen of nineteen models. The magnitudes of Edwards's effects are similar to those of Cheney, at approximately 0.1.

Tables 5.8 and 5.9 present results from a similar analysis of data from the 2000 NAES. Specifically, each table summarizes seven empirical models, first for the Republican ticket (table 5.8) and then for the Democratic ticket (table 5.9). Before discussing these results, we must note some important differences in the 2000 versus 2004 NAES coding of our key variables. In 2000, the presidential and vice presidential candidate favorability ratings are coded from 0 to 100, instead of from 0 to 10, and the presidential candidates' attributes are coded on a scale of 1 to 4 (1 = describes the candidate "extremely well," through 4 = describes the candidate "not well"). Thus, the dependent variables in tables 5.8 and 5.9 (i.e., 2000 NAES) are coded in the opposite direction as those used in tables 5.6. and 5.7 (i.e., 2004 NAES).

In table 5.8, we see that Cheney's favorability ratings are statistically significant predictors of Bush's attributes, and correctly signed, in all seven models. Because we use ordered logistic regression, the coefficients for these estimates cannot be directly interpreted, as in the 2004 data. Therefore, to illustrate these effects in 2004, we estimate the predicted probability of describing Bush as "inspiring" (Model 3).[23] Holding all other variables constant, at their median values, a respondent who rates Cheney at 0 on the 0–100 scale (i.e., least favorable) has a 59.4 percent predicted probability of saying that the word "inspiring" describes Bush either "extremely well" (1) or "quite well" (2). If Cheney's favorability rating increases to 100 (i.e., most favorable), the predicted probability of describing Bush as inspiring increases to 72.2 percent. This constitutes a meaningful, but fairly modest, boost of nearly 13 percentage points. In essence, a radically improved opinion of Dick Cheney will cause voters to see George W. Bush as somewhat more inspiring.

In table 5.9, we see that Lieberman's favorability ratings are statistically significant predictors of Gore's attributes, and correctly signed, in five of seven models. In like fashion, we estimate the predicted probability of describing Gore as "inspiring" (Model 3). Holding all other variables constant, at their median values, a respondent who rates Lieberman at 0 on the 0–100 scale (i.e., least favorable) has a 21.9 percent predicted probability of saying that the word "inspiring" describes Gore either "extremely well" (1) or "quite well" (2).

Table 5.8. Predictors of George W. Bush's Perceived Attributes, 2000 NAES

Variables	Cares	Honest	Inspiring	Knowledge	Hypocritical	Trustworthy	Leadership
Bush favorability	-0.037***	-0.037***	-0.040***	-0.030***	-0.017***	-0.042***	-0.041***
0 = Most unfavorable, to 97 = most favorable	(0.001)	(0.001)	(0.001)	(0.001)	(0.003)	(0.002)	(0.001)
Cheney favorability	-0.006***	-0.008***	-0.006***	-0.007***	-0.012***	-0.007***	-0.005***
0 = Most unfavorable, to 97 = most favorable	(0.001)	(0.001)	(0.001)	(0.001)	(0.003)	(0.002)	(0.001)
Gore favorability	0.007***	0.007***	0.007***	0.003**	-0.001	0.008***	0.006***
0 = Most unfavorable, to 97 = most favorable	(0.001)	(0.001)	(0.001)	(0.001)	(0.003)	(0.002)	(0.001)
Lieberman favorability	0.004***	0.003**	0.007***	0.010***	-0.006+	0.001	0.007***
0 = Most unfavorable, to 97 = most favorable	(0.001)	(0.001)	(0.001)	(0.001)	(0.003)	(0.002)	(0.001)
Reduction in error	38.00%	24.53%	39.88%	23.50%	8.51%	32.65%	28.79%
Observations	9,164	9,135	9,220	9,245	798	3,085	8,382

Entries are ordered logistic regression coefficients. Standard errors are in parentheses.

*** $p < .001$, ** $p < .001$, * $p < .05$, + $p < .10$.

Control variables have been omitted for brevity. They include Republican (0 = no, 1 = yes); Democrat (0 = no, 1 = yes); conservative (0 = no, 1 = yes); liberal (0 = no, 1 = yes); female (0 = no, 1 = yes); age (continuous); household income (1 = less than $10,000, to 9 = more than $150,000); education (1 = no high school degree, to 5 = advanced degree); white (0 = no, 1 = yes); southerner (0 = no, 1 = yes).

Table 5.9. Predictors of Al Gore's Perceived Attributes, 2000 NAES

Variables	Cares	Honest	Inspiring	Knowledge	Hypocritical	Trustworthy	Leadership
Bush favorability	0.006***	0.003**	0.003***	0.005***	−0.004	0.007***	0.008***
0 = Most unfavorable, to 97 = most favorable	(0.001)	(0.001)	(0.001)	(0.001)	(0.003)	(0.002)	(0.001)
Cheney favorability	0.003***	0.007***	0.005***	0.002*	−0.008*	0.005**	0.003*
0 = Most unfavorable, to 97 = most favorable	(0.001)	(0.001)	(0.001)	(0.001)	(0.003)	(0.002)	(0.001)
Gore favorability	−0.037***	−0.042***	−0.038***	−0.025***	0.018***	−0.045***	−0.041***
0 = Most unfavorable, to 97 = most favorable	(0.001)	(0.001)	(0.001)	(0.001)	(0.003)	(0.002)	(0.001)
Lieberman favorability	−0.006***	−0.004***	−0.004***	−0.011***	0.002	−0.003	−0.008***
0 = Most unfavorable, to 97 = most favorable	(0.001)	(0.001)	(0.001)	(0.001)	(0.003)	(0.002)	(0.001)
Reduction in error	35.32%	43.83%	34.01%	11.64%	17.55%	44.90%	42.74%
Observations	9,176	9,165	9,249	9,256	810	3,109	8,401

Entries are ordered logistic regression coefficients. Standard errors are in parentheses.

***$p < .001$, **$p < .01$, *$p < .05$, +$p < .10$.

Control variables have been omitted for brevity. They include Republican (0 = no, 1 = yes); conservative (0 = no, 1 = yes); Democrat (0 = no, 1 = yes); liberal (0 = no, 1 = yes); female (0 = no, 1 = yes); age (continuous); household income (1 = less than $10,000, to 9 = more than $150,000); education (1 = no high school degree, to 5 = advanced degree); white (0 = no, 1 = yes); southerner (0 = no, 1 = yes).

If Lieberman's favorability rating increases to 100 (i.e., most favorable), the predicted probability increases to 29.1 percent. At 7 percentage points, this represents a smaller increase than for Cheney, but a meaningful one, nonetheless. Here, we can say that a radically improved opinion of Joe Lieberman will cause voters to see Al Gore as slightly more inspiring.

Knowledge Networks, 2008 (Panel Data)

To recap, our analyses of the 2000–2008 NAES consistently indicate that vice presidential candidate evaluations significantly influence same-party presidential candidate evaluations (to varying degrees), across a wide range of attributes that are directly relevant to vote choice. But, as in our analysis of favorability ratings in the first half of this chapter, we are not content to base our conclusions solely on pooled, cross-sectional analyses, given the potentially endogenous relationship between same-party candidate evaluations (see Romero 2001, and note 11 in chapter 3).

It is for this reason that we conclude by analyzing panel data from the 2008 Associated Press–Yahoo! News Panel, conducted by KN. As discussed in chapter 4, the KN database is ideal for such analyses because, as a panel study, it allows us to control for the effects of individual-level factors by tracking changes in presidential versus vice presidential candidate evaluations for the *same* respondents, over time. For example, we can see how changes in a respondent's perception of Sarah Palin's experience affected his or her perception of John McCain's experience, from one month to the next. This is unlike the NAES datasets, which use rolling cross-sectional samples (i.e., a *different* sample of respondents, surveyed daily) and therefore cannot completely control for the confounding effects of individual-level differences.

In figures 5.9 and 5.10, we present respondents' average ratings of John McCain and Barack Obama on ten different attributes measured by KN, in 2008 (standard errors are in brackets). These ratings come from five panel waves, or reinterviews of the same respondents, conducted in June (Wave 5), September (Wave 7), early October (Wave 8), and late October (Wave 9) of that year.[24] To be clear, figures 5.9 and 5.10 do not represent direct tests of the relationship between presidential and vice presidential candidate evaluations, nor should they be interpreted as such. Rather, we present them to illustrate an important point: perceptions of McCain and Obama varied over time, and

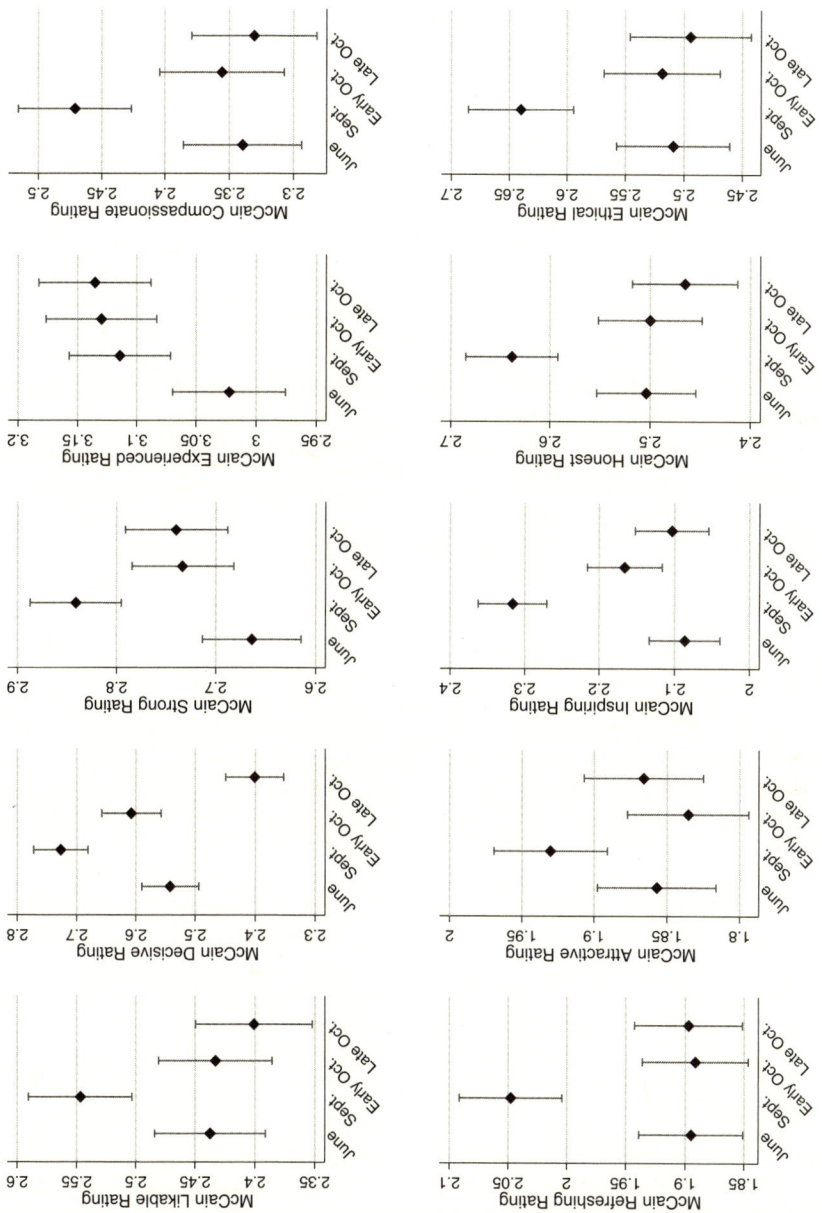

Figure 5.9. Perceptions of John McCain attributes, 2008 KN (Waves 5, 7, 8, and 9)

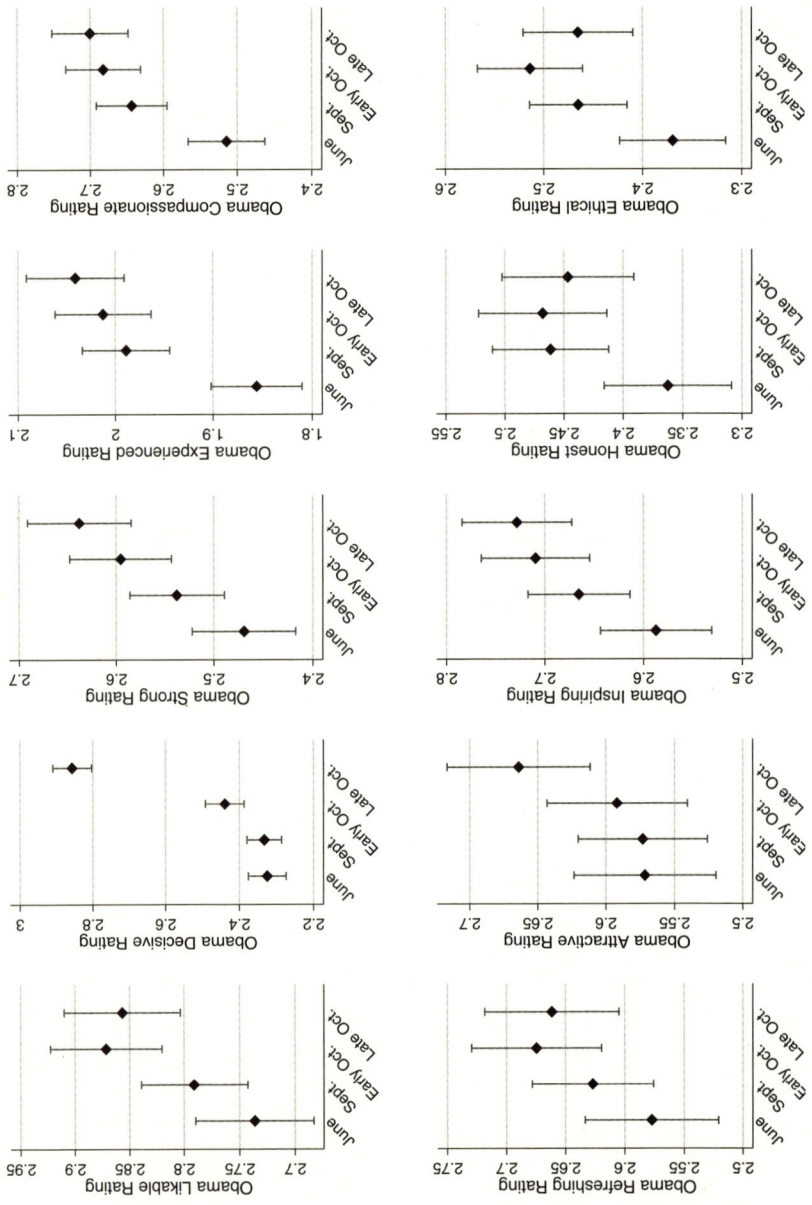

Figure 5.10. Perceptions of Barack Obama attributes, 2008 KN (Waves 5, 7, 8, and 9)

sometimes quite dramatically. McCain, for example, achieved his highest (i.e., most positive) ratings on nine of ten attributes in September, following the selection of Sarah Palin as his running mate.[25] The same is not true for Obama. In fact, six of his highest ratings came in late October. So, it is not the case that perceptions of presidential candidates' attributes vary systematically over time; rather, the nature of that variation was different for McCain and Obama during the same campaign, trending in a negative direction for the former and in a positive direction for the latter.

Because the KN data do not allow us to measure perceptions of Palin and Biden prior to their selection as running mates, in late August, we cannot determine whether those selections, in and of themselves, caused changes in perceptions of McCain and Obama, respectively. However, because subsequent waves included such measures, we can track the dynamic relationship between respondents' evaluations of the vice presidential versus presidential candidates over the course of the campaign. Our question is: To what extent do changes in respondents' perceptions of the running mates cause changes in their perceptions of the presidential candidates? Or, to put it differently, to what extent do voters perceive the running mate to be a direct reflection on who the presidential candidate is, and what he or she stands for? And does a change in their evaluation of the vice presidential candidate also cause them to reevaluate the presidential candidate?

To answer these questions, we return to the three-wave test for panel data, introduced in chapter 4 (see Lenz 2012; Kinder and Kalmoe 2017, 114–115). However, we must note some important differences in the structure of the models presented here. First, we use four—rather than six—panel waves to estimate the effects of perceived vice presidential candidate attributes on perceived presidential candidate attributes, from Waves 5, 7, 8, and 9 (i.e., June through late October) of the 2008 KN panel survey. Second, as noted earlier, KN did not measure perceptions of Palin's and Biden's attributes prior to the time of their selection in late August (of course, because no one knew that they would be the running mates); thus, we cannot directly test how these perceptions contributed to changes in perceptions of the presidential candidates in the pre- versus postselection periods.[26] However, we do have access to various measures of the presidential candidates' attributes during both periods.

Therefore, in each of the postselection waves, we can control for prior perceptions of the presidential candidates as well as their current favorability ratings, when testing how current perceptions of the running mates influence current perceptions of the presidential candidates. For example, we can estimate how perceptions of Sarah Palin's experience influence perceptions of John McCain's experience, in September (Wave 7), *controlling for preexisting perceptions of McCain's experience*, from June (Wave 5). Controlling for perceptions of the presidential candidate, on a given attribute, in the preselection wave essentially provides us with a baseline against which to evaluate changes in perceptions of the same, later in the campaign. This, in turn, allows us to estimate whether, and to what extent, perceptions of the running mate cause changes in perceptions of the presidential candidate. To continue the preceding example, we would consider it affirmative evidence if perceptions of Palin's experience in September were to significantly and positively predict perceptions of McCain's experience in September, independent of the respondent's perception of McCain's experience prior to Palin's selection (i.e., in June).

Formally, the models that we estimate in tables 5.10 and 5.11 may be expressed as follows:

Presidential Attribute

$$= \beta_{oa} \, Cutpoint \, 1 + \beta_{ob} \, Cutpoint \, 2 + \beta_{oc} \, Cutpoint \, 3$$

$+ \beta_1$ *Dependent Variable at Wave 5*

$+ \beta_2$ *Same-Party Presidential Candidate Favorability at Current Wave*

$+ \beta_3$ *Same-Party Vice Presidential Candidate Favorability/Right Experience at Current Wave*

$+ \beta_4$ *Opposite-Party Presidential Candidate Favorability at Current Wave*

$+ \beta_5$ *Opposite-Party Vice Presidential Candidate Favorability/Right Experience at Current Wave* $+ \beta_6$ *Female* $+ \beta_7$ *Evangelical/Catholic*[27]

$+ \beta_8$ *Conservative* $+ \beta_9$ *Liberal* $+ \beta_{10}$ *Republican* $+ \beta_{11}$ *Democrat*

$+ \beta_{12}$ *Household Income* $+ \beta_{13}$ *Education* $+ \beta_{14}$ *Age* $+ \beta_{15}$ *White* $+ \beta_{16}$ *South* $+ \varepsilon$

The dependent variable indicates how well a particular attribute describes McCain or Obama, according to the respondent, on a 4-point scale (1 = not at all well, through 4 = very well). The KN dataset includes ten such attributes. Also, it includes two items measuring perceptions of the vice presidential candidates, in terms of favorability and experience. The former measures favorability on a 4-point scale (1 = least favorable, through 4 = most favorable). The latter is a dichotomous measure ascertaining whether the respondent believes that the running mate has the "right experience to be a good president" (1 = yes, 0 = no).

Table 5.10. Predictors of John McCain's Perceived Attributes, 2008 KN

Variables	Likable	Decisive	Strong	Experienced	Compassionate
DV at Wave 5	0.845***	0.770***	0.852***	0.937***	0.728***
	(0.087)	(0.083)	(0.085)	(0.094)	(0.089)
McCain favorability at Wave 7	1.234***	0.923***	0.932***	0.547***	0.830***
1 = Most unfavorable, to 4 = most favorable	(0.118)	(0.113)	(0.114)	(0.116)	(0.112)
Palin favorability at Wave 7	0.388***	0.519***	0.332***	0.374***	0.418***
1 = Most unfavorable, to 4 = most favorable	(0.098)	(0.097)	(0.097)	(0.102)	(0.095)
Obama favorability at Wave 7	−0.033	−0.180+	−0.189*	−0.313*	−0.212*
1 = Most unfavorable, to 4 = most favorable	(0.094)	(0.094)	(0.097)	(0.100)	(0.093)
Biden favorability at Wave 7	0.056	0.104	0.226*	0.331*	−0.068
1 = Most unfavorable, to 4 = most favorable	(0.097)	(0.099)	(0.100)	(0.104)	(0.097)
Reduction in error	43.98%	38.75%	43.23%	41.14%	44.97%
Observations	953	949	956	953	953

Variables	Refreshing	Attractive	Inspiring	Honest	Ethical
DV at Wave 5	0.879***	1.386***	0.785***	1.058***	1.023***
	(0.091)	(0.096)	(0.082)	(0.092)	(0.090)
McCain favorability at Wave 7	1.149***	0.642***	0.892***	0.974***	1.022***
1 = Most unfavorable, to 4 = most favorable	(0.121)	(0.107)	(0.110)	(0.114)	(0.118)
Palin favorability at Wave 7	0.271***	0.151	0.442***	0.459***	0.390***
1 = Most unfavorable, to 4 = most favorable	(0.099)	(0.095)	(0.094)	(0.095)	(0.096)
Obama favorability at Wave 7	−0.381***	−0.084	−0.242**	−0.235*	−0.230*
1 = Most unfavorable, to 4 = most favorable	(0.095)	(0.091)	(0.091)	(0.096)	(0.096)
Biden favorability at Wave 7	0.058	−0.057	0.066	0.134	0.113
1 = Most unfavorable, to 4 = most favorable	(0.106)	(0.099)	(0.099)	(0.100)	(0.099)
Reduction in Error	45.38%	28.34%	41.09%	52.45%	48.61%
Observations	955	949	951	957	950

(continued on the next page)

Table 5.10. *Continued*

Variables	Likeble	Decisive	Strong	Experienced	Compassionate
DV at Wave 5	0.907***	0.778***	0.916***	0.963***	0.828***
	(0.073)	(0.066)	(0.068)	(0.072)	(0.073)
McCain favorability at Wave 7	1.373***	0.927***	0.985***	0.689***	0.953***
1 = Most unfavorable, to 4 = most favorable	(0.088)	(0.080)	(0.083)	(0.083)	(0.082)
Palin right experience at Wave 7	0.653***	0.867***	0.626***	0.677***	1.123***
0 = No, 1 = yes	(0.135)	(0.133)	(0.136)	(0.147)	(0.134)
Obama favorability at Wave 7	−0.051	−0.207**	−0.188**	−0.221**	−0.193**
1 = Most unfavorable, to 4 = most favorable	(0.071)	(0.067)	(0.070)	(0.073)	(0.069)
Biden right experience at Wave 7	0.052	0.411**	0.372**	0.410**	0.017
0 = No, 1 = yes	(0.129)	(0.126)	(0.130)	(0.138)	(0.125)
Reduction in error	43.07%	34.88%	39.47%	42.25%	43.51%
Observations	1,373	1,368	1,378	1,374	1,375

Variables	Refreshing	Attractive	Inspiring	Honest	Ethical
DV at Wave 5	0.848***	1.292***	0.779***	1.115***	1.095***
	(0.072)	(0.077)	(0.066)	(0.074)	(0.073)
McCain favorability at Wave 7	1.021***	0.610***	1.107***	1.130***	0.945***
1 = Most unfavorable, to 4 = most favorable	(0.084)	(0.075)	(0.081)	(0.086)	(0.085)
Palin right experience at Wave 7	0.816***	0.434***	0.735***	0.891***	0.851***
0 = No, 1 = yes	(0.133)	(0.133)	(0.131)	(0.138)	(0.137)
Obama favorability at Wave 7	−0.286***	0.101	−0.222**	−0.305***	−0.242***
1 = Most unfavorable, to 4 = most favorable	(0.069)	(0.069)	(0.068)	(0.071)	(0.070)
Biden right experience at Wave 7	−0.182	−0.159	−0.103	0.333*	0.251+
0 = No, 1 = yes	(0.126)	(0.125)	(0.125)	(0.132)	(0.131)
Reduction in error	42.24%	30.85%	39.03%	47.34%	42.10%
Observations	1,376	1,369	1,372	1,377	1,367

Entries are ordered logistic regression coefficients. Standard errors are in parentheses.

*** $p < .001$, ** $p < .01$, * $p < .05$, +$p < .10$.

Control variables have been omitted for brevity. They include Republican (0 = no, 1 = yes); Democrat (0 = no, 1 = yes); conservative (0 = no, 1 = yes); liberal (0 = no, 1 = yes); female (1 = no, 2 = yes); age (continuous); household income (1 = less than \$5,000, to 19 = more than \$175,000); education (1 = no high school degree, to 5 = advanced degree); white (0 = no, 1 = yes); southerner (0 = no, 1 = yes).

Table 5.11. Predictors of Barack Obama's Perceived Attributes, 2008 KN

Variables	Likable	Decisive	Strong	Experienced	Compassionate
DV at Wave 5	1.039***	0.975***	0.927***	0.991***	0.995***
	(0.091)	(0.093)	(0.089)	(0.101)	(0.096)
McCain favorability at Wave 7	-0.290**	-0.109	-0.267*	-0.179	-0.283**
1 = Most unfavorable, to 4 = most favorable	(0.110)	(0.103)	(0.107)	(0.110)	(0.107)
Palin favorability at Wave 7	-0.088	-0.175+	-0.068	-0.315**	-0.064
1 = Most unfavorable, to 4 = most favorable	(0.102)	(0.094)	(0.099)	(0.102)	(0.098)
Obama favorability at Wave 7	0.963***	0.937***	1.036***	1.298***	1.018***
1 = Most unfavorable, to 4 = most favorable	(0.111)	(0.104)	(0.109)	(0.117)	(0.110)
Biden favorability at Wave 7	0.116	0.367***	0.316**	0.115	0.166
1 = Most unfavorable, to 4 = most favorable	(0.104)	(0.100)	(0.101)	(0.106)	(0.104)
Reduction in error	48.43%	53.97%	51.54%	61.50%	51.08%
Observations	959	962	952	961	957

Variables	Refreshing	Attractive	Inspiring	Honest	Ethical
DV at Wave 5	0.931***	1.234***	0.917***	0.978***	1.244***
	(0.093)	(0.085)	(0.089)	(0.101)	(0.106)
McCain favorability at Wave 7	-0.214+	-0.299**	-0.194+	-0.197+	-0.176
1 = Most unfavorable, to 4 = most favorable	(0.111)	(0.100)	(0.111)	(0.109)	(0.109)
Palin favorability at Wave 7	-0.059	0.127	-0.073	-0.161+	-0.141
1 = Most unfavorable, to 4 = most favorable	(0.101)	(0.093)	(0.102)	(0.097)	(0.097)
Obama favorability at Wave 7	1.046***	0.687***	1.035***	1.243***	1.057***
1 = Most unfavorable, to 4 = most favorable	(0.116)	(0.102)	(0.114)	(0.115)	(0.117)
Biden favorability at Wave 7	0.013	0.105	0.289**	0.370***	0.374***
1 = Most unfavorable, to 4 = most favorable	(0.108)	(0.096)	(0.105)	(0.104)	(0.106)
Reduction in error	55.81%	41.34%	49.53%	62.43%	63.30%
Observations	955	956	964	952	956

(continued on the next page)

Table 5.11. Continued

Variables	Likable	Decisive	Strong	Experienced	Compassionate
DV at Wave 5	0.996***	0.921***	0.773***	1.058***	0.843***
	(0.073)	(0.075)	(0.071)	(0.083)	(0.076)
McCain favorability at Wave 7	-0.226**	-0.196**	-0.246***	-0.346***	-0.285***
1 = Most unfavorable, to 4 = most favorable	(0.075)	(0.072)	(0.073)	(0.076)	(0.074)
Palin right experience at Wave 7	-0.223+	-0.203	0.127	-0.317*	-0.099
0 = No, 1 = yes	(0.135)	(0.136)	(0.136)	(0.153)	(0.134)
Obama Favorability at Wave 7	1.170***	1.101***	1.276***	1.310***	1.213***
1 = Most unfavorable, to 4 = most favorable	(0.087)	(0.085)	(0.087)	(0.093)	(0.087)
Biden right experience at Wave 7	0.787***	0.446***	0.628***	0.103	0.719***
0 = No, 1 = yes	(0.128)	(0.127)	(0.127)	(0.143)	(0.129)
Reduction in error	49.12%	51.55%	50.04%	58.11%	49.47%
Observations	1,385	1,379	1,369	1,383	1,378

Variables	Refreshing	Attractive	Inspiring	Honest	Ethical
DV at Wave 5	0.880***	1.258***	0.854***	1.071***	1.144***
	(0.072)	(0.070)	(0.070)	(0.083)	(0.084)
McCain favorability at Wave 7	-0.273***	-0.199**	-0.153*	-0.198**	-0.146+
1 = Most unfavorable, to 4 = most favorable	(0.076)	(0.070)	(0.076)	(0.075)	(0.075)
Palin right experience at Wave 7	-0.010	-0.011	-0.202	-0.124	-0.201
0 = No, 1 = yes	(0.136)	(0.131)	(0.136)	(0.140)	(0.139)
Obama Favorability at Wave 7	1.184***	0.707***	1.255***	1.377***	1.301***
1 = Most unfavorable, to 4 = most favorable	(0.089)	(0.076)	(0.088)	(0.094)	(0.093)
Biden right experience at Wave 7	0.466***	0.421***	0.682***	0.671***	0.502***
0 = No, 1 = yes	(0.129)	(0.124)	(0.129)	(0.130)	(0.130)
Reduction in Error	55.32%	43.83%	52.15%	61.52%	59.31%
Observations	1,375	1,375	1,384	1,371	1,373

Entries are ordered logistic regression coefficients. Standard errors are in parentheses.

*** $p < .001$, ** $p < .01$, * $p < .05$, + $p < .10$.

Control variables have been omitted for brevity. They include Republican (0 = no, 1 = yes); conservative (0 = no, 1 = yes); liberal (0 = no, 1 = yes); Democrat (0 = no, 1 = yes); female (1 = no, 2 = yes); age (continuous); household income (1 = less than $5,000, to 19 = more than $175,000); education (1 = no high school degree, to 5 = advanced degree); white (0 = no, 1 = yes); southerner (0 = no, 1 = yes).

Tables 5.10 and 5.11 present the results from twenty ordered logit models regressing each of McCain's or Obama's perceived attributes, respectively, on their running mate's favorability rating (top half) or perceived experience (bottom half). In each case, we measure these variables using data from September (Wave 7). Also, we control for perceptions of the relevant presidential candidate attribute as measured prior to vice presidential selection, in June (Wave 5). Using these waves allows us to estimate the running mate's role in changing perceptions of the presidential candidate immediately following his or her selection.

The results from the McCain-Palin models, in table 5.10, are remarkably consistent. In nineteen of twenty models—excluding only Model 7, predicting perceptions of McCain's "attractiveness" (surely, the least relevant outcome)—perceptions of Palin significantly predict perceptions of McCain, at $p < .001$, and in the expected direction. In other words, independent of the respondent's preexisting views of McCain, Palin's favorability and perceived experience influence his or her view of McCain in the present. This analysis validates one of our central conclusions from the cross-sectional NAES analysis: that vice presidential candidate evaluations influence presidential candidate evaluations.

But what does this mean, in substantive terms? Consider the results from Models 9 and 19, both of which measure perceptions of McCain's honesty. We focus on these models because they yield the greatest proportional reduction in error when it comes to testing the effects of Palin's favorability ratings and her perceived experience, respectively. In Model 9, the probability of rating McCain as 3 or 4 (i.e., the word "honest" describes him somewhat or very well) is 53.5 percent when Palin's favorability is at its lowest level (1 out of 4). However, that probability increases to 82.0 percent when Palin's favorability rating is at its highest level (4 out of 4). In other words, there is a 28.50 percentage-point increase in the predicted probability of describing McCain as honest when Palin's favorability rating moves from its lowest value to its highest value. Similarly, for Model 19, the predicted probability of rating McCain as honest (i.e., this word describes him somewhat or very well) is 70.8 percent when Palin is not perceived as having the right experience to be a good president. But that probability increases to 85.6 percent when Palin is perceived as having the right experience—a 14.8 percentage-point improvement.

The results from table 5.11 indicate that Joe Biden also influenced perceptions of Barack Obama's attributes, in most cases. Indeed, respondents who believed that Biden had the right experience to be a good president were significantly more likely, at $p < .001$, to rate Obama positively on nine of ten attributes—with the only exception being, of all things, perceptions of Obama's experience. Respondents who rated Biden more favorably also were significantly more likely, at $p < .001$, to perceive Obama as decisive, strong, inspiring, honest, and ethical. But in five of ten models, Biden's favorability had no effect on perceptions of Obama.

Once more, to illustrate what these results mean in substantive terms, consider Obama's perceived honesty.[28] For Model 9, when Biden's favorability rating is at its lowest level (1 out of 4), there is a 15.9 percent probability that a respondent would rate Obama as a 3 or 4 in terms of honesty (i.e., this word describes him somewhat well or very well). That probability increases to 36.4 percent when Biden's favorability is at its highest level (4 out of 4)—a 20.5 percentage-point improvement. Next, in Model 19, when a respondent says that Biden does not have the right experience to be a good president (0), there is a 35.4 percent probability that he or she will describe Obama as honest (i.e., this word describes him somewhat well or very well). That probability increases to 51.7 percent when a respondent says that Biden has the right experience to be a good president (1)—a 16.3 percentage-point improvement.[29]

This is strong evidence, indeed, but it cannot tell the full story. After all, each of our time series analyses—from earlier in this chapter, and from chapters 3 and 4—indicates that the running mate's effects on presidential candidate evaluations and vote choice usually fade over the course of a campaign. For that matter, consider that the September wave of the KN panel data, which we analyze earlier, was conducted shortly after the two events that typically give running mates their most extensive and favorable coverage of the entire campaign: the vice presidential announcement and the national party convention (each of which took place in late August or early September 2008). Thus, we cannot be sure that any effects observed in the September wave persisted throughout the campaign; those effects may have weakened, or disappeared altogether, as we have seen previously.

To evaluate potential changes in the running mate's influence over time, next we replicate the models from tables 5.10 and 5.11, using data from each of the subsequent panel waves that included the relevant candidate evaluation measures—specifically, from early October (Wave 8) and late October (Wave 9)—as well as September (Wave 7). For each model, we estimate the relationship between the independent and dependent variables in the present wave, while still controlling for presidential candidate evaluations in the

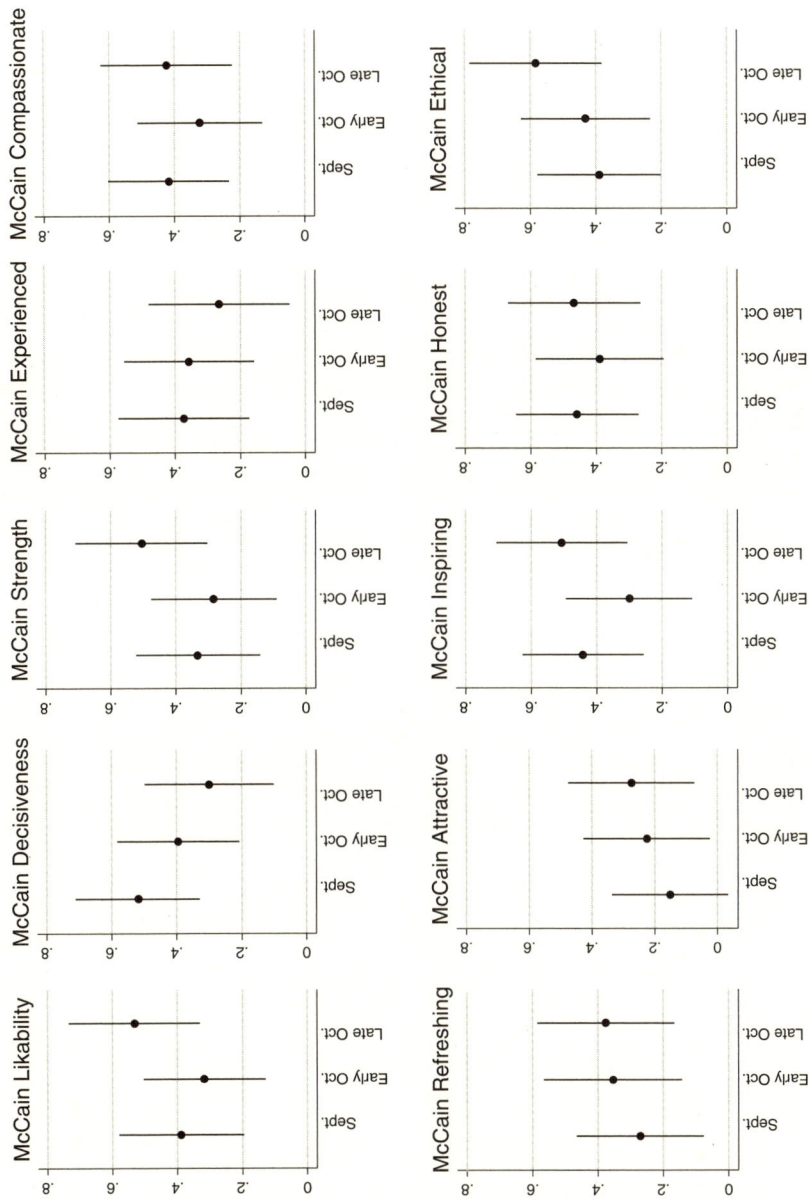

Figure 5.11. The dynamic effect of Palin favorability on McCain attributes, 2008 KN

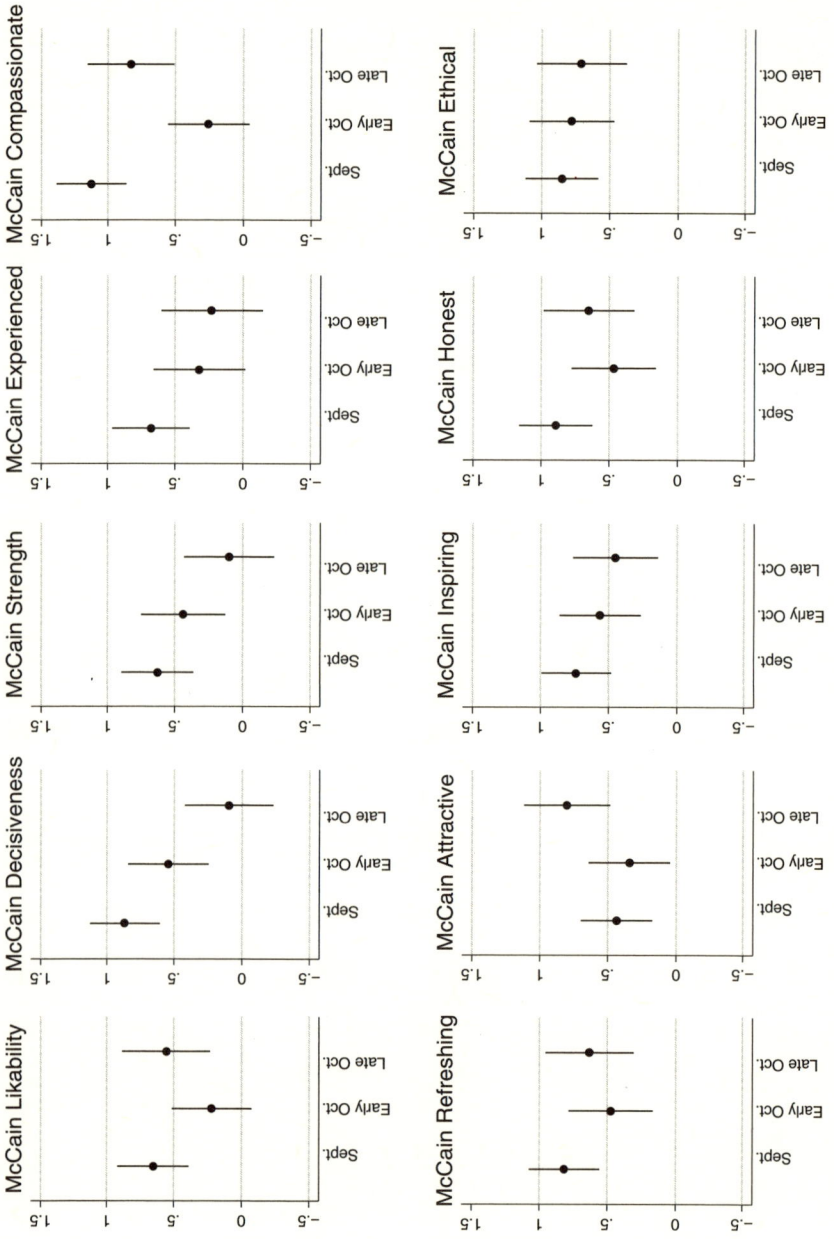

Figure 5.12. The dynamic effect of Palin "right experience" on McCain attributes, 2008 KN

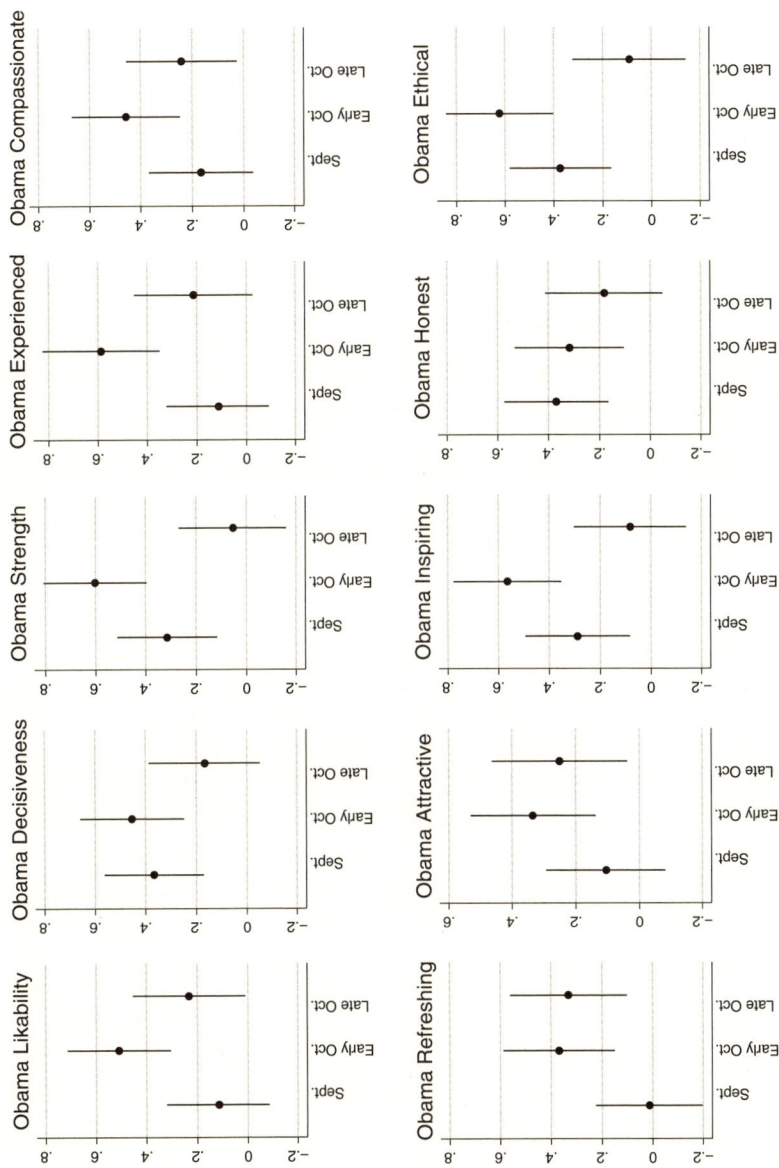

Figure 5.13. The dynamic effect of Biden favorability on Obama attributes, 2008 KN

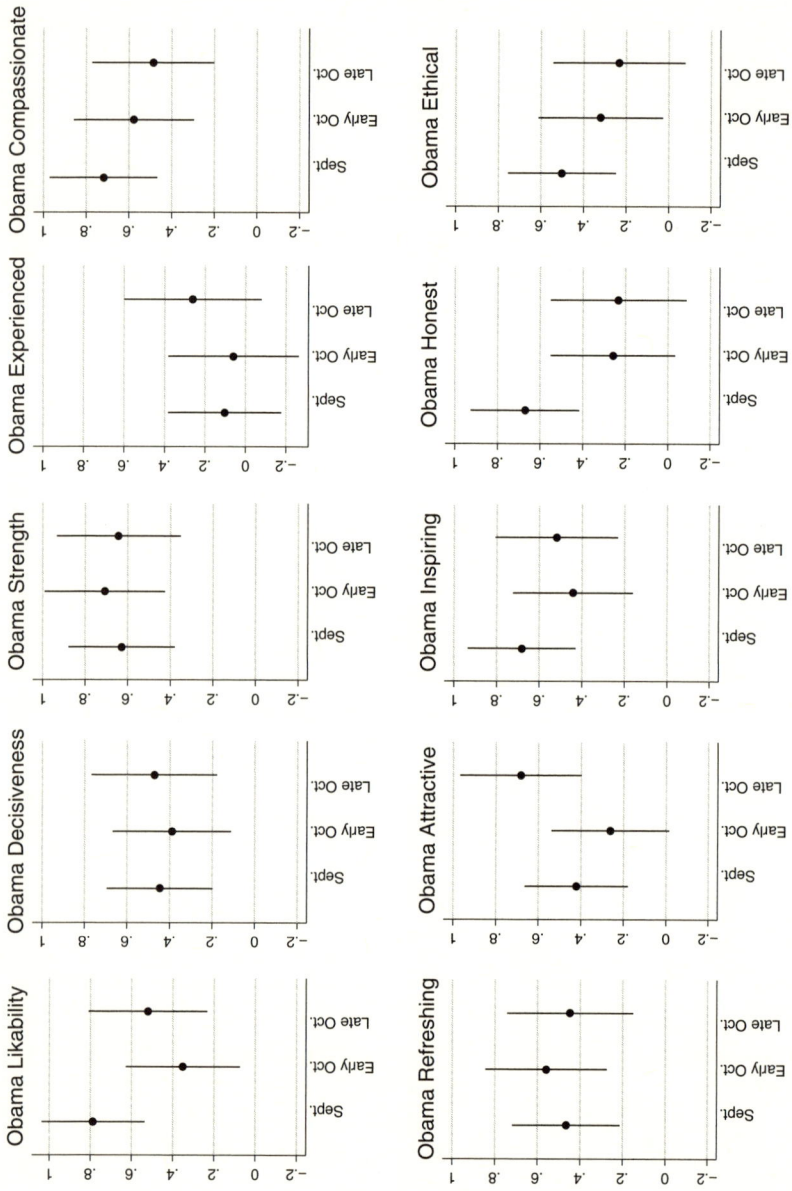

Figure 5.14. The dynamic effect of Biden "right experience" on Obama attributes, 2008 KN

preselection wave (June). Then, we plot the coefficient estimates from each wave, to compare the running mate's influence on perceptions of the same-party presidential candidate, over the course of the campaign. Figures 5.11 and 5.12 present estimates from the McCain-Palin models, for favorability ratings and perceived experience, respectively—and likewise for the Obama-Biden models, in figures 5.13 and 5.14. The continuous lines represent 95 percent confidence intervals for each coefficient estimate.

In figure 5.11, we see that Palin's favorability rating has a relatively consistent effect on perceptions of McCain's attributes across the three panel waves; in fact, the confidence intervals overlap in each case, meaning that the coefficient estimates are statistically indistinguishable from one another. Moreover, in all but one case, these estimates are statistically significant in each wave, and correctly signed. The only exception is for McCain's "attractiveness"; Palin's favorability rating has no effect on this attribute in September, but it has a statistically significant and positive effect in later waves.[30]

In figure 5.12, we observe more variation in the effect of Palin's experience on perceptions of McCain than in figure 5.11. For half of the models, this effect is statistically significant in each wave. Specifically, respondents who believe that Palin has the right experience to be a good president are significantly more likely, throughout the campaign, to view McCain as refreshing, attractive, inspiring, honest, and ethical (and vice versa for those who doubt her experience). Moreover, in each of these cases the effect does not change significantly over time, given the coefficient estimates' overlapping confidence intervals. By the end of the campaign, however, the effect of Palin's experience on perceptions of McCain's decisiveness, strength, and experience becomes indistinguishable from zero. The effect of Palin's experience on McCain's likability and compassion also fades from September to early October, but it reemerges as significant by later that month.

Turning to the Democratic ticket, in figure 5.13, we see that Joe Biden's favorability rating has a weak, and rather variable, effect on perceptions of Barack Obama over the course of the campaign. Indeed, by late October, this variable has no discernible effect on respondents' perceptions of Obama as decisive, strong, experienced, inspiring, honest, or ethical—whereas it had been statistically significant in at least one of the previous waves. For three of these attributes—strong, inspiring, and ethical—we see a statistically significant decline from early to late October, since the coefficients' confidence intervals do not overlap. In other words, these effects fade away over the course of the campaign. However, Biden's favorability rating does have a statistically significant effect on respondents' perceptions of Obama as likable, compassionate, refreshing, and attractive. Each of these effects actually emerges over the course of the campaign; that is to say, they are not statistically significant in September but become so later on.

Figure 5.14, however, suggests that Biden's experience does quite a bit to shape respondents' perceptions of Obama throughout the campaign. In six of ten models, this variable is statistically significant in all three waves, with overlapping confidence intervals. Specifically, Biden's experience has caused respondents to see Obama as more likable, decisive, strong, compassionate, refreshing, and inspiring. Also, it has caused respondents to see Obama as more experienced and attractive in September and in late October but not in early October. In the other two models, we see that the effect of Biden's experience on perceptions of Obama as honest and ethical fades over time, reaching statistical significance in September but not in late October.

By way of summary, let's compare the results for favorability versus experience. Palin's favorability rating significantly influences perceptions of McCain across all three waves, for nine of ten attributes. But Biden's favorability rating does not consistently influence perceptions of Obama; in no case do we find that this effect is statistically significant across all three waves. It is significant in the final wave for four attributes. But for six attributes, the effect of Biden's favorability rating fades over the course of the campaign. In other words, overall evaluations of Palin have a consistent, enduring effect on perceptions of the presidential candidate who selected her; for Biden, they do not.

Contrast this with our results concering whether the running mate "has the right experience to be a good president." In this case, perceptions of the running mate consistently influence perceptions of the presidential candidate's attributes in a majority of cases and for both candidates. For Palin, the effects of her perceived experience are statistically significant across all three waves, for five of ten attributes. For Biden, these effects are statistically significant, across all three waves, for six of ten attributes. Thus, it would appear that perceptions of the running mate's experience have a lasting influence on voters' judgments of *both* presidential candidates, whereas favorability ratings may do so for one and not the other.

Indeed, we have seen throughout this chapter that it *matters* to voters whether the running mate is experienced and is qualified to serve as (vice) president. It matters when they evaluate whether the presidential candidate has good judgment (table 5.3), is too old or too young to be president (table 5.4), or possesses any number of relevant personal or professional attributes (tables 5.10 and 5.11). It matters when they reevaluate those attributes over the course of the campaign (figures 5.12 and 5.14). And it matters when deciding how to vote for president (figures 5.5 through 5.8).

But *why* does the running mate's experience matter? Is it because voters fear that the president, if elected, soon will die, resign, be removed from office, or become incapacitated, then to be succeeded by the vice president? Or is it because they take the vice presidency very seriously, after all, and resolve to elect someone who will wield the awesome powers of that office with the utmost skill? Probably neither. A more plausible explanation is the one that we introduce at the beginning of this chapter: in the words of voters and presidential candidates alike, the choice of a running mate is a "window" into a future presidency—a "message" or a "signal" about who we are electing to the nation's highest office, and what he or she will do once in power. It is not only vice presidential selection itself that seems to influence voters' perceptions of the presidential candidate but also—judging by these results—the running mate's performance over the course of the campaign. Voters reevaluate the presidential candidate as they learn more about the person with whom he or she has chosen to campaign, and possibly to govern. They use this information to make inferences about the values, priorities, and judgment of a potential president who would make such an important decision so (ir)responsibly. And, in turn, they may reconsider whether this is the candidate who deserves their vote.

CONCLUSION

This chapter provides overwhelming evidence that running mates influence voters' perceptions of presidential candidates on a wide range of evaluative dimensions, with direct bearing on presidential vote choice. To reach this conclusion, we estimated more than two hundred statistical models, based on cross-sectional, rolling cross-sectional, and panel data from five nationally representative databases, and a sophisticated, multimethod approach. Moreover, our data include a diverse range of candidate evaluations, including favorability, experience, ideology, and other personal or political attributes.

In short, we find that voters perceive running mates to be a reflection on the presidential candidates who selected them. Thus, running mates matter not only in terms of their ability to *directly* influence vote choice among voters at large or among targeted groups (as we find, to a limited extent, in chapters 3 and 4) but also, if not more important, in terms of their ability to *indirectly* influence vote choice by causing voters to reevaluate who the presidential candidate is, what he or she stands for, and how he or she will govern, if elected. Indeed, there is every reason to believe that voters take seriously the notion that vice presidential selection is a presidential candidate's "first presidential act." Their reaction to this selection, and to the running mate's performance during the campaign, provides valuable information about the presidential candidate that can directly inform their voting calculus.

To be clear, though, vice presidential candidate evaluations are not so influential as to be *determinative* of presidential candidate evaluations and vote choice. In other words, vice presidential selection should not be considered an opportunity to totally remake a candidate's image before entering the final months of the presidential campaign—such that an ideologue will come to be seen as a moderate, or an inexperienced candidate as experienced. To this point, recall the predicted probablity estimates presented earlier in this chapter. We found that running mates did a great deal to shape some perceptions of the presidential candidate—for example, the probability of rating McCain as "very conservative" dropped by 22.5 percentage points when Palin's perceived ideology shifted from "very conservative" to "moderate"—but less so for other perceptions (e.g., age-related concerns). In short, there is variation in the extent to which running mates influence perceptions of the presidential candidate. Nonetheless, perceptions of the running mate clearly matter, to some degree, and presidential candidates and their staff would be wise to take that into account when selecting a partner for the campaign (and, perhaps, for the White House). As our evidence suggests, for example, an ideologically extreme running mate could change how voters preceive the ideology of the presidential candidate. That, in turn, could alienate moderate voters, or attract ideologues (see Elis, Hillygus, and Nie 2010; Court and Lynch 2015; also see chapter 4).

There is another important lesson to be learned from these data. As we show in chapter 2, voters' most evident criterion for vice presidential candidates is that they be qualified to serve in office as president, if necessary. This, probably not coincidentally, is the main criterion that presidential candidates cite when publicly discussing vice presidential selection (chapter 1). To the extent that voters perceive the running mate to be a window into the presidential candidate who selected him or her, presidential candidates have a strong incentive to select a credible partner who will help to persuade or reassure voters of their good judgment, leadership skills, and potential to serve effectively as president. Conversely, if they select a running mate who is not qualified for office, or who will perform poorly on the campaign trail, presidential candidates risk undermining their own credibilty with voters and, in turn, their chances of being elected.

To illustrate this point, consider some examples presented earlier in the chapter. In 2008, a 5-point increase in Sarah Palin's or Joe Biden's perceived readiness to be president generally resulted in a 1-point increase (on an 11-point scale) in voters' perception of John McCain or Barack Obama, respectively, as having the judgment necessary to be president (see table 5.3). Indeed, evaluations of the running mate's experience had a consistent, statistically significant effect on the perceived characteristics of the same-party presidential candidate in all ten of the relevant models from table 5.10 (McCain/Palin), and in nine of ten models from table 5.11 (Obama/Biden). If presidential candidates heed the familiar advice to pick a running mate who shall "do no harm," then selecting someone who clearly possesses the requisite experience to serve as (vice) president is only prudent, from an electoral standpoint—and from a governing standpoint, to boot. Choosing someone who does not meet that standard, in contrast, may prove to be a risk that the campaign—and the nation—cannot afford.

Given these considerations, it makes little sense to select a "high-risk/high-reward" running mate who is not clearly qualified for office, in hopes of transforming the presidential candidate's public image or the trajectory of the campaign. Clearly, running mates influence voters' perceptions of the presidential candidates. But running mates make their mark on the margins—not on a blank page. Moreover, the running mate's influence is most evident when he or she is exceptionally popular (or unpopular). And yet presidential candidates rarely have the opportunity to enlist such talent; after all, if a potential running mate were so appealing to voters, and willing to engage in a national campaign, probably he or she would have run for president in the first place. Thankfully for presidential candidates, while superstar running mates are hard to come by, well-qualified ones are not. Selecting a running mate who is qualified and ready to serve as (vice) president therefore should be a presidential candidate's top priority—as it is for voters.

6. Why Does This Matter?

By March 7, 2019, thirteen Democrats had entered the race for their party's presidential nomination in 2020—with many more soon to follow. But Sherrod Brown would not be one of them. The announcement, on that morning, that he would not run for president came as a surprise to nearly everyone. Just days before, Brown had completed a monthlong tour of several early primary and caucus states, built around his blue-collar message: "The Dignity of Work." It was the same message that he had used to win reelection to the US Senate, from Ohio, the previous fall, at a time when Republicans swept all other partisan, statewide offices. Brown's impressive performance in that election bolstered the rationale for his presidential candidacy—that he was a progressive Democrat, with working-class appeal, who could win back Ohio and the other midwestern states that had carried Donald Trump to victory in 2016. In fact, Brown wondered whether he could have helped to defeat Trump that year, as Hillary Clinton's running mate (see the introduction). But she passed him over. And now that Brown had passed on the upcoming presidential campaign, it looked like he would not have the opportunity to defeat Trump and return a Democrat to the White House in 2020. Or would he?

Immediately after Sherrod Brown announced that he would forgo a run for the presidency, reporters began asking whether he wanted to run for *vice* president instead. "I'm not even interested in thinking about that," he responded dismissively, while taking questions at the US Capitol that day (Ember and Martin 2019). Later, in a conference call with Ohio reporters, the question came up again. "I'm not thinking about that," Brown insisted. "It's just not a concern of mine right now." But would he soon have a change of heart, as had been the case in 2016? Apparently not. "I want to stay in the arena and fight," Brown added, referring to his role in the US Senate. "I don't aspire to be vice president" (Gomez 2019). Now, this sounded more definitive. But, of course, it also sounded a lot like his proclamation in 2015 that "I have zero interest in being vice president" (Terris 2015). And we know how that turned out.

If Sherrod Brown was not thinking about the vice presidency in March 2019, plenty of other people were. Two weeks after his announcement, a headline in the *New York Times*' "On Politics" newsletter read: "Vice President Season Starts

Early for 2020 Democrats" (Lerer 2019). Just that morning, the news (or the rumors, at least) broke that former vice president Joe Biden was planning to announce his presidential candidacy with a running mate, former Georgia legislator Stacey Abrams, already at his side. Picking Abrams—a young, progressive, African American woman from a potential battleground state—would seem to balance out Biden's apparent weaknesses and strengthen his chances of winning the Democratic primary. Other Democrats had similar ideas in mind. For example, two men seeking the Democratic nomination for president—New Jersey senator Cory Booker and former Texas congressman Beto O'Rourke—recently had promised that they would select a woman as their running mate.

Vice presidential speculation was not limited to the Democratic Party, either. Indeed, there was some question whether Vice President Mike Pence would rejoin President Trump on the Republican ticket in 2020. At a press conference on November 7, 2018, Trump seemed to put these rumors to rest when a reporter asked, point-blank: "Will the Vice President be your running mate?" At first, Trump responded, weakly: "Well, I haven't asked, but I hope so." Then, decisively, the president turned to his left, where Pence was seated in the East Room, and extended the offer: "Mike will you be my running mate? . . . Will you?" Pence stood and seemed to affirm his acceptance. "Thank you," Trump replied. "The answer is yes, okay?" (Haberman and Rogers 2018).

But, over the next month, some reports suggested that Trump was having second thoughts. At a 2020 strategy session, in early December 2018, several advisers reportedly raised the idea of dumping Pence from the ticket. According to one source who was briefed on the meeting, the advisers presented Trump with polling data showing that Pence's candidacy would have no effect, positive or negative, on his reelection campaign; in essence, "He doesn't detract from it, but he doesn't add anything either" (Sherman 2018). Other advisers, mostly from outside the White House, reportedly "suggested that . . . [Pence] may have used up his utility" with evangelical voters, since Trump had built his own rapport with them while in office. Instead, these advisers argued, "What [Trump] might benefit from more is a running mate who could help him with female voters" (Haberman and Rogers 2018). In other words, he needed a running mate who could help him *win*.

The preceding examples illustrate just how salient vice presidential selection is in 2020 (indeed, in all modern presidential elections)—even nearly one year before the first primaries and caucuses! Furthermore, they illustrate many of this book's central themes. First, Sherrod Brown exemplifies what is—among political elites and Americans, generally—a common, conflicted view of the vice presidency and vice presidential candidacies, whereby the same person who dismisses the importance of these roles (as outside of "the arena" and thus unworthy of one's aspirations) at other times signals quite the opposite ("By the end, I really wanted it" [Terris 2017]). Second, in Donald Trump and Joe Biden, we find—if the reports are correct—yet more examples of presidential candidates who have publicly dismissed electoral considerations as irrelevant to vice presidential selection (Trump, "History has said nobody ever helps. I've never seen anybody that helps" [Cillizza 2016]; Biden, "The only thing that vice president[ial candidate]s can do is hurt you" [Rees 2000]), only to privately entertain notions that a strategically targeted pick could help their campaign and perhaps even lead them to victory. Third, we see evidence of the many ways in which presidential candidates and their advisers, as well as voters, tend to think that running mates can influence the outcome of an election—particularly, by winning over key groups of voters, such as women (Biden, Booker, O'Rourke, Trump). Thus, there is no question as to the perception of running mate effects in 2020. The question is whether those perceptions match reality.

HERE'S WHY IT MATTERS

Our objective in this book has been to test perceptions of the running mate's influence on voting in presidential elections against the relevant empirical evidence. In short, we ask: Do running mates matter, in the way that people (i.e., presidential candidates and voters) *think* they matter? But why bother asking this question, in the first place? Why should the *answer* matter? And to whom?

First, this research should matter to scholars who study the (vice) presidency, as well as campaigns and elections. Indeed, many previous studies—cited throughout this book—have analyzed vice presidential selection and the vice presidential candidate's influence on voting behavior. This book represents the most comprehensive study of running mate effects to date in that we use a multimethod approach to analyze cross-sectional, rolling cross-sectional, and panel data from many different surveys and election years, in order to evaluate not one but three distinct pathways whereby these effects might occur (i.e., direct, targeted, and indirect). Also, we use qualitative evidence to evaluate the role of electoral, versus governing, considerations in vice presidential selection processes during the era of the "modern vice presidency" (1976–present), and then to test perceptions of running mate effects against the relevant empirical evidence. Our research therefore makes an essential contribution to scholars' understanding of the running mate's perceived versus actual influence on voting in presidential elections. More broadly, our research contributes to the scholarly literature on presidential campaigns and elections, particularly with respect to the influence of campaign strategy or events, versus electoral fundamentals (including partisanship, economic conditions, and incumbency), in shaping presidential vote choice and electoral outcomes (e.g., J. Campbell et al. 2017; Holbrook 1996; Lazarsfeld, Berelson, and Baudet 1948; Sides and Vavreck 2013).

Second, our research has a practical purpose. That is to say, as political scientists, our goal is not just to speak to other political scientists but also to speak to the wider public and to political practitioners and decision makers, in hopes of better informing their deliberations on such important matters as vice presidential selection. Indeed, political scientists have made great strides toward increased public engagement in recent years (e.g., Sides 2011; see also the special issue of *PS: Political Science & Politics* 48 [2015]). And, there is evidence to suggest that political campaigns (e.g., Issenberg 2012) and commentators (e.g., Rove 2012), for instance, have begun taking notice and putting scientific evidence into practice. In that case, it is fitting to conclude this analysis by asking: What advice would we give to presidential candidates and their campaign advisers, as they consider choosing a running mate? In essence, what are the takeaway points from this book that might help decision makers to make informed judgments about the electoral consequences of vice presidential selection? What are the myths, as it were, and what are the empirical realities? For that matter, how should journalists, political commentators, and you, the reader, engage in and respond to public discourse on this topic?

We have five recommendations.

1. Pick Someone Who Can Be a Good Vice President

By constitutional design, the vice president is nearly powerless. In fact, vice presidents exercise their only formal powers in the legislative, rather than executive, branch, by presiding over the US Senate and casting tie-breaking votes in that body, when necessary. This has the perverse consequence of making presidential succession—upon the president's death, resignation, incapacity, or removal from office—the primary means by which a vice president may hope to exercise substantial, formal power. In the (ironic) words of Harry Truman, "The Vice President simply presides over the Senate and sits around hoping for a funeral" (McCullough 1992, 298–299). Indeed, the vice presidency has been the butt of jokes throughout US history. As former vice president Walter Mondale once put it, "The office is handmade for ridicule and for dismissal" (Woodward and Broder 1992, 196).

But over the past forty years—beginning (also ironically) with Walter Mondale—the vice president's powers have grown substantially. This is not because the US Constitution has changed during that time. Rather, as Joel K. Goldstein explains in his definitive work on the subject, this is due to a series of *informal* changes that constitute "the most impressive development in American political institutions during the past four decades" (2016, 301). In particular, Goldstein cites the "Mondale Model" implemented during Jimmy Carter's presidential administration as the genesis of these changes. In short, Carter and Mondale agreed that the vice president should be fully integrated into White House operations, with nearly unlimited access to the president, and freed from tedious and often fruitless "line-item assignments" that tied him to a particular interest, or piece of bureaucratic turf, within the administration. Instead, the vice president would aid the president by serving as "a senior, across-the-board adviser and troubleshooter on significant matters" (302)—for instance, as a liaison to Congress in domestic affairs, and as a foreign ambassador in international affairs. Also, to realize the vice president's integration into White House operations, Mondale secured an office in the West Wing, increased staffing and resources, and regular access to intelligence briefings and to the president, including weekly lunches and the right to sit in on major presidential meetings.

Subsequent presidential administrations have adopted the Mondale Model, with minor modifications, because it has proved helpful to the president. In short, it has provided the president with a well-resourced, well-informed, governing partner of his choosing, who serves with the administration's general interests in mind and has the potential to carry on the president's legacy if elected to succeed him. Indeed, as Goldstein (2016) documents, recent vice presidents including Dick Cheney and Joe Biden have served critical roles in the George W. Bush and Barack Obama administrations, respectively. For instance, Cheney helped to shape the Bush administration's national security and foreign policies, particularly during his first term, with respect to domestic antiterrorism efforts and the Iraq War (see also Baker 2013). Biden, for his part, was a key adviser on foreign policy matters such as the war in Afghanistan (see also Woodward 2010) and was the Obama administration's liaison to Congress during the 2011 budget negotiations (see also Woodward 2012). Hence, Goldstein (2016, 5) concludes, in stark contrast to historical realities and the institution's beleaguered reputation, "most vice-presidential work now is significant."[1]

So, what does this have to do with vice presidential selection? Quite simply, as Goldstein (2016, 307) puts it: "A presidential candidate who chooses poorly sacrifices a substantial governing asset." That is to say, presidential candidates may choose a running mate who is unqualified, or less qualified than other viable alternatives, in order to win an election. And it is possible—yet unlikely, according to our research—that this strategy will succeed and essentially "deliver" the ticket to victory. But, if it does, the new president surely will pay for it in the long run. Instead of a well-qualified partner in government who can contribute to the administration's successes, the vice president will be a hindrance, at worst, and a nonentity, at best. Moreover, a vice president's poor performance in office may create conflict in the administration and hurt the president's reputation, thereby adversely affecting his or her chances of reelection. History also may judge the president poorly for making such an irresponsible decision. In that case, choosing an electoral "game changer" could—at least, theoretically—serve the purposes of a presidential candidate who simply wants to get elected. But if the candidate's goal is to be a successful president, then his or her "first presidential act" should be to select the best possible governing partner.

2. Don't Just Say It; Mean It

To hear presidential candidates tell it, they don't need our first recommendation; they're already saying the same thing. This is evident in our analysis of the "VP Formula," from chapter 1. Every presidential nominee since 1976 has stated publicly that his or her primary criterion for vice presidential selection is to choose someone who is qualified to serve as president, if needed. As Walter Mondale put it in 1984: "My choice will be guided by the need to select someone totally qualified to assume the office of the President should that be necessary" (Weinraub 1984). Beyond that, many presidential candidates have cited the need for political and/or personal compatibility, and some have acknowledged electoral considerations—albeit, usually as something of a potentially fortuitous coincidence.

The problem is that many presidential candidates who publicly forswear electoral calculations privately give them some, if not a great deal of, credence and attention when actually choosing a running mate. Indeed, some candidates who faithfully invoked the VP Formula during the campaign clearly made their eventual selections for strategic reasons. Gerald Ford, for instance, later admitted: "The selection of [Bob] Dole [in 1976] was purely a pragmatic political one."[2] Walter Mondale and John McCain both cited steep polling deficits to explain their selections of Geraldine Ferraro, in 1984, and Sarah Palin, in 2008, respectively. Mondale recalled: "We were looking for running mates who could help us, and we were looking at polls. We were down 10–15 points, and another white male wasn't interesting the public an awful lot."[3] McCain recalled: "We felt, and polling confirmed, that there were moderate and conservative Democrats who had voted for Hillary Clinton and might be persuaded to vote for a Republican presidential candidate with . . . the female chief executive he had picked as his running mate" (McCain and Salter 2018, 53–54). And, in 2000, according to the *New York Times*: "[Al] Gore's search was shaped by gritty political concerns that had little bearing on what he had repeatedly described as his single most important criterion for choosing a running mate: someone possessed of the experience and ability to assume the presidency if necessary" (Barstow with Seelye 2000).

This is not to say that all, or even most, vice presidential selections come down to crass electoral calculations. Indeed, most running mates, and every vice president (e.g., Gore, Cheney, Biden, Pence), in recent years clearly has been qualified to hold the office. But the qualitative evidence that we present in chapter 1 indicates that most, if not all, presidential candidates and/or their top advisers believe that the running mate can influence voters and perhaps decide an election. And under certain electoral conditions—particularly when the presidential candidate is well behind in the polls and in need of a game changer—these perceptions of running mate effects may shape decisions about the vice presidential "short list," or even the eventual selection. In that case, the fact that a presidential candidate recites the VP Formula, perhaps even sincerely, hardly guarantees that he or she will choose a running mate based on qualifications, first and foremost, as advertised.

The question is: What's wrong with this? We have already made the case that it is in the presidential candidate's long-term interest to select someone who can serve effectively as vice president. But if the candidate is willing to accept that risk, and just wants to get elected, then why not select a less qualified but strategically advantageous running mate? Is there any reason to think that this will not pay off in the short term, either? In fact, there are two reasons to think so. First, voters care about the running mate's qualifications. Second, they will judge the presidential candidate more negatively for choosing an unqualified running mate.

To the first point, in chapter 2 we see that survey respondents consistently cite as their most important criterion the running mate's qualifications, or experience, and they assign little importance to demographic or electoral considerations. When evaluating the qualities of a generic running mate, seven in ten respondents cite political or business experience as a strength, while the same number say that gender and ethnicity are irrelevant (table 2.5). And when asked about Donald Trump's or Hillary Clinton's choice of a running mate, in 2016, respondents cited political or business experience as one of the most important qualities for either candidate (table 2.6). In fact, the five top-ranked qualities for Trump's potential running mate included each of the four that pertained to qualifications or experience, as did three for Clinton. None of the items pertaining to demography (i.e., gender and ethnicity) or geography (i.e., "From a swing state") ranked in the top five for either candidate. Voters also seem to prefer a ticket that is balanced, in terms of experience. In a 2008 poll, most respondents said that it was particularly important for Barack Obama to select a running mate with experience in military and foreign affairs, and for John McCain to select one with economic expertise—both of which countered the presidential candidates' greatest weaknesses, as indicated in the same poll.

To the second point, in chapter 5 we see that voters' perceptions of the presidential candidates were shaped by voters' judgments of the running mate's qualifications. In 2008, for instance, survey respondents who saw Palin or Biden as ready to be president consistently rated McCain or Obama, respectively, more favorably on a wide range of political and personal attributes (tables 5.10 and 5.11). Moreover, as respondents reassessed the running mate's credentials throughout the campaign, they also reevaluated the presidential candidate who selected him or her, accordingly (figures 5.12 and 5.14). And this, in turn, influenced vote choice. For instance, respondents who came to believe in (doubt) Palin's qualifications over the course of the campaign also came to believe in (doubt) McCain's judgment, and as a result they were more (less) likely to vote for the Republican ticket (figure 5.5).

This evidence illustrates the dangers of choosing a running mate who is not clearly qualified and ready to take over as (vice) president. In short, voters are likely to notice when the running mate's credentials are lacking, and to hold the presidential candidate accountable for making such a reckless decision. Conversely, voters are likely to reward a presidential candidate for selecting a well-qualified running mate, perhaps even more so if this serves to "balance the ticket" (e.g., Obama-Biden, Trump-Pence). In that case, vice presidential selection rarely, if ever, represents a choice between the presidential candidate's long-term versus short-term interests—between a running mate who can help, *if elected*, and one who can help *get elected*. Simply put, choosing a well-qualified running mate is not just a matter of responsible governance; it is also a good campaign strategy.

3. Ask Whether the Running Mate Will Matter Enough

By this point, it should be clear that, yes, running mates matter. This is not just because one of the running mates will become the next vice president (although we think that is the ultimate reason). It is also because vice presidential candidates influence presidential vote choice. The most significant way that they do so, according to our analysis, is via indirect effects—that is, by shaping perceptions of the presidential candidate, which, in turn, affect voting behavior. In the preceding section, we discuss these effects in terms of the running mate's qualifications. In chapter 5, we also demonstrate that the vice presidential candidate's favorability ratings influence the presidential candidate's favorability ratings, among respondents to the 1952–2016 American National Election Studies (ANES). This, in turn, has a significant effect on vote choice (figures 5.1 and 5.2).

Our analysis also indicates that vice presidential candidates often have a direct effect on voting behavior. That is to say, if voters (dis)like the running mate, they are more (less) likely to vote for his or her presidential ticket. But this effect is limited in several respects. For instance, in our pooled analysis of the 1952–2016 ANES data, from chapter 3, we find that vice presidential candidate feeling thermometer ratings have a statistically significant and positive effect on a respondent's likelihood of voting for that candidate's ticket (table 3.2). But the predicted probability of doing so increases by only 2 to 3 percentage points in response to a 5-point increase in the running mate's thermometer ratings (table 3.3). Presidential candidates have three to four times this effect. Also, such effects vary across election years, and by party. Ten of thirteen Democratic running mates included in our ANES data had a statistically significant effect on vote choice in a given election year, but this was the case for only seven of thirteen Republican running mates (figure 3.1). Moreover, our vector autoregression analysis of rolling cross-sectional data from the 2000 and 2004 National Annenberg Election Surveys (NAES) indicates that the running mate's effect on intended vote choice usually fades away very quickly, if it occurs at all (figures 3.2 and 3.3). Only for John Edwards, in 2004, do we find that a one-unit positive shock to his favorability ratings had an enduring effect on voters' preferences for the Democratic ticket. In short, we conclude that only the most popular running mates—as Edwards was that year—are likely to change voters' minds over the course of an election.

Thus, we find that running mates have indirect, as well as direct, effects on voting behavior. But, according to our analysis of pooled 1952–2016 ANES data, from chapter 5, the former far exceeds the latter. That is to say, running mates have a much greater *indirect* effect on vote choice, by shaping presidential candidate evaluations, than they do a *direct* effect, via vice presidential candidate evaluations (table 5.2). This evidence is consistent with the notion that voters cast their ballots primarily to elect a president, rather than a vice president. In essence, running mates matter most when causing voters to reevaluate the presidential candidates who are, in fact, the principal objects of their voting decision. To our minds, this only makes sense, given that presidents exercise far more power—formally and informally—than vice presidents. As a result, voters can more easily weigh the costs and benefits associated with electing one person versus another as president, rather than vice president. Furthermore, the choice among presidential candidates is much more salient to voters during a campaign, since presidential candidates attract the lion's share of media coverage and, by way of a more formal indicator, engage in three debates, versus one for the vice presidential candidates.

All of this is to say that running mates have a real, but *marginal,* effect on voting behavior. Their direct effects are quite limited in terms of size, consistency, and duration. And their indirect effects are limited by the fact that presidential candidate evaluations necessarily depend on the presidential candidate's characteristics and performance, first and foremost. Also, consider that voters expect a running mate to be at least reasonably likable and qualified—as, in fact, they tend to be. In that case, how much can a presidential candidate really do to exceed voters' expectations when choosing a running mate? Is it possible even to imagine a running mate *so* beloved or *so* experienced that voters would flock to support the ticket on which he or she runs? In hopes of gaining what, exactly? If the running mate were to have a dramatic effect on voting behavior, it seems much more likely that this would be because he or she has *failed* to meet the public's expectations—as someone who is decidedly *un*popular or *un*qualified—and thus represents some risk to voters, while also undercutting the presidential candidate's credibility.

This is why the notion of a vice presidential game changer, frankly, is foolish (and reckless, to boot). Running mates simply do not influence voting behavior enough to rescue a presidential ticket from certain defeat. Yes, they influence voting behavior to some extent—and, therefore, they could make the difference in a very close election. But that is not what game changers are for; by definition, their role is to change a game that already seems lost. Also, we must note, if a presidential campaign seems doomed, this is probably because the electoral fundamentals are working against it, or voters simply do not like the presidential candidate. In either case, no running mate can radically alter these dynamics. And throwing a vice presidential "Hail Mary" just might make things worse, by causing voters to doubt the presidential candidate's character and judgment.

In short: Ask not whether running mates matter. (They do.) Ask whether any running mate could matter *enough* to make the difference in this election. (Probably not. But, if so, it is because the presidential candidate has a decent shot at winning already, anyway.)

4. Don't Expect the Running Mate to "Deliver" a Key Voting Bloc

Then again, why should the running mate have to appeal to *everyone* in order to make the difference in an election? Aren't running mates most effective at winning over *targeted* groups of voters? Indeed, this has been the dominant understanding of running effects throughout US history. For example, prior to the implementation of the McGovern-Fraser Commission reforms, in the 1970s, the vice presidential nomination was more likely to go to finalists who came from a competitive state (Baumgartner 2012; Hiller and Kriner 2008). Since that time, experience has emerged as a significant predictor of selection, and home state competitiveness no longer predicts selection (Baumgartner 2016; Hiller and Kriner 2008). Nonetheless, prospects of a home state advantage continue to dominate the news media's coverage of the vice presidential selection process, while also apparently influencing the allocation of campaign resources (i.e., candidate visits and advertisements) in some recent elections (see Devine and Kopko 2016). And in chapter 1 we see that most presidential candidates and their campaigns since the 1970s have seemed to believe that the choice of a running mate could help them appeal to a key voting bloc—most often with respect to geography, but also ideology, race or ethnicity, gender, religion, and age.

In chapter 4, we present the most comprehensive analysis of targeted effects to date. The results are underwhelming, to say the least. First, in terms of geography, we find no clear evidence of a vice presidential home state advantage among 1952–2016 ANES respondents, in general (table 4.1). Nor do we find evidence of a geographic advantage at the US Census divisional or regional levels, or when focusing on southern running mates, in particular (figure 4.1). This includes the most recent southern running mate, Tim Kaine. Our analysis of panel data, from 2016, indicates that southerners did not become more likely to vote for the Democratic ticket at any point following Kaine's selection (figure 4.10). Nor did midwesterners become more likely to vote for the Republican ticket following Mike Pence's selection that year (figure 4.9). At best, we see a temporary increase in midwesterners' preferences for the Republican ticket following Paul Ryan's selection in 2012, but this fades away almost immediately and has no effect on vote choice, in the end (figure 4.8).

Demographic effects are more variable but still quite weak. In terms of gender, we do not find any evidence that women running mates increase support for their party's ticket among women voters. Women were no more likely to vote for these tickets in 1984 or 2008 than in other election years, according to our pooled ANES analysis (figure 4.2). And, according to our 2008 panel data analysis, women were no more likely to vote for the Republican ticket at any point following Palin's selection than they were beforehand (figure 4.6). In terms of religion, our research indicates that no Catholic running mate has influenced vote choice among Catholics since the 1960s (figure 4.3). Nor do we find that Joe Lieberman's vice presidential candidacy had a significant effect on Jewish voters, in 2000. (However, this is only one candidacy, and the 2000 ANES included very few Jewish respondents.) Only evangelical Christians show some evidence of targeted religious effects in recent elections. In particular, panel data indicate that evangelical support for the Republican ticket increased significantly, but only temporarily, in 2008 and 2016, following the selections of fellow evangelicals Sarah Palin and Mike Pence, respectively.

Evangelical respondents exhibited no change in voting preferences, as compared with the preselection period, by late October for Palin, and almost immediately, by August, for Pence.

It is only in terms of ideology that we find clear evidence of targeted running mate effects in a recent presidential election—but just once, in 2012. In that year, panel data indicate that conservatives' support for the Republican ticket increased significantly after Mitt Romney selected Paul Ryan as his running mate, in August. And this effect persisted throughout the campaign, into November. For Palin, in 2008, we see only a temporary increase in conservatives' support following her selection, in September and again in late October. But this effect fades away by the time of the election. For Pence, in 2016, we see no significant change in conservatives' support for the Republican ticket, at any point following his selection.

Probably, there is no more seductive element of "veepstakes" speculation than the notion of targeted running mate effects. How easy and how brilliant, it seems, to purchase a bloc of voters on the cheap, with one essentially symbolic act: by picking a running mate who they will see as "one of us." But if this seems too good to be true, for the campaign operative or the political junkie, that's probably because it is. Indeed, we find very little evidence of targeted running mate effects, particularly in terms of geography and gender (which, ironically, may be the two most commonly cited target groups). When these effects occur, usually they are temporary and do not end up influencing vote choice. Only in terms of ideology do we find evidence of a promising opportunity for targeted effects.

This conclusion may be surprising; but, actually, it shouldn't be. For one thing, does it really make sense to think of a group of voters as a "bloc?" Individual interests vary within any social group, and social identities tend to be complex (Roccas and Brewer 2002). Some groups, however, are particularly cohesive and may even share a sense of "linked fate" (see chapter 4). Identification with such a group therefore may be more salient, and perceived interests within the group may be more homogeneous, than for other groups. But if this is the case, then—as we see for African Americans and, increasingly, Latinos—probably the group will have aligned itself with one party, already. In that case, the groups that are most likely to vote as a bloc, as it were, also seem least likely to detach from one political party in order to support an in-group running mate on the other party's ticket. To "deliver" a purported voting bloc probably would require redefining the relationship between the party and the group in question, so as to address the underlying rationale for its members' alienation. Policy changes can do that. Presidential candidates probably can, too. Running mates surely cannot.

5. Don't Just Take Our Word for It

This is what the evidence tells us, at least. But why should anyone believe it? Because, as we have argued, this is the most comprehensive analysis of running mate effects to date. Yet our analysis also is limited in at least two important respects that future research ought to address.

First, much of our analysis focuses on only the most recent presidential elections. For instance, our analysis of rolling cross-sectional data, in chapter 3, is limited to two elections (2000, 2004); panel data, in chapter 4, three elections (2008, 2012, 2016); and panel data, in chapter 5, one election (2008). This is not deliberate, on our part; rather, it reflects the limited range of rolling cross-sectional and (three-wave) panel datasets that are available for analysis—particularly when that analysis requires direct vice presidential candidate evaluation measures, as ours does. The problem, of course, is that focusing on a relatively small number of elections may limit the generalizability of some of our research findings. For instance, when we determine that perceptions of the running mate's readiness to be president have a dynamic effect on perceptions of the presidential candidate's attributes, over the course of a campaign, this is based on data from one panel survey (Knowledge Networks), in one election year (2008), and two vice presidential candidacies (Palin and Biden). If we had been able to use comparable data from another survey or another election year, we would have done so. But, to our knowledge, no such data exist (or, at least, they are not publicly accessible). Aside from conducting our own, original rolling cross-sectional or panel survey—a massive undertaking, to be sure—there is little that we can do to address this concern directly. We do, however, supplement our analyses whenever possible with cross-sectional data from a much wider range of elections. While these data are more limited for the purposes of establishing causal inference, by and large they confirm the results from our rolling cross-sectional and panel data analyses.

The best way to address this limitation, though, is for researchers to conduct surveys—particularly, rolling cross-sectional and panel surveys—in future elections that directly measure voters' impressions of the vice presidential candidates, as well as the presidential candidates. For a model, consider the

2008 KN survey that we analyze in chapter 5. It includes three vice presidential candidate evaluation measures: favorability ratings, ideological placements, and perceptions of the running mate's readiness to be president. It also includes ten items that measure perceptions of the presidential candidate's professional or personal attributes (e.g., decisiveness, experience, honesty). If similar items were included in future surveys, one could replicate or extend our analyses to determine whether the results that we describe here are generalizable across election years and vice presidential candidacies, and perhaps whether they vary under certain appropriately defined conditions.[4]

Second, our ability to test for targeted running mate effects is limited by the range of available candidacies. While our data include a fairly diverse set of vice presidential candidates in terms of geography, ideology, and some religious affiliations (particularly, for Catholics and evangelical Christians), they include only two women and one Jewish candidate. Moreover, our estimate of Lieberman's targeted effect, in 2000, is based on a very small sample of Jewish respondents. This makes it difficult to draw firm conclusions about targeted effects among these groups of voters. For other social groups—including African Americans, Latinos, Asian Americans, Muslims, and gays and lesbians—we cannot estimate targeted running mate effects because (at the time of this writing) no in-group member has run for the vice presidency on a major party ticket. Given the relative salience and cohesiveness of some of these group identities, it is entirely possible that such an analysis would yield clearer evidence of targeted effects than what we find in chapter 4.

It is also possible that we may find clearer evidence of targeted effects by focusing on the *intersection* of multiple in-group identities. Indeed, social identity encompasses membership in multiple groups, and it is at the intersection of these identities that individuals often define themselves and feel the strongest sense of in-group attachment (see Brewer 1991; Roccas and Brewer 2002). We do not analyze intersectional targeted effects here, but it would be possible to do so using the same data sources. For instance, one could use the ANES data to analyze Geraldine Ferraro's effect on voting among Catholic women in 1984. Or one could use the KN panel data to analyze Sarah Palin's dynamic effect on conservative women over the course of the 2008 campaign. Also, one could conduct such analyses in the future, if, say, an African American woman (e.g., Stacey Abrams) or a Latino/a conservative (e.g., Marco Rubio) were to run for vice president.

This is a promising opportunity for future research, and we encourage other scholars to pursue it. However, we must caution that conducting such an analysis will be complicated by issues of sample size and statistical power. That is to say, defining respondents in terms of an intersectional identity requires dividing the sample into ever-smaller segments. For instance, African Americans represent approximately 14 percent of the US population. But African American women represent approximately half of that (i.e., 7 percent of the US population). Reducing the respondent sample in this way necessarily makes it more difficult to precisely estimate the statistical relationship between in-group identification and vote choice, thus increasing the likelihood of committing a type II error (i.e., failing to reject a null hypothesis that is, in fact, false). Using large-sample surveys, such as the Cooperative Congressional Election Study, may help to alleviate this concern.

Indeed, the emergence of more diverse running mates and survey data sources in future years will be critical to evaluating—and hopefully validating—the results of this analysis. Ours will not be the last word as to whether, and how, running mates matter; nor should it be. But for now, of course, you could just take our word for it.

CODA

Or you could take Dick Cheney's word for it.

This book begins with an excerpt from an April 2012 interview with the former vice president. We find Cheney's comments to be particularly striking, for two reasons. First, there may be no one alive who has more experience or insight with respect to vice presidential candidacies and the office of the vice presidency than Dick Cheney. Indeed, Cheney led two vice presidential searches, for Gerald Ford in 1976 and for George W. Bush in 2000. After being selected as Bush's running mate, Cheney successfully campaigned for the vice presidency in 2000, and again as an incumbent in 2004. And, of course, he served two full terms as vice president. Reflecting on his decision to lead Bush's search, Cheney wrote: "When I thought about it, I realized I'd been observing or participating in the vice presidential selection process for nearly a quarter century" (Cheney with Cheney 2011, 255). And that was before he was selected, elected, and served in office.

Cheney's take on vice presidential selection also is remarkable, particularly given his wealth of experience, because it so closely aligns with the contents of this book. Indeed, it could function as a thematic summary of our substantive chapters. Here goes.

Perceptions of Running Mate Effects (Chapters 1 and 2)

"The decision you make as a presidential candidate on who your running mate is going to be is the first presidential-level decision that the public sees you make. It's the first time you're making a decision that you're going to have to live with. It gives the public a chance to watch you operate and see what you think is important, what kind of individual you choose to serve as your running mate, what are the criteria.

"And I think the single most important criteria [*sic*] has to be the capacity to be president. That's why you pick them. Lots of times in the past that has not been the foremost criteria [*sic*]. It really varies [from] administration to administration."

Direct and Targeted Effects (Chapters 3 and 4)

"As you watch the talking heads out there now, they're talking about, 'Well, gee, you better get a woman or you better get a Hispanic or you better pick somebody from a big state.' Those are all interesting things to speculate about, but it's pretty rare that an election ever turns on those kinds of issues."

Indirect Effects (Chapter 5)

"It's much more likely to turn on the kind of situation where they'll judge the quality of your decision-making process based on whether or not this individual is up to the task of taking over and serving as president of the United States should something happen to the president."[5]

This sounds about right to us. And now there is evidence to back it up.

Notes

INTRODUCTION

1. US Constitution, Article I, Section 3.

2. US Constitution, Article I, Section 3. Vice President Joe Biden (2009–2017) cast eight tie-breaking votes during his eight years in office. With a more evenly divided Senate, Vice President Mike Pence (2017–present) cast thirteen tie-breaking votes just during his first two years in office (see https://www.senate.gov/pagelayout/reference /four_column_table/Tie_Votes.htm [accessed June 1, 2019]).

3. US Constitution, Article II, Section 1.

4. US Constitution, Amendment 25. No vice president has succeeded to the presidency on a permanent basis due to presidential incapacitation. However, once during Ronald Reagan's presidency (1985) and twice during George W. Bush's presidency (2002, 2007) the vice president temporarily served as acting president when Reagan and Bush, respectively, underwent a surgical procedure and a pair of colonoscopies. The current practice, established during George H. W. Bush's administration, is for presidents to invoke the Twenty-Fifth Amendment when they are put under general anesthesia, but not for localized anesthesia (Goldstein 2016, 258–259).

5. US Constitution, Amendment 20.

6. See https://www.whitehouse.gov/1600/presidents/johnadams (accessed June 1, 2019).

7. Interview, Bob Hartmann with Nelson Rockefeller, December 2, 1977, folder "Rockefeller, Nelson (1)," Box 199, Bob Hartmann Papers, Gerald R. Ford Library, Ann Arbor, Michigan.

8. Interview, Hartmann with Rockefeller.

9. Available at https://www.c-span.org/video/?407325-1/role-vice-president (accessed January 10, 2020).

10. Interview, Hugh Morrow with Nelson Rockefeller, February 22, 1978, folder "Rockefeller, Nelson—Interviews, 1977–78/2," Box 199, Bob Hartmann Papers, Gerald R. Ford Library.

11. *Meet the Press*, March 3, 2000, transcript accessed via the Lexis/Nexis database.

12. See http://www.cnn.com/2007/POLITICS/11/28/debate.transcript.part2 (accessed June 1, 2019).

13. Available at https://millercenter.org/the-presidency/presidential-oral-histories /j-danforth-quayle-oral-history-vice-president-united (accessed January 10, 2020).

14. For perspective on the Garner quote, see https://www.cah.utexas.edu/news /press_release.php?press=press_bucket (accessed June 1, 2019).

15. Indeed, as anyone who closely follows presidential politics knows, the news media devote an enormous amount of attention to vice presidential selection. For

example, the Pew Research Center's Project for Excellence in Journalism found that, during the week of August 18–24, 2008, 41 percent of all presidential campaign media coverage was devoted to the Democratic and Republican "veepstakes." Thirty-seven percent of all campaign coverage was devoted to Barack Obama's imminent selection of a running mate, and then its aftermath. The next most popular topic received less than one-third of that amount of coverage (available at www.journalism.org/node /12514 [accessed January 10, 2020]). And, in mid-August 1988, Dan Quayle's recently announced vice presidential candidacy attracted two-thirds to four-fifths of the three major television networks' political coverage (Woodward and Broder 1992, 71).

16. During the 2000 veepstakes, former presidential candidate and future vice president Joe Biden expressed a version of this sentiment when he said: "The only thing vice president[ial candidate]s can do is hurt you" (Rees 2000). Presumably, he did not reiterate this philosophy while being vetted by the Obama campaign, in 2008.

17. George W. Bush endorsed this view in his memoirs. To explain his choice of a running mate in 2000, he wrote that Cheney's "lack of impact on the electoral map did not concern me either. I believe voters base their decision on the presidential candidate, not the VP" (Bush 2010, 67).

18. That is not to say that it is the first book-length treatment of vice presidential candidates, in any respect. As noted previously, Ulbig (2013) analyzes running mates in relation to media coverage. And Devine and Kopko (2016) analyze running mates in relation to the home state advantage.

PART I: PERCEPTIONS OF RUNNING MATE EFFECTS

1. We can only speculate as to why this is the case. One possibility is that the development of online polling has increased the number of polls and polling firms that are amenable to asking such questions. In essence, there simply may be more "space" available to ask about a relatively narrow or niche topic such as vice presidential selection in this new polling environment. While this reality is not ideal for the purposes of comparing results across chapters 1 and 2, proceeding with our analysis, as described, is appropriate for two reasons in particular. First, the nature of the qualitative evidence that we rely on in chapter 1 makes it impractical to restrict our analysis to the 2000–2016 elections; as our research indicates, often it takes decades to learn the truth about the inner workings of a campaign, and so the most recent elections provide the most limited and least reliable evidence on which to base our conclusions. Second, to the extent that public opinion has become more polarized since the 1990s, and the parties more ideologically sorted, modern voters may ascribe less importance to vice presidential selection than in past elections because they feel more attached to their party and thus are less likely to defect in the election. If so, then it is preferable for our analysis to focus on the most recent elections in order to discern, in the most contemporaneous sense, whether running mates matter in the way that voters think they matter. Finally, it is also the case that, due to data limitations, the empirical evidence of

running mate effects that we present in part II of this book primarily comes from the 2000–2016 elections. In that case, voters' perceptions of running mate effects (chapter 2) may be directly compared with their actual voting behavior (chapters 3–5).

2. We present these results by year, rather than aggregating across the entire 1952–2004 period. Therefore, given the concerns raised in the previous note, interested readers may draw some comparisons to other results from chapter 2, as well as part II, across the most relevant time frames.

CHAPTER 1. (WHY) DO PRESIDENTIAL CANDIDATES THINK THAT RUNNING MATES MATTER?

1. Adler and Azari (2018) do, however, find quantitative and qualitative evidence of ideological ticket balancing, particularly since 1972.

2. In a similar vein, Baumgartner (2012) finds that home state competitiveness significantly predicted vice presidential selection, and political experience did not, during what he calls the "convention era" (1832–1928). Conversely, he finds that political experience (in the US House, US Senate, or other national offices) significantly predicted selection from 1960 to 2016, while home state competitiveness did not (Baumgartner 2016).

3. This critique is not intended to challenge the studies cited earlier, each of which represents a major contribution to scholars' understanding of vice presidential selection, in terms of their research methodologies or substantive conclusions. Rather, our purpose is to identify these studies' limitations with respect to the present research objectives. Specifically, the cited studies evaluate presidential candidates' *behavior*, i.e., which characteristics determine their selection of a running mate. Our study, in contrast, evaluates presidential candidates' *perceptions*, i.e., whether they think running mates influence presidential vote choice in the first place, and, if so, which running mate characteristics they think have the potential to influence voting in elections, generally, or in this election, particularly.

4. Available at https://www.c-span.org/video/?405439-1/donald-trump-regent-universitys-presidential-candidate-forum&start=2634 (accessed January 10, 2020).

5. Available at https://charlierose.com/videos/28464 (accessed January 10, 2020).

6. Available at http://transcripts.cnn.com/TRANSCRIPTS/1607/23/cnr.04.html (accessed January 10, 2020).

7. Press Release, Statement by President Gerald R. Ford, July 31, 1976, folder "Vice Presidential Selection—1976: General," Box 64, Philip Buchen Files, Gerald R. Ford Library.

8. Article, *Washington Post*, March 21, 1976, folder "Vice President (2)," Box H34, President Ford Committee Records 1975–77, Gerald R. Ford Library.

9. Available at https://www.c-span.org/video/?3329-1/republican-candidates-forum&start=1650 (accessed January 10, 2020).

10. Available at https://www.c-span.org/video/?26971-1/clinton-vice-presidential-announcement (accessed January 10, 2020).

11. Available at https://www.c-span.org/video/?154150-1/republican-candidates -debate (accessed January 10, 2020).

12. Available at http://transcripts.cnn.com/TRANSCRIPTS/0401/04/se.01.html (accessed January 10, 2020).

13. Available at http://transcripts.cnn.com/TRANSCRIPTS/0808/22/cnr.02.html (accessed January 10, 2020).

14. Available at http://www.foxnews.com/transcript/2012/06/19/exclusive-mitt-and -ann-romney-talk-vp-decision-us-economy.html (accessed January 10, 2020).

15. Available at http://www.nbcnews.com/id/25004682/ns/msnbc-morning_joe/t /verdict-dan-abrams-wednesday-june/#.WwiMd3ovyMp (accessed January 10, 2020).

16. This concern seems to have influenced Bill Clinton's campaign, in 1992, for instance. Pollster Stanley Greenberg recalled that Clinton did not want the public, or even many members of the campaign team, to know that Greenberg was conducting polling on potential running mates. "I don't think they wanted it to be thought they were polling the Vice Presidential selection," he said later. "I'm not sure why that should be thought to be different than other things, but there was a sense that one shouldn't be polling it." Available at https://millercenter.org/the-presidency/presidential-oral-histo ries/stanley-greenberg-oral-history-2005-pollster (accessed January 10, 2020).

17. A dissenting voice on this point comes from former New Mexico governor Bill Richardson, who sought the vice presidential nomination, unsuccessfully, on multiple occasions. "At the very end, what makes the final decision is a bunch of white guys that are polling," Richardson said. "They are not, in my judgment, sensitive about national security or ethnicity. They are looking for additional votes for the presidential candidates." In the same interview, Richardson "recalled the raw political nature of the vice-presidential selection process for Al Gore, John F. Kerry and Barack Obama" (O'Keefe 2016).

18. Perhaps one reason for reporters' persistence is the fact that Ford had decided not to run with his incumbent vice president, Nelson Rockefeller. Indeed, Rockefeller clearly met Ford's stated vice presidential criteria. He was eminently qualified, as a four-term governor of New York with two years already under his belt as vice president. Moreover, the fact that Ford had nominated Rockefeller for the vice presidency in 1974, following President Nixon's resignation and then vice president Ford's succession to the presidency, and that he had a good relationship with Ford while serving as vice president, certainly suggested that he was sufficiently compatible with the president. But Rockefeller, a relatively liberal Republican, was very unpopular with conservatives in the Republican Party, particularly those who supported Ronald Reagan's primary challenge that year, and so Ford dropped Rockefeller from the ticket clearly for electoral purposes—that is, to win the party's nomination and then to shore up the conservative base for the general election.

19. Available at https://www.fordlibrarymuseum.gov/library/document/0204/1512185 .pdf (accessed January 10, 2020).

20. Ford's press secretary, Ron Nessen, also repeated these criteria ad nauseum in response to reporters' questions at press conferences throughout that summer. His most expansive statement on the matter came on August 17:

The President's first consideration in picking a Vice Presidential running mate will be to pick the person who he considers to be the best qualified to take over as President should that need arise.

As I said before, the second consideration would be someone who is compatible with the President both in terms of his policies—domestic and foreign policies—and also personally compatible. . . . The third factor, or the least important of these factors, would be someone who would contribute to the President's election campaign. . . . That is the way he has set out his priorities for selecting a running mate.

Available at https://www.fordlibrarymuseum.gov/library/document/0151/1671705.pdf (accessed January 10, 2020).

21. Raoul-Duval also was a leading campaign adviser in 1976, whose duties included developing Ford's famous "Rose Garden strategy," at chief of staff Dick Cheney's request.

22. Memo, Anonymous, n.d., folder "Vice President Selection," Box 24, Michael Raoul-Duval Papers, Gerald R. Ford Library.

23. Memo, Robert Teeter to Gerald Ford, August 16, 1976, folder "Political Affairs—Ford (8)," Box 37, Presidential Handwriting File, Gerald R. Ford Library.

24. Interview, James M. Cannon with Gerald Ford, April 27, 1990, folder: "Ford, Gerald—Interview, April 27, 1990," Box 1, James M. Cannon Research Interviews and Notes, Gerald R. Ford Library.

25. Interview, James M. Cannon with Gerald Ford, April 29, 1990, folder: "Ford, Gerald—Interview, April 29, 1990," Box 1, James M. Cannon Research Interviews and Notes, Gerald R. Ford Library.

26. Available at https://docs.google.com/gview?url=http://dolearchivecollections.ku.edu/collections/oral_history/pdf/dole_bob_2007-09-07.pdf (accessed January 10, 2020).

27. Interview, Cannon with Ford, April 27, 1990.

28. Article, *Los Angeles Times*, July 16, 1976, folder: "Vice President (2)," Box H34, President Ford Committee Records, Gerald R. Ford Library.

29. Available at https://docs.google.com/gview?url=http://dolearchivecollections.ku.edu/collections/oral_history/pdf/mondale_walter_2007-11-28.pdf (accessed January 10, 2020).

30. Available at https://www.ozy.com/2016/watch-episode-7-of-the-contenders-16-for-16/73676 (accessed January 10, 2020).

31. Available at https://millercenter.org/the-presidency/presidential-oral-histories/walter-mondale-oral-history-vice-president-united-states (accessed January 10, 2020).

32. Available at https://docs.google.com/gview?url=http://dolearchivecollections.ku.edu/collections/oral_history/pdf/baker_james_2007-05-21.pdf (accessed January 10, 2020).

33. Available at https://digitalcommons.bowdoin.edu/mitchelloralhistory/173 (accessed January 10, 2020).

34. Available at https://digitalcommons.bowdoin.edu/mitchelloralhistory/173 (accessed January 10, 2020).

35. Available at https://search.alexanderstreet.com/preview/work/bibliographic _entity%7Cvideo_work%7C3229884 (accessed June 1, 2019).

36. Available at http://transcripts.cnn.com/TRANSCRIPTS/0406/24/lkl.00.html (accessed January 10, 2020). Also, see Clinton 2004, 414.

37. Available at https://docs.google.com/gview?url=http://dolearchivecollections. ku.edu/collections/oral_history/pdf/ellsworth_bob_2007-08-08.pdf (accessed January 10, 2020).

38. Available at https://docs.google.com/gview?url=http://dolearchivecollections. ku.edu/collections/oral_history/pdf/reed_scott_2007-11-08.pdf (accessed January 10, 2020). For additional evidence based on extensive archival research, see Adler and Azari (2018).

39. Available at https://archive.org/details/FOXNEWS_20120421_020000_Greta _Van_Susteren/start/480/end/540 (accessed January 10, 2020).

40. Ironically, when considering Lieberman for the vice presidential nomination in 1992, the Bill Clinton campaign conducted just such a poll. According to the campaign's pollster, Stanley Greenberg, "We did look at Lieberman to see what the effect might be of a Jewish Vice President. I did a poll on that. It was just a poll devoted to that question." And, for the record, "we didn't find an impact." Available at https://millercenter.org/the-presidency/presidential-oral-histories/stanley-greenberg -oral-history-2007-pollster (accessed January 10, 2020).

41. Anecdotally, Bill Richardson also recalls that, when he was notified that he had been passed over for Edwards, "Kerry said something like, 'Well, we have a shot at North Carolina'" (O'Keefe 2016).

42. Available at http://transcripts.cnn.com/TRANSCRIPTS/0401/04/se.01.html (accessed January 10, 2020).

43. Available at https://www.c-span.org/video/?328827-1/walter-mondale-joe-biden -reflections-office-vice-president (accessed January 10, 2020).

44. Devine and Kopko (2016, chap. 5) find that Johnson did not help Kennedy in Texas or the South in 1960. In fact, survey data from the 1960 American National Election Study and internal Kennedy campaign polls indicate that Johnson was significantly less popular in Texas than in other southern states, and less popular in the South than in other regions.

45. Available at https://wikileaks.org/podesta-emails/emailid/15616 (accessed June 1, 2019).

CHAPTER 2. (WHY) DO VOTERS THINK THAT
RUNNING MATES MATTER?

1. As noted in the introduction to part I, this search yielded many more polls from the 2000–2016 period than beforehand. Thus, we have chosen to focus our analysis on

this time period. While it may be fruitful to analyze earlier polls, in order to identify possible differences in earlier perceptions of running mate effects, the more recent results are most relevant to this book's analysis since we are primarily concerned with explaining, in a contemporaneous sense, whether and how running mates matter.

2. Indeed, there may be an element of social desirability in these responses. That is to say, many respondents may tell pollsters that the running mate's qualifications are important—and, for that matter, that demographic considerations such as race/ethnicity and gender are unimportant—simply because they wish to project a positive, socially acceptable image. While this explanation is entirely plausible, the available data do not allow us to evaluate it empirically.

3. Available at http://www.rasmussenreports.com/public_content/politics/elections/election_2016/gingrich_carson_are_early_gop_veep_favorites (accessed January 10, 2020).

4. Response patterns were similar across parties, with at least 70 percent of Democratic, Republican, and unaffiliated respondents answering "Very important" or "Important."

5. Available at https://poll.qu.edu/2008-presidential-swing-state-polls/release-detail?ReleaseID=2195 (accessed January 10, 2020).

6. Available at https://poll.qu.edu/2008-presidential-swing-state-polls/release-detail?ReleaseID=1188 (accessed January 10, 2020).

7. Available at http://www.publicpolicypolling.com/pdf/2008/PPP_Release_NCVP.pdf (accessed January 10, 2020).

8. Available at http://www.washingtonpost.com/wp-srv/politics/documents/post poll_071408.html (accessed January 10, 2020).

9. Specifically, 15 percent of respondents answered "Extremely important"; 33 percent, "Very important"; and 35 percent, "Somewhat important."

10. This poll used a split-sample design for some measures, including the one described in the corresponding text. Half of the respondent sample rated the importance of nine items, including vice presidential selection, while the other half rated the importance of eight other items, none of which pertained to vice presidential selection. Direct comparison across samples is problematic, in part because of priming effects—that is to say, respondents might rate an item's importance differently depending on what other issues are made salient to them at the same time. Bearing this caveat in mind, it is still the case that vice presidential selection performs poorly in comparison to the full list of potential election influences. Of the seventeen items, in total, "The candidates' choices for vice presidential running mates" finished last in terms of extremely important responses. When combining extremely and very important responses, though, one item—"Social issues such as abortion and gay civil unions"—was selected less often (by 9 percentage points).

11. Jones and Carroll (2005) list the results for "Because he is a Republican" (Bush voters) and "Because he is a Democrat" (Kerry voters) separately. No other results are disaggregated by party or candidate preference. To make our analysis more intuitive, here we report the average percentage of respondents saying that party affiliation was extremely

important or very important. This is reasonable, given that the sample was nearly evenly split between Bush (47 percent) and Kerry (48 percent) voters. If party influence is not combined across Bush and Kerry voters, the running mate's influence ranks tenth out of thirteen items in terms of "Extremely important" ratings, and ninth out of thirteen items in terms of combined "Extremely important" and "Very important" ratings.

12. For related evidence regarding individuals' frequent inability to identify the factors that shape their decisions, in general or in political contexts, see, respectively, Nisbett and Wilson 1977; Cohen 2003.

13. Available at https://www.scribd.com/document/326355825/10-4-16-CBS-News -poll-toplines-views-of-the-vice-presidential-candidates-Tim-Kaine-and-Mike -Pence#from_embed (accessed January 10, 2020).

14. Available at http://www.pollingreport.com/wh2vp.htm (accessed January 10, 2020).

15. Available at https://morningconsultintelligence.com/media/mc/160701_topline _Topicals_VP_v2_AP.pdf (accessed June 1, 2019).

16. Available at https://www.monmouth.edu/polling-institute/reports/Monmouth Poll_US_062316 (accessed January 10, 2020).

17. Available at https://www.monmouth.edu/polling-institute/reports/Monmouth Poll_US_071816 (accessed January 10, 2020).

18. Available at http://www.pollingreport.com/wh16b.htm (accessed January 10, 2020).

19. Pence also showed a slight advantage in this poll, when the same question was asked about his candidacy: 14 percent, "More likely"; 7 percent, "Less likely"; and 79 percent, "Not much effect."

20. Available at http://ssrs.com/abc-news-ssrs-opinion-poll-week-seven-topline (accessed January 10, 2020).

21. Available at https://www.scribd.com/document/326355825/10-4-16-CBS-News -poll-toplines-views-of-the-vice-presidential-candidates-Tim-Kaine-and-Mike -Pence#from_embed (accessed January 10, 2020).

22. The percentage of respondents who do not express a positive or negative opinion of the running mates varies not only across candidates and election years but also for the same candidate in the same election year due to elements of survey design. For instance, the CBS News poll cited in the corresponding text elicited a higher percentage of neutral or nonopinions about Kaine and Pence, probably because the "Undecided" and "Haven't heard enough" options are worded so as to be welcoming, rather than alienating, to respondents who know little or nothing about the running mate but may not want to admit this in stark terms. Other polls, such as the Gallup series noted earlier, use less forgiving "Never heard of" and "No opinion" options. It seems likely that many respondents would resist choosing these options in order not to appear entirely ignorant or indifferent, and instead claim "Favorable" or "Unfavorable" attitudes that they do not actually have. Thus, even while the percentage of respondents expressing substantive opinions in many polls is low, we suspect that the actual percentage often is even lower—essentially, along the lines of what we see in the CBS results.

23. Available at http://www.electionstudies.org (accessed January 2, 2018).

24. Available at https://electionstudies.org/wp-content/uploads/2018/12/anes_time series_cdf_codebook_var.pdf (accessed January 2, 2018).

25. Available at https://electionstudies.org/wp-content/uploads/2018/12/anes_time series_cdf_codebook_app.pdf (accessed January 2, 2018).

26. The latter includes "Mondale; good/bad choice for nominee" (10); "Gore, Al" (19); "Lieberman, Joseph" (20); "Edwards, John" (22); "Shriver; good/bad choice for nominee [in 1972]"; "Eagleton [in 1972]" (24); "Agnew; good/bad choice for nominee" (33); "Rockefeller" (34); "Bush, Sr., George . . . [in 1980 and 1984]" (37); "Dole, Robert . . ." (42); and "Cheney, Dick" (44). In the subsequent analysis, we treat these codes as vice presidential references only when they occur in the same year that the individual in question was running for the vice presidency. For example, the Al Gore code qualified as a vice presidential reference only in 1992 and 1996, when he was a vice presidential candidate, and not in 2000, when he was a presidential candidate.

27. This methodology probably overestimates the proportion of respondents who referenced the vice presidential candidate. First, that is because the numerator represents the total number of vice presidential *responses*, while the denominator represents the total number of *respondents* with any valid responses. This approach assumes that someone who references the running mate as a reason for dis/liking the presidential candidate will not repeat him- or herself while continuing to answer with likes or dislikes about the same presidential candidate. However, if some respondents made such references multiple times (to the running mate's experience as well as character, for example), then our estimates will be inflated. Second, the denominator excludes respondents who did not provide a valid response when asked for their dis/likes about the presidential candidate. If they were included in the denominator—and there is a reasonable case for doing so, if we take them at their word as not having a reason (vice presidential candidacies, included) for voting for/against the candidate—then this would deflate our estimates quite dramatically. Indeed, about half of all respondents, on average, and the majority of them in 2000, did not provide any valid dis/likes for a given presidential candidacy.

28. Available at http://surveys.ap.org/data/KnowledgeNetworks/AP_Election_Wave5 _Topline_070208%20wrd%20codes.pdf (accessed January 10, 2020).

29. The two remaining variables in their models, identifying whether the vice presidential finalist ran against the presidential candidate for the party's nomination or never had done so, are closely related to ideological balancing. After all, presidential rivals often represent competing party factions, and those factions often are grounded in ideological difference.

30. Available at https://morningconsultintelligence.com/media/mc/160409_cross tabs_TOPICALS_v4_KD_stacked.pdf (accessed June 1, 2019).

31. Specifically, the poll asked respondents: "If [Hillary Clinton/Donald Trump] is selected as the [Democratic/Republican] nominee for President, how important is it for [her/his] Vice Presidential running mate to be [insert attribute]?" Response options included "Very important," "Somewhat important," "Not too important," "Not at all important," and "Don't know/No opinion."

32. Available at http://s.wsj.net/public/resources/documents/WSJ_Poll_072308.pdf (accessed January 10, 2020).

33. Available at https://web.archive.org/web/20160717100711/http://www.suffolk.edu:80/documents/SUPRC/7_11_2016_complete_national_tables.pdf (accessed January 10, 2020).

34. Of course, in the Morning Consult poll discussed earlier, respondents were more mixed on whether Clinton should choose an ideological liberal or a moderate as her running mate. However, the sample for that poll consisted of registered voters, across all parties, whereas this poll sampled only Democratic primary voters. Naturally, Democrats would be least inclined to see Clinton as too liberal and thus in need of a moderate to balance her ticket; presumably, such responses would come from Republicans and Independents who were included in the Morning Consult sample. Democrats, particularly following Bernie Sanders's challenge to Clinton in the 2016 primaries, from her left, would have been most likely to see her as too moderate and thus in need of a liberal, or progressive, running mate to provide ideological balance.

35. Available at http://i2.cdn.turner.com/cnn/2016/images/06/21/rel7c.-.vp.selections.pdf (accessed January 10, 2020).

36. With respect to business experience, these results differ somewhat from those found in the Morning Consult poll described earlier. Our explanation for this discrepancy is analogous to the one we provide in note 34, concerning the ideology of Hillary Clinton's running mate.

37. Available at http://www.pollingreport.com/wh12c.htm (accessed January 10, 2020).

PART II. EVIDENCE OF RUNNING MATE EFFECTS

1. While we would prefer to analyze the same set of elections in each chapter, so as to maximize comparability, this is not possible given the available data. Specifically, we are not aware of any rolling cross-sectional datasets from prior to 2000, or any three-wave panel datasets from prior to 2008, that could be used to estimate running mate effects in the same way and with the same methodological rigor as what we present here. Thus, our quantitative analysis of running mate effects in part II—much like our qualitative analysis of perceptions of running mate effects in part I—most directly pertains to the 2000–2016 elections, while also incorporating evidence from previous elections, whenever possible. As stated in part I, our essential objective is to evaluate whether running mates matter in a contemporaneous sense. It is therefore appropriate—albeit not ideal—that our empirical evidence primarily comes from the most recent elections. We do, however, make full use of the 1952–2016 ANES data. This is for three reasons, in particular. First, it is in keeping with our goal to make this the most comprehensive empirical analysis of running mate effects possible. Second, in some cases (e.g., the descriptive analysis of direct effects in chapter 3), we seek to replicate and extend findings from previous studies that use ANES data from these

earlier periods. Third, when estimating targeted running mate effects in chapter 4, the earlier ANES data allow us to include several important cases, including Geraldine Ferraro's vice presidential candidacy in 1984, that would be excluded otherwise. While such cases may have less bearing on contemporaneous running mate effects, nonetheless they provide useful insights into the generalizability of our findings from the 2000–2016 period (e.g., Sarah Palin's effect on women voters in 2008).

CHAPTER 3. DIRECT EFFECTS

1. Available at https://www.youtube.com/watch?v=BjpUQJCCXso (accessed January 10, 2020).

2. Available at https://www.youtube.com/watch?v=2PN7Sa9QtgQ (accessed January 10, 2020).

3. Previous iterations of the ANES did, however, include open-ended items asking respondents to identify up to two things that they liked, as well as disliked, about each of the vice presidential candidates. This can be used to create a scale ranging from the most negative evaluation (two dislikes, no likes), to the most positive evaluation (two likes, no dislikes), of each running mate. But, clearly, this is a more limited measure of candidate evaluations than feeling thermometers, and the two are not directly comparable in such a way that we could integrate them into our analysis. While it may be appropriate to use such measures when studying an election, or a set of elections, prior to the introduction of the ANES feeling thermometers (see, e.g., Devine and Kopko 2016, chap. 6), we exclude those election years from this analysis.

4. While ANES respondents were asked to rate feeling thermometer targets on a scale of 0 to 100, these ratings are truncated to range from 0 to 97 in the ANES Cumulative File.

5. In a separate analysis, we find no substantive differences when restricting the data to include only the most recent set of presidential elections, from 2000 to 2016.

6. As in the case for table 3.1, in a separate analysis, we find no substantive differences when restricting the data to include only the most recent set of presidential elections, from 2000 to 2016.

7. Of the three models from table 3.2, Model 1 yields the greatest proportional reduction in error (88.74 percent) and the highest percentage of outcomes correctly predicted (94.55 percent).

8. Given that all three models from table 3.2 are very similar in terms of their predictive power (i.e., proportional reduction in error and percentage of cases correctly predicted), there is no reason to expect that the results would differ significantly had we used Model 2 or Model 3 to generate the predicted probabilities. To elaborate on this point, consider that Model 2 employs only the four thermometer ratings for each ticket's presidential and vice presidential candidates. In Model 1, we include eleven additional control variables after the thermometer ratings. These additional variables in Model 1 improve the proportional reduction in error only by about 2 percentage

points, and the percentage of observations correctly predicted improves by less than 1 percentage point. From this, we conclude that candidate evaluations drive most of the variation in the dependent variable. Likewise, in Model 3, which includes only the presidential candidate feeling thermometers, the proportional reduction in error and percentage correctly predicted are within a few percentage points of the estimates for Model 1 (even though Model 1 includes thirteen additional variables). This provides further evidence that presidential candidate evaluations exert, by far, the greatest influence in determining presidential vote choice, even if vice presidential candidate evaluations also have an independent effect.

9. Disaggregating by election year also allows us to observe potential changes in direct effects over time. For instance, if recent increases in partisan polarization have weakened the running mate's influence on vote choice, we should see that in more recent elections the relationship between vice presidential candidate evaluations and vote choice is less often statistically significant and, when significant, tends to be smaller in magnitude, in comparison to previous election years. However, the evidence does not clearly indicate any such pattern.

10. This approach is similar to that of several previous studies of direct running mate effects, by Ulbig (2010), Knuckey (2012), and Burmila and Ryan (2013).

11. Specifically, due to data availability issues, it is usually impossible to estimate a two-stage model with an instrumental variable that applies to presidential or vice presidential candidate favorability ratings. However, there is one exception in the scholarly literature: Romero's (2001) use of the 1972–1976 ANES panel survey. Romero's objective, in this study, is to account for "rationalization" effects—i.e., "whether voter rationalization of their intended vote exaggerates the influence of vice presidential nominees . . . on presidential vote" (455). Romero uses the respondent's party identification and favorability ratings of Gerald Ford and Walter Mondale, each from the 1974 panel wave, as instrumental variables to predict vote choice in 1976. (Ford was the Republican presidential candidate, and Mondale the Democratic vice presidential candidate, in that year's election.) In the context of that election, Romero finds that presidential candidate evaluations significantly predict vote choice, but—after accounting for rationalization effects—vice presidential candidate evaluations do not. While this is an important scholarly contribution, it has methodological limitations that we seek to address in this study. First, Romero's model does not account for the distinct favorability ratings of all four candidates on a presidential ticket; rather, his model's independent variables are index measures of both vice presidential and presidential candidates, respectively. Second, as Romero notes, his model does not account for "the reverse endogenous relation, the intended vote's influence on candidate evaluations" (459n5). The VAR model that we present in this chapter specifically accounts for such effects. Finally, Romero's analysis is cross-sectional. Our analysis, in contrast, captures the dynamic influence of candidate evaluations over the course of a campaign.

12. However, favorability ratings tend to be highest—and probably artificially high—immediately following vice presidential selection, in part because media scrutiny of the candidate intensifies thereafter. Since Palin was introduced as McCain's

running mate on August 29, using her September favorability ratings as a baseline for this analysis may bias these estimates toward indicating a loss of votes.

13. While the data allow us to analyze only two elections, at worst these can be seen as case studies for evaluating the extent to which vice presidential candidate and presidential candidate evaluations influence each other (which we explore in more detail in chapter 5), and how these ratings independently affect intended vote choice *over time* (which is the focus of our analysis in this chapter). Here, we are not generally testing how running mate evaluations may influence vote choice, but, instead, we assess how these evaluations result in changes from a baseline level over a period of several days; that is an important distinction compared with the previous cross-sectional analyses.

14. We do not analyze the 2008 NAES because—in contrast to the 2000 and 2004 NAES—it does not include a sufficient number of observations, with respect to vice presidential candidate evaluations, for the purposes of conducting VAR. The reason for this discrepancy is simple: the running mates were chosen much later in 2008 (late August) than in 2000 (late July/early August) or 2004 (early July). The 2000 NAES included feeling thermometers for both major party vice presidential candidates beginning on August 7, resulting in 92 days of observations, while the 2004 NAES included these measures beginning on July 15, resulting in 110 days of observations. The 2008 NAES, however, began including these measures only on August 29, resulting in 66 days of observations. It is inadvisable to conduct VAR analysis with fewer than 70 observations. Indeed, the statistical models do not converge in Stata when using the same methodology in 2008 as in 2000 and 2004. Finally, it is important to note that the NAES was discontinued after 2008; thus, we cannot conduct similar analyses of more recent elections.

15. For information on VAR models, see Box-Steffensmeier, Freeman, and Hitt (2014, 106–124).

16. "Granger causality" refers to the process of estimating a model in which the dependent variable (y) is regressed on lagged values (i.e., past values) of itself ($y-1$, $y-2$, $y-3$, . . . etc.) and other lagged independent variables (x, $x-1$, $x-2$, $x-3$, . . . etc.) (see Granger 1969). As Freeman (1983, 328) explains, "A variable x is said to 'Granger cause' another variable y, if y can be better predicted from the past of x and y together than the past of y alone, other relevant information being used in the prediction."

17. However, in this chapter, we assess the effect of candidate thermometer ratings only on intended vote choice; in chapter 5 we explore the interdependence of same-party candidate thermometer ratings.

18. Using the 2004 NAES as an example, this means that for lag 13, the cumulative effect is the summation of all effects from days one through twelve.

19. The scales for figures 3.2 and 3.3 are different because the thermometer rating codes changed from the 2000 to 2004 NAES. In 2000, the thermometer was coded from 0 to 100, while in 2004 the variable was coded from 0 to 10.

20. It is unclear why a positive shock to Cheney's favorability rating, or that of any running mate, would end up hurting his ticket at any point in the time series. One possibility is that, because Cheney generally was unpopular, the very fact that he

was attracting attention ultimately led to more negative evaluations of the Republican ticket. This explanation is entirely speculative, however. Further research is necessary to clarify this effect for Cheney or, for that matter, any other presidential or vice presidential candidate.

21. Edwards's estimated CIRF actually suggests that a one-unit positive shock to his favorability rating caused intended Democratic vote choice to increase by approximately 20 percentage points! This effect may seem enormous, but it is important to keep in mind that the range of thermometer ratings in the 2004 NAES is 0 to 10. Thus, a one-unit positive change constitutes an extraordinary increase in favorability, of approximately 9 percentage points. Also, there was little variation in the candidates' favorability ratings over the course of the campaign. In Edwards's case, his average thermometer rating ranged from approximately 4.75 to 5.75 throughout the campaign. Such minimal variation, combined with the limited scale for the NAES feeling thermometers, helps to account for the size of Edwards's CIRF estimates.

22. NAES data indicate that between July and August 2004, Edwards was the least recognized candidate on either presidential ticket, despite being the runner-up in that year's Democratic presidential primary. In fact, during that time between 6 percent and 9 percent of respondents did not know Edwards or did not know enough about him to rate him in terms of favorability. For the other presidential or vice presidential candidates, only 2 to 4 percent of respondents answered "don't know" when asked to rate them during the same period.

23. As Box-Steffensmeier, DeBoef, and Lin (2004, 522–523) explain: "In general, a time series process may exhibit both long-term, persistent memory, which is captured by the fractional parameter d, and short-term, transient memory, which is captured by the stationary auto-regressive and moving average parameters p and q." This constitutes the autoregressive fractionally integrated moving average process (ARFIMA [p, d, q]) (see Box-Steffensmeier, Darmofal, and Farrell 2009, 315).

24. To execute this transformation, we use Christopher Baum's (2000) "fracdiff" Stata command.

25. The Osama bin Laden tape was broadcast on Al Jazeera on October 29, 2004. It was the first video of bin Laden to appear in more than a year. In it, he took credit for the September 11 terrorist attack and warned the United States against threatening the security interests of Muslims worldwide (Jehl and Johnston 2004). In identifying these significant events, we adhere as closely as possible to the examples of Johnston, Hagen, and Jamieson (2004) and Box-Steffensmeier, Darmofal, and Farrell (2009), who also identified significant electoral events in the 2000 presidential election.

CHAPTER 4. TARGETED EFFECTS

1. Notably, some people pushed back against the notion that Kaine's bilingualism somehow qualified him as an honorary member of the Latino community—even portraying this as a form of "pandering." As Roque de la Fuente, a Latino presidential

candidate who ran against Hillary Clinton in the 2016 Democratic primaries, said: "Speaking Spanish doesn't mean that he understands the issues. That doesn't mean that he knows what it means to be discriminated [against]" (Peralta 2016).

2. Trump campaign pollster Tony Fabrizio reportedly confirmed this presumption. In contrast to vice presidential finalists Newt Gingrich and Chris Christie, who, Fabrizio's polling indicated, did nothing to help the ticket, "Pence was the only candidate he'd run numbers on who helped lift Trump with evangelical voters and conservatives" (LoBianco 2019, 242).

3. Indeed, Pence often played on his rural and midwestern roots when trying to connect with voters, as in this quote from a rally in rural Pennsylvania: "Lancaster is—my gosh, you know, I grew up with a cornfield in my backyard. I know how sturdy, how important a family farm is to the vitality and the character of this nation" (Hillyard 2016).

4. We do not examine targeted effects in terms of partisan identity because each presidential ticket in the modern era has featured a presidential and vice presidential candidate from the same party. However, this does not have to be the case. For example, in 2004, Democratic presidential nominee John Kerry seriously considered selecting Republican John McCain as his running mate (Hiller and Kriner 2008). And, in 2008, McCain seriously considered selecting Joe Lieberman, a Democrat-turned-Independent, as his running mate on the Republican ticket (McCain and Salter 2018). Had either of these running mates been selected, or if such a selection were to be made in a future election, it would be appropriate to conduct a similar analysis of targeted partisan effects.

5. Specifically, this refers to the literature on ticket balancing, including studies by Baumgartner with Crumblin (2015), Goldstein (2016), Hiller and Kriner (2008), and Sigelman and Wahlbeck (1997). We do not analyze targeted effects in terms of governing experience because this category does not correspond to an identifiable electoral subgroup.

6. Specifically, this includes identities based on geography (e.g., Cuba and Hummon 1993; Paasi 1986, 2003, 2009), gender (e.g., Burn 1995; Burn, Aboud, and Moyles 2000), religion (e.g., Deaux et al. 1995, 288; Kopko 2012; Ysseldyk, Matheson, and Anisman 2010), and ideology (e.g., Devine 2015; Malka and Lelkes 2010).

7. There are, of course, other reasons why voters might favor in-group candidates. Most notably, they might expect such candidates to better understand and advocate for issues that are particularly important to their group. Social identity theory in no way excludes such a possibility. However, it does not rely on policy motivations to explain in-group favoritism; rather, as indicated earlier, mere self-categorization within an in-group is sufficient to trigger such behavioral responses. This approach is particularly appropriate in the context of the present study, since vice presidents have almost no direct influence over public policy (the most obvious exception being to cast tie-breaking votes in the US Senate, which occurs rarely). If we were to explain targeted running mate effects strictly in terms of expected policy outcomes, surely this would overstate voters' expectations regarding the powers and influence of the

vice presidency (see the introduction and chapter 1). Our emphasis on social identity theory, instead, allows us to capture in a much more comprehensive way the perceived benefits of an in-group member's success, whether symbolic or substantive.

8. A limited exception is found in Brox and Cassels's (2009) analysis of the 2008 election. Specifically, they use favorability ratings and reports of intended vote choice from six CNN/Opinion Research Corporation polls conducted between late August and Election Day to evaluate Sarah Palin's effect on vote choice among women and conservatives, as well as other target groups.

9. This also allows interested readers to draw comparisons across time periods—for instance, to see whether targeted effects have become stronger or weaker in recent years.

10. Lenz (2012, 31–40; see also 242–245) establishes a three-wave test of priming, using panel data, to determine how prior positions on a given policy matter influence later evaluations of the same, following the occurrence of an intervening—and potentially influential—event. We follow a similar approach using multiple waves. According to Lenz, his method differs in two significant ways from what he calls the "conventional test" for analyzing panel data, whereby researchers compare differences in an independent variable's coefficient at Wave 1 versus Wave 2 to determine whether the intervening event caused a change in the dependent variable. As Lenz (2012, 243) explains, his "three-wave test":

> measures policy views or performance assessments in a prior wave; that is, it measures the cause before the effect, eliminating bias from reverse causation. Second, it models change in prior votes or candidate evaluations (y) by including what researchers call the lagged dependent variable. By modeling change it addresses problems that can arise when measuring variables in prior panel waves. Specifically, without controlling for lagged vote or candidate evaluations, regression to the mean on these variables can bias issue-weight estimates downward because prior vote or candidate evaluations are often moderately or even strongly correlated with prior issue attitudes.

In addition, Lenz (2012, chap. 4) employs a prior-persuasion test to assess changes in candidate performance over time. We do not follow that approach here because, as Lenz notes, the prior-persuasion test "can miss the persuasion effects it is meant to detect. . . . The prior-persuasion test is therefore a conservative test of policy and performance judgements; it will likely underestimate any effect" (92). Thus, our approach, while informed by Lenz, should increase the probability that we detect running mate effects. However, as we discuss later in this chapter, and also in chapter 5, we find little evidence of these effects changing over time.

11. The panel data models can be expressed as Intended Vote Choice = β_0Constant + β_1Intended Vote Choice in Previous, Pre-Selection Wave + β_2Republican + β_3Democratic + β_4Conservative + β_5Liberal + β_6Female + β_7Age + β_8Income + β_9Education + β_{10}White + β_{11}South + β_{12}Catholic + ε.

12. For each model that uses data from a postselection wave, we control for intended vote choice in the last wave conducted prior to vice presidential selection (e.g., June for Palin's announcement in 2008).

13. We use the US Census Bureau's classification scheme to determine whether respondents lived in the same region or division as a given running mate. For more information, see "Census Regions and Divisions of the United States": https://factfinder.census.gov/help/en/region.htm and https://factfinder.census.gov/help/en/division.htm (accessed January 10, 2020).

14. This methodological approach also allows us to test the effect of moving from a smaller to a larger geographic area. Home states are nested within census divisions, which, in turn, are nested in census regions.

15. Likewise, many of these elections featured a southerner as the Democratic (1964, 1976, 1980, 1992, 1996, 2000) or Republican (1988, 1992, 2000, 2004) presidential candidate.

16. For the purposes of this analysis, we define the US South as including the eleven states of the Old Confederacy: Alabama, Arkansas, Florida, Georgia, Louisiana, Mississippi, North Carolina, South Carolina, Tennessee, Texas, and Virginia. This coding scheme more precisely captures southern identity—among candidates and voters—than the broad US Census designation that classifies states such as Delaware, Maryland, and West Virginia as being in the South. However, readers will note that we use the census coding scheme in the analysis from table 4.1. There, it makes sense to do so for two reasons. First, in table 4.1, we analyze geographic effects for every US region, and others—such as the West or Midwest—have no alternative regional classifications comparable to the Old Confederacy. Second, in table 4.1, we estimate geographic effects at the US Census region *and* division levels. Thus, if our use of the broader South designation obscures the effects of southern identity, we should observe different effects at the division level (which we do not).

17. Formally, the 1952–2016 ANES vote choice model, which we use to analyze southerners and women, is: Vote Choice = β_0Constant + β_1Republican + β_2Democratic + β_3Female + β_4Age + β_5Income + β_6Education + β_7White + β_8South + ε.

18. It is important to note that we cannot draw causal inferences from this analysis due to the cross-sectional nature of the data. However, we could be more confident in making a causal claim by relying on this analysis *and* others presented later in this chapter regarding the potential for targeted regional effects. In other words, we could assume there is a causal relationship if multiple analyses throughout this chapter all provide support for this type of electoral effect. For the purposes of this analysis, if there is variation in estimates from year to year that coincide with in-group running mate selection in a given presidential election year, that *could* be attributable to the electoral effect of a running mate. However, absent variation and absent further evidence from other models presented in this chapter, it would be reasonable to conclude that the candidate did not have a targeted effect on the group of voters in question (e.g., southerners).

19. This is not to say that Johnson and Kaine necessarily had a *negative* effect on southerners. Again, we cannot make causal inferences based on the cross-sectional

data presented here. Rather, these results most directly demonstrate that the candidates in question did not have a positive effect on vote choice among southerners. It is also possible, and perhaps most likely, that these candidates simply had no distinct, regional effect on vote choice.

20. One limitation of this analysis is that, in order to directly compare the South variable's effect across election years, our models must include only those variables for which we have data from each of the 1952–2016 ANES. Thus, in figure 4.1, we do not control for ideological (i.e., liberal or conservative) and religious (i.e., Catholic, Jewish, Evangelical) self-identification. However, adding each of these variables to our models (for those years in which the ANES reports measures for each: 1964–1968; 1980–2012) has almost no effect on our substantive conclusions. Only in 1968—when no southern candidate, by our definition, appeared on the ballot—do we see any difference, with the South variable's effect going from statistically significant, in favor of Republican voting, to null. In every other election year, the statistical significance and direction of the South variable remain the same. For that matter, the conclusions regarding targeted ideological and religious effects that we report next also change minimally when analyzing only those election years in which the ANES measured the full range of variables featured in this chapter. In seventy-two out of seventy-seven cases (93.5 percent), we observe no change in the statistical significance of the independent variable—South, gender, Catholic, Jewish, evangelical, liberal, or conservative—or the direction of its effect on vote choice, if any. Most important, we observe no such change in any of the twenty-one potential targeted running mate effects tested during the relevant period of analysis (e.g., Catholicism's effect on vote choice in those years when a Catholic ran for vice president, or gender's effect when a woman ran for vice president).

21. At the time they ran for vice president, Sarah Palin attended an Assembly of God church in Wasilla, Alaska (Johnson and Severson 2008), and Mike Pence attended College Park Church in Indianapolis, Indiana (Mahler and Johnson 2016). Other recent vice presidential candidates also have identified or attended churches associated with what are commonly considered "evangelical" denominations ("Appendix B: Classification" 2015). For example, at the time of their vice presidential candidacies, Dan Quayle (1988, 1992) and Jack Kemp (1996) attended the Fourth Presbyterian Church in Washington, DC, which has been affiliated with the Evangelical Presbyterian Church since 1986 (see Broder and Woodward 1992; Christian 1996; "Our History" 2020). Also, Al Gore had a long-standing affiliation with the Southern Baptist Convention prior to his vice presidential candidacies in 1992 and 1996. However, these candidates were not as closely identified with evangelical Christianity, or as willing to invoke their faith on the campaign trail, as Palin and Pence. For example, in 1992, Quayle's pastor said: "His negative is his Christianity is not high-profile." Quayle, when asked directly about this criticism, did not disagree but rather said that his faith was a "very private" matter and that "as long as I'm in public life, I'll never [proselytize]" (Broder and Woodward 1992). As for Al Gore, in 2000 the *New York Times* reported that he "has not been active in church for a decade, and acknowledges a new distance from his larger faith community" (Hennebarger 2000). Even if we were to treat Quayle, Gore, and Kemp as evangelicals for the

purposes of this analysis, the presence of an evangelical running mate on both tickets in 1992 and 1996 should have canceled out any potential targeted effects.

22. Formally, the Catholic vote choice model is: Vote Choice = β_0Constant + β_1Republican + β_2Democratic + β_3Female + β_4Age + β_5Income + β_6Education + β_7White + β_8South + β_9Catholic + ε. The Jewish vote choice model is: Vote Choice = β_0Constant + β_1Republican + β_2Democratic + β_3Female + β_4Age + β_5Income + β_6Education + β_7White + β_8South + β_9Jewish + ε. Also, note: As of this writing, the ANES cumulative file does not include measures of Catholic or Jewish identification in the 2016 sample. Therefore, we estimate models of Catholic and Jewish effects only through 2012.

23. Formally, the Evangelical vote choice model is: Vote Choice = β_0Constant + β_1Republican + β_2Democratic + β_3Female + β_4Age + β_5Income + β_6Education + β_7White + β_8South + β_9Evangelical + ε.

24. Using this measure of biblical literalism, or fundamentalism, as a proxy for evangelical Christianity, is reasonable given the data limitations described earlier, but certainly it is not optimal. Most notably, that is because biblical literalism measures a person's theological beliefs, and not necessarily his or her identification with a religious group (i.e., evangelical Christian). Elsewhere in this chapter, we use a direct measure of evangelical identification when analyzing data from KN, in 2008. However, we must use biblical literalism as a proxy for evangelicalism, again, when analyzing data from TAPS, in 2012 and 2016.

25. Of course, one might interpret this as evidence that Miller helped to neutralize the advantage among Catholics that Democrats had developed as a result of Kennedy's historic election in 1960, and his presidency.

26. We cannot provide estimates for 1996 because, in that year's ANES, only one Jewish respondent who voted for president did not vote for the Democratic ticket. The Jewish variable drops out of our logistic regression model because, when controlling for other factors, it does not predict any variation in the dependent variable.

27. It is also possible that Lieberman had a targeted effect on Orthodox Jews, in particular. There is some, rather limited, evidence to indicate that this might have been the case (Fingerhut 2008; Rocklin 2017).

28. It is unlikely that evangelical voters' support for the Republican ticket in 1992 can be attributed to Dan Quayle's affiliation with an evangelical church since, as we discuss in note 21 of this chapter, his Democratic opponent, Al Gore, identified as a Southern Baptist, and both of these candidates were not particularly vocal about their evangelical associations. Additionally, it is worth noting that evangelical identification did not have a statistically significant effect on vote choice in 1988, when Quayle first ran for vice president, or in 1996, when Gore ran for reelection against Republican Jack Kemp, who attended the same evangelical church as Quayle.

29. Formally, the ideological vote choice model is: Vote Choice = β_0Constant + β_1Conservative + β_2Liberal + β_3Republican + β_4Democratic + β_3Female + β_4Age + β_5Income + β_6Education + β_7White + β_8South + ε.

30. To maximize comparability across the time series, in 1964 and 1968 we created 7-point ideological identification scales based on respondents' relative feeling

thermometer ratings of liberals versus conservatives (variable VCF0801 in the ANES Cumulative File). Specifically, we divided these 0–97 ratings into seven equal categories, ranging from "extremely liberal" (a score of 0 to 13 on VCF0801) to "extremely conservative" (a score of 84 to 97 on VCF0801).

31. This represents Waves 5, 7, 8, 9, and 10, respectively. Like Elis, Hillygus, and Nie (2010, 584), who also use the 2008 KN database to analyze Palin's effect on vote choice in that election, we do not analyze Wave 6 because it was a separately commissioned study.

32. The model for Sarah Palin is specified as: Intended Republican Vote Choice = β_0Constant + β_1Vote Choice Past Wave + β_2Republican + β_3Democratic + β_4Conservative + β_5Liberal + β_6Female + β_7Age + β_8Income + β_9Education + β_{10}White + β_{11}South + β_{12}Evangelical + ε.

33. Formally, the 2008 Catholic vote choice model is: Vote Choice = β_0Constant + β_1Vote Choice Past Wave + β_2Republican + β_3Democratic + β_4Conservative + β_5Liberal + β_6Female + β_7Age + β_8Income + β_9Education + β_{10}White + β_{11}South + v_{12}Catholic + ε.

34. Did Biden's selection temporarily hurt the Democratic ticket among Catholic voters? We believe this is unlikely to be the case. But even if that were true, the effect dissipates by Election Day because the coefficient is not statistically distinguishable from zero in later waves, again suggesting there is no meaningful effect on vote choice.

35. Available at https://taps.wustl.edu (accessed March 29, 2019). We modified the 2012 and 2016 TAPS datasets to include additional respondent demographic data contained in a separate TAPS data file. By merging responses and additional respondent demographic variables, we are able to estimate models consistent with our analysis of the 2008 KN panel.

36. Formally, the model estimating Paul Ryan's targeted effects in 2012 is: Intended Republican Vote Choice = β_0Constant + β_1Vote Choice Past Wave + β_2Republican + β_3Democratic + β_4Conservative + β_5Liberal + β_6Female + β_7Age + β_8Income + β_9Education + β_{10}White + β_{11}South + β_{12}Catholic + β_{13}Midwesterner + ε.

37. Formally, the model estimating Mike Pence's targeted effects in 2016 is: Intended Republican Vote Choice = β_0Constant + β_1Vote Choice Past Wave + β_2Republican + β_3Democratic + β_4Conservative + β_5Liberal + β_6Female + β_7Age + β_8Income + β_9Education + β_{10}White + β_{11}South + β_{12}Catholic + β_{13}Midwesterner + β_{14}Evangelical + ε.

38. Formally, the model estimating Tim Kaine's targeted effects, in terms of geography and religion, in 2016 is: Intended Democratic Vote Choice = β_0Constant + β_1Vote Choice Past Wave + β_2Republican + β_3Democratic + β_4Conservative + β_5Liberal + β_6Female + β_7Age + β_8Income + β_9Education + β_{10}White + β_{11}South + β_{12}Catholic + β_{13}Midwesterner + β_{14}Evangelical + ε. When estimating Kaine's effect on Latinos, we add the dichotomous variable described earlier to this model.

CHAPTER 5. INDIRECT EFFECTS

1. This participant, by the way, did not describe himself as being predisposed to dislike Kaine; to the contrary, in fact. After calling Kaine a "jerk" for the first time,

he quickly noted: "I actually liked that guy, and I was really disappointed in him this time."

2. Available at https://www.youtube.com/watch?v=2PN7Sa9QtgQ (accessed January 10, 2020).

3. Available at https://www.youtube.com/watch?v=BjpUQJCCXso (accessed January 10, 2020).

4. Available at http://www.nbcnews.com/id/25004682/ns/msnbc-morning_joe/t/verdict-dan-abrams-wednesday-june/#.WwiMd3ovyMp (accessed January 10, 2020).

5. Available at https://digitalcommons.bowdoin.edu/mitchelloralhistory/173 (accessed January 10, 2020).

6. However, we are not the first scholars to explore the potential for indirect running mate effects. Romero (2001) also did so, using panel data from the 1972–1976 ANES. Indeed, he finds that vice presidential candidate evaluations significantly influenced vote choice, via presidential candidate evaluations, in the 1976 presidential election (Romero 2001, 461–462). Romero's analysis is groundbreaking. But it is also limited in that it examines data only from a single election, which took place more than forty years ago; see chapter 3, note 11. Kenski, Hardy, and Jamieson (2010) also examine the effects of vice presidential selection on perceptions of the presidential candidates' experience (figure 6.1), judgment (figure 6.2), and readiness to be commander in chief (figure 6.3), in 2008. However, they provide only a rough estimate of the running mate's indirect effect, by comparing perceptions of the presidential candidate's attributes in the periods before and after vice presidential selection.

7. Given the exceptional circumstances that we describe here, however, it is quite possible that the evidence of indirect effects is stronger in 2008 than what we would find—if similar evidence were available—in other election years with more traditional running mates who attracted less media coverage and public attention. That is to say, most running mates probably are less capable of defining the presidential candidates— and the presidential election itself—than Sarah Palin and Joe Biden were in 2008. In that sense, we view the 2008 data primarily as an ideal indicator of the *potential* for indirect running mate effects, rather than providing a representative estimate of those effects. We do believe, based on the evidence from other election years presented later in this chapter, that it is typical for running mates to exert an indirect effect on voting behavior. But the magnitude of these effects is likely to vary across election years and in all probability it was greater in 2008 than in most other elections.

8. We use Model 2 over Model 1 because the former resulted in the highest percentage of variation explained by the model in terms of the adjusted R^2 statistic.

9. We employ Stata's maximum likelihood estimation method for all SEMs in this chapter. For more information on SEMs, see Acock (2013).

10. This approach is preferable, given our intention to present this chapter's findings in a concise and intuitive manner (see earlier discussion). However, it is important to note that the results from our SEM models do not substantively change after adding other control variables. Of course, given the difference in model specification, there will be some variation in effect size compared with the results presented earlier

in this chapter and in chapter 3. Nonetheless, our substantive conclusions regarding indirect effects are not dependent on model specifications. Our substantive conclusions also do not change when restricting our analysis to the most recent presidential elections, from 2000 to 2016. In fact, the indirect effect coefficient estimates for both Republican and Democratic vice presidential candidate feeling thermometers are virtually identical when restricting our analysis to the 2000–2016 elections, in comparison to the 1968–2016 elections.

11. After estimating the SEMs, we used Stata's "teffects" postestimation command to derive the indirect effect of the vice presidential candidate thermometer ratings.

12. It is important to note that these changes in predicted probabilities refer to the respondent's *likelihood* of voting for a given ticket, not a change in the percentage of votes cast for that ticket (i.e., party vote share). Thus, a nearly 9 percentage-point increase in the predicted probability of a Democratic vote, for instance, is substantial but not as dramatic as it may sound; some respondents already were likely to vote for that ticket anyway, and others were very unlikely to do so and still would not. These effects are most likely to cause a change in vote choice among persuadable voters (e.g., those voters who started with a 40 to 60 percent likelihood of voting for the ticket in question). In that sense, such a change in predicted probabilities would gain votes among some, but certainly not all, respondents.

13. For further information on Granger causality, see note 16 in chapter 3.

14. This means that for an eleven-day lag (as is the case for the 2000 data), the cumulative effect is the summation of all preceding days' effects.

15. While it is not the focus of our analysis, it is worth noting that three of the four presidential candidates did not have a positive effect on their running mates' favorability, at any point in the time series. The only exception is Al Gore, who had a statistically significant and positive effect on Lieberman's favorability on days three and four.

16. We do not conduct the same analysis for perceptions of ideology because, whereas the other two items represent valence issues (i.e., having good judgment is a good thing, being "too young/old" to be president is a bad thing), the electoral implications of a candidate's ideology will vary across individuals. In other words, being perceived as conservative will appeal to conservative voters while repelling liberals. Thus, we cannot model these effects consistently across the full sample of survey respondents. We do, however, model the effects of Palin's perceived ideology on perceptions of McCain's ideology, later in this chapter. This is appropriate because the question at hand is a factual one (e.g., Is McCain conservative? How much so?) and thus something on which people should agree, regardless of their political views or affiliations.

17. In the interest of brevity, we do not include results for the control variables in table 5.3. However, at the bottom of the table, we identify these variables and explain how they are coded.

18. In the interest of brevity, we describe these results here in the text and do not detail them in a table. We do the same for the next SEM, regarding the presidential candidates' age.

19. We use the estimates from Models 2 and 3 for this analysis, since these models

yielded the greatest proportional reduction in error for McCain and Obama, respectively. To estimate predicted probabilities, we set all control variables to their median values. We follow the same procedure in later models.

20. The predictive power of Models 3 and 4, however, is abysmal. In fact, the standard battery of control variables and the presidential candidate favorability ratings do not reduce the model's error prediction at all.

21. Although these models provide evidence for the hypothesis that running mates influence perceptions of presidential candidate ideology, it is important to note that Model 1, in particular, does not perform very well. In fact, that model yields only a 5.46 percent proportional reduction in error, while the model predicting Obama's ideology (Model 2) performs markedly better with a proportional reduction in error of 38.13 percent. This suggests that Model 1 does not include some factors that significantly influence perceptions of McCain's ideology.

22. This is because, to our knowledge, no dataset from 2012 or 2016 includes measures of the presidential *and* vice presidential candidates' perceived ideologies.

23. We rely on Model 3 because it yields the highest proportional reduction in error (39 percent).

24. Consistent with Elis, Hillygus, and Nie (2010, 584n10) we do not analyze Wave 6. That wave was commissioned separately from the other waves, and sampling began prior to Sarah Palin's selection as John McCain's running mate, on August 29, then continued through September. Our analysis uses essentially the same waves as those used by Elis, Hillygus, and Nie (2010).

25. But, of course, many factors could have contributed to McCain's exceptional performance in September—for instance, he may have been enjoying a postconvention "bump" (see J. Campbell, Cherry, and Wink 1992; see also J. Campbell 2000). Also, the September panel wave was conducted just before the beginning of the 2008 financial collapse. This may be the main reason that McCain's rating are worse in the October and November waves, and Obama's better, than they were in September.

26. This is in contrast to our analysis of targeted effects from chapter 4, where we were able to measure the independent variable's value (i.e., whether respondents identified with a particular group such as Catholics or conservatives) in the preselection wave.

27. We include control variables for Catholic and evangelical affiliation because Biden and Palin, respectively, were members of these religious groups and thus might have appealed to their coreligionists. The evidence from chapter 4 indicates that Biden's selection did not increase Catholic support for the Democratic ticket. However, Palin's selection did seem to have a temporary, positive effect on evangelical support for the Republican ticket.

28. This model yields the second-greatest proportional reduction in error of any that uses Biden's favorability rating as its independent variable, and the greatest proportional reduction in error for those models that use perceptions of Biden's experience.

29. Tables 5.10 and 5.11 also indicate that running mates influence perceptions of

the *opposite* party's presidential candidate—albeit, to a lesser extent than the opposite-party running mate. Consider the evidence from table 5.10. As a reminder, in nineteen of twenty models, the Palin variable influenced perceptions of McCain's attributes, and in the expected direction. But, using the conventional $p < .05$ threshold, so did Obama's favorability rating in fifteen of those models, and Biden's in six models. Curiously, though, in each of these cases the Obama variable is correctly signed (i.e., more favorable ratings of Obama cause more negative evaluations of McCain), while the Biden variable is not (i.e., more favorable ratings of Biden cause more positive evaluations of McCain). Compare this to table 5.11. There, we see that the Biden variables influenced perceptions of Obama's attributes in fourteen of twenty models. But so did McCain's favorability rating in thirteen of those models, and Palin in just two models. In this case, each of the McCain and Palin variables is correctly signed (i.e., more positive evaluations of the Republican candidates cause more negative evaluations of Obama).

30. Should we even hazard a guess as to what is going on here? The most obvious interpretation would be that having a positive view of Palin literally made McCain appear more physically attractive to voters. Another possibility is that respondents interpreted "attractiveness" in a more general sense, as going beyond physical appearance. For instance, respondents might have been expressing that McCain was a more *appealing* or *compelling* candidate, if they liked Palin. The ambiguity of this term is such that either interpretation may be plausible. And, frankly, the obvious interpretation is so bizarre that we cannot help but root against it.

CHAPTER 6. WHY DOES THIS MATTER?

1. But, Goldstein stresses, as long as the vice president's expanded powers rest on informal institutional changes, they can always be rolled back by a president who, as a matter of policy or practice, chooses not to adhere to the Mondale Model. Indeed, Goldstein (2019) characterizes Mike Pence's vice presidency as "more challenging—and less meaningful—than those of recent vice presidents because of the president he serves."

2. Interview, James M. Cannon with Gerald Ford, April 27, 1990, folder: "Ford, Gerald—Interview, April 27, 1990," Box 1, James M. Cannon Research Interviews and Notes, Gerald R. Ford Library.

3. Available at https://millercenter.org/the-presidency/presidential-oral-histories /walter-mondale-oral-history-vice-president-united-states (January 10, 2020).

4. Also, similar analyses of running mate effects could be conducted at the state level, with respect to lieutenant gubernatorial candidates, or internationally, in a comparative context. Indeed, Baumgartner and Evans Case (2009, 156) find that twenty-one democratic countries "link the selection of the VP to that of the president, either by way of popular election (as in the U.S.) or by allowing the president to select the VP after the election (with or without legislative approval)." Furthermore,

one could extend the present analysis to coalition partners in parliamentary systems, which, if announced in advance of an election, may serve a similar function to vice presidential candidates in the United States.

5. Available at https://www.c-span.org/video/?305595-1/interview-former-vice -president-dick-cheney&start=1655 (accessed January 10, 2020).

Bibliography

Acock, Alan C. 2013. *Discovering Structural Equation Modeling Using Stata*. College Station, TX: Stata Press.

Adkison, Daniel M. 1982. "The Electoral Significance of the Vice Presidency." *Presidential Studies Quarterly* 12 (3): 303–336.

Adler, William D., and Julia Azari. 2018. "The Party Decides (Who the Vice President Will Be)." Paper presented at the annual meeting of the American Political Science Association, Boston, August 30–September 2.

Alberta, Tim. 2016. "Life on the Inside: Mike Pence's Turbulent Trip with Donald Trump." *National Review*, November 3. https://www.nationalreview.com/2016/11/mike-pence-2016-campaign-inside-view-profile (accessed January 10, 2020).

———. 2019. *American Carnage: On the Front Lines of the Republican Civil War and the Rise of President Trump*. New York: Harper.

Aldrich, John H., and John D. Griffin. 2018. *Why Parties Matter: Political Competition and Democracy in the American South*. Chicago: University of Chicago Press.

Allen, Jonathan, and Amy Parnes. 2017. *Shattered: Inside Hillary Clinton's Doomed Campaign*. New York: Crown.

"Appendix B: Classification of Protestant Denominations." Pew Research Center, May 12. https://www.pewforum.org/2015/05/12/appendix-b-classification-of-protestant-denominations/#fnref-23336-27 (accessed January 10, 2020).

Asher, Herb. 2017. *Polling and the Public: What Every Citizen Should Know*. 9th ed. Thousand Oaks, CA: Sage.

Axelrod, David. 2015. *Believer: My Forty Years in Politics*. New York: Penguin.

Baker, Peter. 2013. *Days of Fire: Bush and Cheney in the White House*. New York: Doubleday.

Barstow, David, with Katharine Q. Seelye. 2000. "In Selecting a No. 2, No Detail Too Small." *New York Times*, August 9. https://www.nytimes.com/2000/08/09/us/the-2000-campaign-the-selection-in-selecting-a-no-2-no-detail-too-small.html (accessed January 10, 2020).

Baum, Christopher F. 2000. "FRACDIFF: Stata Module to Generate Fractionally-Differenced Timeseries." IDEAS. https://ideas.repec.org/c/boc/bocode/s413901.html (accessed January 10, 2020).

Baum, Christopher F., and Vince Wiggins. 2000. "Utility for Time Series Data." *Stata Technical Bulletin* 57 (10): 2–4.

Baumgartner, Jody C. 2008. "The Veepstakes: Forecasting Vice Presidential Selection in 2008." *PS: Political Science & Politics* 41 (4): 765–772.

———. 2012. "Vice Presidential Selection in the Convention Era: Experience or Electoral Advantage?" *Congress & the Presidency* 39 (3): 297–315.

———. 2016. "Rejecting More of the Same? The 2016 Veepstakes." *PS: Political Science & Politics* 49 (4): 775–781.

Baumgartner, Jody C., and Rhonda Evans Case. 2009. "Constitutional Design of the Executive: Vice Presidencies in Comparative Perspective." *Congress & the Presidency* 36 (2): 148–163.

Baumgartner, Jody C., with Thomas F. Crumblin. 2015. *The American Vice Presidency: From the Shadow to the Spotlight.* Lanham, MD: Rowman & Littlefield.

Beaumont, Tom. 2016. "Some See Pence, Post-debate, as Top-of-Ticket Material." Associated Press, October 5. https://apnews.com/ff938630c20341c98605a7cdfa8afac8 (accessed January 10, 2020).

Bettencourt, B. Ann, Norman Miller, and Deborah L. Hume. 2010. "Effects of Numerical Representation within Cooperative Settings: Examining the Role of Salience in In-Group Favouritism." *British Journal of Social Psychology* 38 (3): 265–287.

Box-Steffensmeier, Janet M., David Darmofal, and Christian A. Farrell. 2009. "The Aggregate Dynamics of Campaigns." *Journal of Politics* 71 (1): 309–323.

Box-Steffensmeier, Janet M., Suzanna DeBoef, and Tse-Min Lin. 2004. "The Dynamics of the Partisan Gender Gap." *American Political Science Review* 98 (3): 515–528.

Box-Steffensmeier, Janet M., John R. Freeman, Matthew P. Hitt, and Jon C. W. Pevehouse. 2014. *Time Series Analysis for the Social Sciences.* New York: Cambridge University Press.

Bradburn, Norman, Seymour Sudman, and Brian Wansink. 2004. *Asking Questions: The Definitive Guide to Questionnaire Design—For Market Research, Political Polls, and Social and Health Questionnaires.* San Francisco: Jossey-Bass.

Brewer, Marilynn B. 1991. "The Social Self: On Being the Same and Being Different." *Personality and Social Psychology Bulletin* 17 (5): 475–482.

Broder, David S., and Bob Woodward. 1992. "What If Dan Quayle Were to Become President?" *Washington Post,* January 12. https://www.washingtonpost.com/archive/politics/1992/01/12/what-if-dan-quayle-were-to-become-president/63c9742c-e948-4d01-b344-a10633d4bd6d/ (accessed January 10, 2020).

Brox, Brian J., and Madison L. Cassels. 2009. "The Contemporary Effects of Vice-Presidential Nominees: Sarah Palin and the 2008 Presidential Campaign." *Journal of Political Marketing* 8 (4): 349–363.

Burmila, Edward M., and Josh M. Ryan. 2013. "Reconsidering the 'Palin Effect' in the 2008 U.S. Presidential Election." *Political Research Quarterly* 66 (4): 952–959.

Burn, Shawn M. 1995. *The Social Psychology of Gender.* New York: McGraw Hill.

Burn, Shawn M., Roger Aboud, and Carey Moyles. 2000. "The Relationship between Gender Social Identity and Support for Feminism." *Sex Roles* 42 (11–12): 1081–1089.

Bush, George W. 2010. *Decision Points.* New York: Crown.

Campbell, Angus, Philip E. Converse, Warren E. Miller, and Donald E. Stokes. 1960. *The American Voter.* Chicago: University of Chicago Press.

Campbell, James E. 1992. "Forecasting the Presidential Vote in the States." *American Journal of Political Science* 36 (2): 386–407.

———. 2000. *The American Campaign: U.S. Presidential Campaigns and the National Vote.* College Station: Texas A&M University Press.

Campbell, James E., Syed Ali, and Farida Jalalzai. 2006. "Forecasting the Presidential Vote in the States, 1948–2004: An Update, Revision, and Extension of a State-Level Presidential Forecasting Model." In *Campaigns and Political Marketing,* edited by Wayne Steger, Mark Kelly, and Sean Wrighton, 33–58. New York: Routledge.

Campbell, James E., Lynna L. Cherry, and Kenneth A. Wink. 1992. "The Convention Bump." *American Politics Quarterly* 20 (3): 287–307.

Campbell, James E., Helmut Norpoth, Alan I. Abramowitz, and Michael S. Lewis-Beck. 2017. "A Recap of the 2016 Election Forecasts." *PS: Political Science & Politics* 50 (2): 331–338.

Cannon, Lou. 1980. "Reagan Campaign Looks to Running Mate." *Washington Post,* May 13. Accessed via LexisNexis.

———. 1980. "The Republicans in Detroit: A Foretaste of a Reagan Presidency; Television Melodrama Gives a Glimpse of Reagan Concept of the Presidency; News Analysis." *Washington Post,* July 18. Accessed via LexisNexis.

Cheney, Dick, with Liz Cheney. 2011. *In My Time: A Personal and Political Memoir.* New York: Threshold Editions.

Christian, Sue Ellen. 1996. "On the Sidelines." *Chicago Tribune,* September 29. https://www.chicagotribune.com/news/ct-xpm-1996-09-29-9609290282-story.html (accessed January 10, 2020).

Cillizza, Chris. 2016. "Donald Trump Will Make His Mind Up on VP Pick in 'Next Three to Four Days.'" *Washington Post,* July 11. https://www.washingtonpost.com/news/the-fix/wp/2016/07/11/donald-trump-will-make-his-mind-up-on-vp-pick-in-next-three-to-four-days/?utm_term=.2f5920e20462 (accessed January 10, 2020).

Clinton, Bill. 2004. *My Life.* New York: Alfred A. Knopf.

Cohen, Geoffrey L. 2003. "Party over Policy: The Dominating Impact of Group Influence on Political Beliefs." *Journal of Personality and Social Psychology* 85 (5): 808–822.

"Comments from Dukakis, Bentsen and Jackson." 1988. *New York Times,* July 13. https://www.nytimes.com/1988/07/13/us/comments-from-dukakis-bentsen-and-jackson.html (accessed January 10, 2020).

"A Conversation with Jimmy Carter." 1992. ABC News, *Nightline,* July 14. Accessed via LexisNexis.

Converse, Philip E. 1964. "The Nature of Belief Systems in Mass Publics." In *Ideology and Discontent,* edited by David E. Apter, 206–261. New York: Free Press of Glencoe.

Court, Whitney Lauraine. 2012. "The Risks and Rewards of Selecting Vice Presidential Nominees." PhD diss., University of Kansas. https://kuscholarworks.ku.edu/bitstream/handle/1808/10431/Court_ku_0099D_12001_DATA_1.pdf?sequence=1 (accessed January 10, 2020).

Court, Whitney L., and Michael S. Lynch. 2015. "How Presidential Running Mates Influence Turnout: The Risks and Rewards of Revving up the Base." *American Politics Research* 43 (5): 897–918.

"A Crisis Named Eagleton." 1972. *Newsweek*, August 7, 12–16.

Cuba, Lee, and David M. Hummon. 1993. "A Place to Call Home: Identification with Dwelling, Community, and Region." *Sociological Quarterly* 34 (1): 111–131.

Dawson, Michael C. 1995. *Behind the Mule: Race and Class in African-American Politics.* Princeton, NJ: Princeton University Press.

Deaux, Kay, Anne Reid, Kim Mizrahi, and Kathleen A. Ethier. 1995. "Parameters of Social Identity." *Journal of Personality and Social Psychology* 68 (2): 280–291.

Devine, Christopher J. 2015. "Ideological Social Identity: Psychological Attachment to Ideological In-Groups as a Political Phenomenon and a Behavioral Influence." *Political Behavior* 37 (3): 509–535.

Devine, Christopher J., and Kyle C. Kopko. 2011. "The Vice Presidential Home State Advantage Reconsidered: Analyzing the Interactive Effect of Home State Population and Political Experience, 1884–2008." *Presidential Studies Quarterly* 41 (1): 1–17.

———. 2013. "Presidential versus Vice Presidential Home State Advantage: A Comparative Analysis of Electoral Significance, Causes, and Processes, 1884–2008." *Presidential Studies Quarterly* 43 (4): 814–838.

———. 2016. *The VP Advantage: How Running Mates Influence Home State Voting in Presidential Elections.* Manchester, UK: Manchester University Press.

———. 2019. "Bringing Voters into the Equation: An Individual-Level Analysis of the Vice Presidential Home State Advantage." *Presidential Studies Quarterly* 49 (4): 827–854.

Dinan, Stephen. 2008. "Dukakis: McCain's Palin Pick 'Pretty Pathetic.'" *Washington Times*, October 17. https://www.washingtontimes.com/news/2008/oct/17/dukakis -mccains-palin-pick-pretty-pathetic (accessed January 10, 2020).

Dudley, Robert L., and Ronald B. Rapoport. 1989. "Vice-Presidential Candidates and the Home State Advantage: Playing Second Banana at Home and on the Road." *American Journal of Political Science* 33 (2): 537–540.

Elis, Roy, D. Sunshine Hillygus, and Norman Nie. 2010. "The Dynamics of Candidate Evaluations and Vote Choice in 2008: Looking to the Past or Future?" *Electoral Studies* 29 (4): 582–593.

Ember, Sydney, and Jonathan Martin. 2019. "Sherrod Brown Won't Run for President in 2020." *New York Times*, March 7. https://www.nytimes.com/2019/03/07/us/poli tics/sherrod-brown-2020-president.html (accessed January 10, 2020).

Enten, Harry. 2016. "Trump Is More Unpopular Than Clinton Is—And That Matters." *FiveThirtyEight*, September 30. http://fivethirtyeight.com/features/trump -is-more-unpopular-than-clinton-is-and-that-matters (accessed January 10, 2020).

Felix, Melvin, and Brandon Shaik. 2016. "Why It Matters That Tim Kaine Speaks Spanish." *Univision*, July 28. https://www.univision.com/univision-news/why-it -matters-that-tim-kaine-speaks-spanish (accessed January 10, 2020).

Fingerhut, Eric. 2008. "Some Stats on the Orthodox Jewish Vote." *Jewish Telegraphic Agency*, November 26. https://www.jta.org/2008/11/26/culture/some-stats-on-the -orthodox-jewish-vote (accessed January 10, 2020).

Freedland, Jonathan. 2008. "US Elections: 'I Think It'd Be the Worst Mistake That

Could Be Made." *The Guardian*, June 4. https://www.theguardian.com/world/au dio/2008/jun/04/freedland.carter (accessed January 10, 2020).

Freeman, John R. 1983. "Granger Causality and the Times Series Analysis of Political Relationships." *American Journal of Political Science* 27 (2): 327–358.

Gallup, George H., Jr. 2003. "How Many Americans Know U.S. History? Part I." Gallup, October 21. http://www.gallup.com/poll/9526/how-many-americans-know -us-history-part.aspx (accessed January 10, 2020).

Garand, James C. 1988. "Localism and Regionalism in Presidential Elections: Is There a Home State or Regional Advantage?" *Political Research Quarterly* 41 (1): 85–103.

Glover, Mike. 2000. "Gore Has 'Short List' of VP Possibilities." Associated Press, July 26. Accessed via LexisNexis.

Goldstein, Joel K. 2016. *The White House Vice Presidency: The Path to Significance, Mondale to Biden.* Lawrence: University Press of Kansas.

———. 2019. "Mike Pence Has Lasted 2 Years as Trump's VP. That May Be His Main Accomplishment." *Washington Post*, January 18. https://www.washingtonpost.com /news/monkey-cage/wp/2019/01/18/mike-pence-has-lasted-2-years-as-trumps-vp -that-may-be-his-main-accomplishment (accessed January 10, 2020).

Gomez, Henry J. 2019. "Sherrod Brown Won't Run for President, after Months of Planning for the 2020 Race." *BuzzFeed News*, March 7. https://www.buzzfeednews.com /article/henrygomez/sherrod-brown-2020-decision-president (accessed January 10, 2020).

Goodstein, Laurie. 2016. "Religious Right Believes Donald Trump Will Deliver on His Promises." *New York Times*, November 11. https://www.nytimes.com/2016/11/12/us /donald-trump-evangelical-christians-religious-conservatives.html (accessed January 10 2020).

Granger, Clive W. J. 1969. "Investigating Causal Relations by Econometric Models and Cross-Spectral Methods." *Econometrica* 37 (3): 424–438.

Grofman, Bernard, and Reuben Kline. 2010. "Evaluating the Impact of Vice Presidential Selection on Voter Choice." *Presidential Studies Quarterly* 40 (2): 303–309.

Haberman, Maggie, and Katie Rogers. 2018. "Is Mike Pence Loyal? Trump Is Asking, Despite His Recent Endorsement." *New York Times*, November 16. https://www .nytimes.com/2018/11/16/us/politics/mike-pence-trump-administration.html (accessed January 10, 2020).

Halbfinger, David M. 2004. "McCain Is Said to Tell Kerry He Won't Join." *New York Times*, June 12. http://www.nytimes.com/2004/06/12/us/mccain-is-said-to-tell -kerry-he-won-t-join.html?_r=1 (accessed January 10, 2020).

Halperin, Mark, and John Heilemann. 2013. *Double Down: Game Change 2012.* New York: Penguin.

Heersink, Boris, and Brenton D. Peterson. 2016. "Measuring the Vice-Presidential Home State Advantage with Synthetic Controls." *American Politics Research* 44 (4): 734–763.

Heilemann, John, and Mark Halperin. 2010. *Game Change: Obama and the Clintons, McCain and Palin, and the Race of a Lifetime.* New York: HarperCollins.

Henneberger, Melinda. 2000. "The 2000 Campaign: Spiritual Seeker; Gore Has Explored A Range of Beliefs from Old Time to New Age." *New York Times*, October 22. https://www.nytimes.com/2000/10/22/us/2000-campaign-spiritual-seeker-gore-has-explored-range-beliefs-old-time-new-age.html (accessed January 10, 2020).

Hiller, Mark, and Douglas Kriner. 2008. "Institutional Chance and the Dynamics of Vice Presidential Selection." *Presidential Studies Quarterly* 38 (3): 401–421.

Hillyard, Vaughn. 2016. "Mike Pence Carves Familiar Path across Swing States for Donald Trump." NBC News, August 27. https://www.nbcnews.com/politics/2016-election/mike-pence-carves-familiar-path-across-swing-states-donald-trump-n638756 (accessed January 10, 2020).

Hoffman, John P., and John P. Bartkowski. 2008. "Gender, Religious Tradition and Biblical Literalism." *Social Forces* 86 (3): 1245–1272.

Holbrook, Thomas M. 1991. "Presidential Elections in Space and Time." *American Journal of Political Science* 35 (1): 91–109.

———. 1996. *Do Campaigns Matter?* Thousand Oaks, CA: Sage.

Issenberg, Sasha. 2012. *The Victory Lab: The Secret Science of Winning Campaigns*. New York: Crown.

Jamieson, Kathleen Hall, ed. 2013. *Electing the President, 2012: The Insider's View*. Philadelphia: University of Pennsylvania Press.

Jehl, Douglas, and David Johnston. 2004. "In Video Message, Bin Laden Issues Warning to U.S." *New York Times*, October 30. https://www.nytimes.com/2004/10/30/world/middleeast/in-video-message-bin-laden-issues-warning-to-us.html (accessed January 10, 2020).

Jelen, Ted G. 2018. "'Can We Get the Catholic Vote?' The Effects of Catholic Running Mates in Presidential Elections." In *Catholics and US Politics after the 2016 Elections: Understanding the "Swing Vote,"* edited by Marie Gayte, Blandine Chelini-Pont, and Mark J. Rozell, 193–207. Cham, Switzerland: Palgrave Macmillan.

Johnson, Kirk, and Kim Severson. 2008. "In Palin's Life and Politics, Goal to Follow God's Will." *New York Times*, September 5. https://www.nytimes.com/2008/09/06/us/politics/06church.html (accessed January 10, 2020).

Johnston, Richard, Michael G. Hagen, and Kathleen Hall Jamieson. 2004. *The 2000 Presidential Election and the Foundations of Party Politics*. Cambridge: Cambridge University Press.

Jones, Jeffrey M., and Joseph Carroll. 2005. "Changing Minds in the 2004 Election?" Gallup, June 4. http://www.gallup.com/poll/16576/changing-minds-2004-election.aspx (accessed January 10, 2020).

Kahane, Leo H. 2009. "It's the Economy, and Then Some: Modeling the Presidential Vote with State Panel Data." *Public Choice* 139 (3–4): 343–356.

Keeter, Scott. 1985. "Public Opinion in 1984." In *The Election of 1984: Reports and Interpretations*, edited by Gerald E. Pomper, 91–111. Chatham, NJ: Chatham House.

Kenski, Kate, Bruce W. Hardy, and Kathleen Hall Jamieson. 2010. *The Obama Victory: How Media, Money, and Message Shaped the 2008 Election*. Oxford: Oxford University Press.

Kerry, John. 2018. *Every Day Is Extra*. New York: Simon & Schuster.

Kertscher, Tom. 2016. "Picking Paul Ryan Ended Mitt Romney's Chances of Winning the White House in 2012, Donald Trump Says." *PolitiFact*, February 26. https://www.politifact.com/wisconsin/statements/2016/feb/26/donald-trump/picking-paul-ryan-ended-mitt-romneys-chances-winni (accessed January 10, 2020).

Key, V. O. 1949. *Southern Politics in State and Nation*. New York: Random House.

Kiefer, Francine. 2016. "Clinton Picks Tim Kaine, Devout Catholic and Bridge-Builder." *Christian Science Monitor*, July 22. https://www.csmonitor.com/USA/Politics/2016/0722/Clinton-picks-Tim-Kaine-devout-Catholic-and-bridge-builder (accessed January 10, 2020).

Kinder, Donald R., and Nathan P. Kalmoe. 2017. *Neither Liberal nor Conservative: Ideological Innocence in the American Public*. Chicago: University of Chicago Press.

Knuckey, Jonathan. 2012. "The 'Palin Effect' in the 2008 U.S. Presidential Election." *Political Research Quarterly* 65 (2): 275–289.

———. 2013. "Comments on 'Reconsidering the Palin Effect.'" *Political Research Quarterly* 66 (4): 960–963.

Kopko, Kyle C. 2012. "Religious Identity and Political Participation in the Mennonite Church USA." *Politics and Religion* 5 (2): 367–393.

Krauze, Leon. 2016. "Tim Kaine, en Espanol." *New Yorker*, July 24. https://www.newyorker.com/news/news-desk/tim-kaine-en-espanol (January 10, 2020).

Kreisher, Otto, and John Marelius. 1988. "Dukakis Focuses on Running Mate; Thorough Search Pledged; Jackson Indicates Interest." *San Diego Tribune*, September 9. Accessed via LexisNexis.

Krumel, Thomas P., and Ali Enami. 2017. "Balancing the Ticket While Appealing to the Base: The Game Theory behind Mitt Romney's Selection of Paul Ryan as His Presidential Running Mate." *Party Politics* 23 (5): 498–506.

Lalonde, Richard N., and Randy A. Silverman. 1994. "Behavioral Preferences in Response to Social Injustice: The Effects of Group Permeability and Social Identity Salience." *Journal of Personality and Social Psychology* 66 (1): 78–85.

Lazarsfeld, Paul F., Bernard Berelson, and Hazel Baudet. 1948. *The People's Choice: How the Voter Makes Up His Mind in a Presidential Campaign*. 2nd ed. New York: Columbia University Press.

Lenz, Gabriel. 2012. *Follow the Leader? How Voters Respond to Politicians' Policies and Performance*. Chicago: University of Chicago Press.

Lerer, Lisa. 2019. "Vice President Season Starts Early for 2020 Democrats." *New York Times*, March 21. https://www.nytimes.com/2019/03/21/us/politics/on-politics-2020-vice-president.html (accessed January 10, 2020).

Levendusky, Matthew. 2009. *The Partisan Sort: How Liberals Became Democrats and Conservatives Became Republicans*. Chicago: University of Chicago Press.

Lewis-Beck, Michael S., William G. Jacoby, Helmut Norpoth, and Herbert F. Weisberg. 2008. *The American Voter Revisited*. Ann Arbor: University of Michigan Press.

Lewis-Beck, Michael S., and Tom W. Rice. 1983. "Localism in Presidential Elections: The Home State Advantage." *American Journal of Political Science* 27 (3): 548–556.

Lieberman, Joe, and Hadassah Lieberman, with Sarah Crichton. 2003. *An Amazing Adventure: Joe and Hadassah's Personal Notes on the 2000 Campaign.* New York: Simon & Schuster.

Lightman, David. 2016. "VP Debate Creates a Rising Star—Perhaps for 2020." *McClatchy DC Bureau,* October 5. https://www.mcclatchydc.com/news/politics-go vernment/election/article106057727.html (accessed January 10, 2020).

Lipka, Michael. 2013. "How Many Jews Are There in the United States?" Pew Research Center, October 2. https://www.pewresearch.org/fact-tank/2013/10/02/how-many -jews-are-there-in-the-united-states (accessed January 10, 2020).

LoBianco, Tom. 2019. *Piety & Power: Mike Pence and the Taking of the White House.* New York: Dey Street Books.

Mahler, Jonathan, and Dirk Johnson. 2016. "Mike Pence's Journey: Catholic Democrat to Evangelical Republican." *New York Times,* July 20. https://www.nytimes .com/2016/07/21/us/politics/mike-pence-religion.html (accessed January 10, 2020).

Malcolm, Andrew. 2008. "Dick Cheney: How I Became Vice President." *Los Angeles Times,* June 12. http://latimesblogs.latimes.com/washington/2008/06/cheney-se crets.html (accessed January 10, 2020).

Malka, Ariel, and Yphtach Lelkes. 2010. "More Than Ideology: Conservative-Liberal Identity and Receptivity to Political Cues." *Social Justice Research* 23 (2–3): 156–188.

Margolis, Michael. 1977. "From Confusion to Confusion: Issues and the American Voter (1956–1972)." *American Political Science Review* 71 (1): 31–43.

Markus, Gregory B. 1982. "Political Attitudes during an Election Year: A Report on the 1980 NES Panel Study." *American Political Science Review* 76 (3): 538–560.

Markus, Gregory B., and Philip E. Converse. 1979. "A Dynamic Simultaneous Model of Electoral Choice." *American Political Science Review* 73 (4): 1055–1070.

Mason, Jeff. 2008. "How to Choose a VP? For McCain, Rule One Is 'Do No Harm.'" Reuters, July 29. http://blogs.reuters.com/talesfromthetrail/2008/07/28/how-to -choose-a-vp-for-mccain-rule-one-is-do-no-harm (accessed January 10, 2020).

Mason, Lilliana. 2018. *How Politics Became Our Identity.* Chicago: University of Chicago Press.

McCain, John, and Mark Salter. 2018. *The Restless Wave: Good Times, Just Causes, Great Fights, and Other Appreciations.* New York: Simon & Schuster.

McCullough, David. 1992. *Truman.* New York: Simon & Schuster.

McKee, Seth C. 2018. *The Dynamics of Southern Politics: Causes and Consequences.* Washington, DC: CQ Press.

McPherson, Lindsey. 2016. "Pence Could Build Bridges to Social Conservatives, GOP Lawmakers Say." *Roll Call,* July 14. http://www.rollcall.com/news/politics/gop-law makers-say-pence-build-bridges-social-conservatives (accessed January 10, 2020).

Meacham, Jon. 2015. *Destiny and Power: The American Odyssey of George Herbert Walker Bush.* New York: Random House.

Milkis, Sidney M., and Michael Nelson. 2011. *The American Presidency: Origins & Development, 1776–2011.* 6th ed. Los Angeles: Sage.

Miller, Arthur. 1988. "Gender and the Vote, 1984." In *The Politics of the Gender Gap:*

The Social Construction of Political Influence, edited by Carol Mueller, 258–282. Newbury Park, CA: Sage.

Mills, Terrence D. 1992. *Time Series Techniques for Economists*. New York: Cambridge University Press.

Mixon, Franklin, and J. Matthew Tyrone. 2004. "The 'Home Grown' Presidency: Empirical Evidence on Localism in Presidential Voting, 1972–2000." *Applied Economics* 36 (16): 1745–1749.

Mondale, Walter F., with Dave Hage. 2010. "'The Good Fight': Mondale Picks Ferraro—'A Nation Is Stronger When It Can Tap All Its Talents.'" *MinnPost.com*, November 18. https://www.minnpost.com/politics-policy/2010/11/good-fight-mon dale-picks-ferraro-nation-stronger-when-it-can-tap-all-its-tal (accessed January 10, 2020).

Morin, Rebecca. 2016. "Kaine Delivers Entire Speech in Spanish at Miami Church." *Politico*, October 16. https://www.politico.com/story/2016/10/tim-kaine-delivers -entire-speech-in-spanish-at-miami-church-229866 (accessed January 10, 2020).

Morini, Marco. 2015. "Vice Presidential Candidates in the American Presidential Elections: Strategies for Selection and Effects." *Epiphany: Journal of Transdisciplinary Studies* 8 (1): 83–100.

Mullen, Brian, Rupert J. Brown, and Colleen Smith. 1992. "Ingroup Bias as a Function of Salience, Relevance, and Status: An Integration." *European Journal of Social Psychology* 22 (2): 103–122.

Mullin, Barbara-Ann, and Michael A. Hogg. 1998. "Dimensions of Subjective Uncertainty in Social Identification and Minimal Ingroup Discrimination." *British Journal of Social Psychology* 37 (3): 345–365.

Nelson, W. Dale. 1980. "Dole Says Reagan Will Need Running Mate Experienced in Washington." Associated Press, April 5. Accessed via LexisNexis.

"Newt Gingrich: Mike Pence Would Have 'Midwestern Appeal.'" 2016. *Time*, July 14. http://time.com/4406836/donald-trump-running-mate-mike-pence-newt-ging rich (accessed January 10, 2020).

Nisbett, Richard E., and Timothy DeCamp Wilson. 1977. "Telling More Than We Can Know: Verbal Reports on Mental Processes." *Psychological Review* 84 (3): 231–259.

O'Keefe, Ed. 2016. "Once Again, Hispanics Were Considered for VP. Once Again, They're Expecting to Be Passed Over." *Washington Post*, July 20. https://www.wash ingtonpost.com/politics/once-again-hispanics-were-considered-for-vp-once -again-theyre-expecting-to-be-passed-over/2016/07/20/e8dfobc8-4e91-11e6-a7d8 -13d06b37f256_story.html?utm_term=.2a075d44eedd (accessed January 10, 2020).

"Our History." 2020. Fourth Presbyterian Church. https://4thpres.org/about/history (accessed January 10, 2020).

Paasi, Anssi. 1986. "The Institutionalization of Regions: A Theoretical Framework for the Understanding of the Emergence of Regions and the Constitutions of Regional Identity." *Fennia* 164 (1): 105–146.

———. 2003. "Region and Place: Regional Identity in Question." *Progress in Human Geography* 27 (4): 475–485.

————. 2009. "The Resurgence of the 'Region' and 'Regional Identity': Theoretical Perspectives and Empirical Observations on Regional Dynamics in Europe." *Review of International Studies* 35 (supp. S1): 121–146.

Page, Benjamin I., and Calvin C. Jones. 1979. "Reciprocal Effects of Policy Preferences, Party Loyalties and the Vote." *American Political Science Review* 73 (4): 1071–1089.

Page, Susan. 2008. "5 Lessons for Picking a Running Mate." *USA Today*, June 11. http://usatoday30.usatoday.com/news/politics/election2008/2008-06-10-veeps_n.htm (accessed January 10, 2020).

Peralta, Eyder. 2016. "Kaine en Espanol: Pandering or a Symbol of Understanding for Latinos?" *National Public Radio*, July 27. https://www.npr.org/2016/07/27/487491607/kaine-en-espa-ol-pandering-or-a-symbol-of-understanding-for-latinos (accessed January 10, 2020).

Pierce, David A., and Larry D. Haugh. 1977. "Causality in Temporal Systems: Characterizations and a Survey." *Journal of Econometrics* 5 (3): 265–293.

Pittman, David. 1996. "Dole's VP 'Short List' Includes McCain." *Tucson Citizen*, July 19. https://web.archive.org/web/20151005064331/http://tucsoncitizen.com/morgue/1996/07/19/217579-dole-s-vp-short-list-includes-mccain (accessed January 10, 2020).

Quaid, Libby. 2008. "McCain Sees No Need for VP Regional Balance." Associated Press, February 9. https://tucson.com/news/national/govt-and-politics/elections/mccain-sees-no-need-for-vp-regional-balance/article_3b4e76ae-045c-56ea-8e27-da52143eac93.amp.html (accessed January 10, 2020).

Rahn, Will, and Emily Schultheis. 2016. "Veepstakes: Who Could Hillary Clinton Pick as Her Running Mate?" CBS News, May 17. https://www.cbsnews.com/news/democratic-veepstakes-who-could-hillary-clinton-pick-as-her-running-mate (accessed January 10, 2020).

Raju, Manu, and Theodore Schleifer. 2016. "Sherrod Brown: I'm Not Interested in Being Hillary Clinton's Vice President." CNN, April 25. http://www.cnn.com/2016/04/25/politics/sherrod-brown-hillary-clinton-vice-president/index.html (accessed January 10, 2020).

Raum, Tom. 1980. "Reagan Refusing to Predict Victories in South." Associated Press, March 8. Accessed via LexisNexis.

————. 1988. "Bush Blames Poor Poll Showing on Democratic Criticisms." Associated Press, June 15. Accessed via LexisNexis.

Rees, Matthew. 2000. "The Veep's Veep." *Weekly Standard*, March 20. http://www.weeklystandard.com/the-veeps-veep/article/12345 (accessed January 10, 2020).

"The Religious Affiliations of the Candidates." 1988. *St. Petersburg Times*, November 5. Accessed via LexisNexis.

Roccas, Sonia, and Marilynn B. Brewer. 2002. "Social Identity Complexity." *Personality and Social Psychology Review* 6 (2): 88–106.

Rocklin, Mitchell. 2017. "Are American Jews Shifting Their Political Affiliation?" *Mosaic*, January 18. https://mosaicmagazine.com/observation/politics-current-affairs/2017/01/are-american-jews-shifting-their-political-affiliation (accessed January 10, 2020).

Romano, Andrew. 2011. "How Ignorant Are Americans?" *Newsweek,* March 20. http://www.newsweek.com/how-ignorant-are-americans-66053 (accessed January 10, 2020).

Romero, David W. 2001. "Requiem for a Lightweight: Vice Presidential Candidate Evaluations and the Presidential Vote." *Presidential Studies Quarterly* 31 (3): 454–463.

Rosenstone, Steven J. 1983. *Forecasting Presidential Elections.* New Haven, CT: Yale University Press.

Rosentiel, Tom. 2008. "The Candidates: In a Word." Pew Research Center, September 25. https://www.pewresearch.org/2008/09/25/the-candidates-in-a-word (accessed January 10, 2020).

Rove, Karl. 2012. "I Was Wrong about Dick Cheney . . . and Other Lessons I Learned from Vetting Vice-Presidential Candidates." *Wall Street Journal,* April 25. https://www.wsj.com/articles/SB10001424052702304811304577365870484193362 (accessed January 10, 2020).

Saad, Lydia. 2000. "Pro-choice VP Selection Carries Risks for Bush." Gallup, July 21. http://www.gallup.com/poll/2713/prochoice-selection-carries-risks-bush.aspx (accessed January 10, 2020).

———. 2016. "Tim Kaine Matches Mike Pence in Lackluster Initial Ratings." Gallup, July 25. http://www.gallup.com/poll/193907/tim-kaine-matches-mike-pence-lackluster-initial-ratings.aspx (accessed January 10, 2020).

Scher, Bill. 2016. "The Left's Beef with Tim Kaine." *Politico,* June 29. https://www.politico.com/magazine/story/2016/06/hillary-clinton-2016-vp-pick-tim-kaine-213997 (accessed January 10, 2020).

Schultz, David. 2016. "(Un)Conventional Wisdom and Presidential Politics: The Myth of Convention Locations and Favorite-Son Vice Presidents." *PS: Political Science & Politics* 49 (3): 420–425.

Shaw, Daron. 2006. *The Race to 270: The Electoral College and Campaign Strategies of 2000 and 2004.* Chicago: University of Chicago Press.

Sherman, Gabriel. 2018. "'They're Beginning to Think about Whether Mike Pence Should Be Running Again': As the Mueller Fire Nears, Trump Ponders Jettisoning His Loyal V.P." *Vanity Fair,* December 5. https://www.vanityfair.com/news/2018/12/mike-pence-2020-mueller-trump (accessed January 10, 2020).

Shirley, Craig. 2009. *Rendezvous with Destiny: Ronald Reagan and the Campaign That Changed America.* Wilmington, DE: Intercollegiate Studies Institute.

Short, Aaron. 2016. "Trump Offered Christie His VP Slot—Then Rescinded It." *New York Post,* October 30. https://nypost.com/2016/10/30/trump-offered-christie-his-vp-slot-then-rescinded-it (accessed January 10, 2020).

Shrum. Robert. 2007. *No Excuses: Concessions of a Serial Campaigner.* New York: Simon & Schuster.

Siddiqui, Sabrina. 2016. "Who Will Be Hillary Clinton's Running Mate? Five of the Most Likely Choices." *The Guardian,* July 18. https://www.theguardian.com/us-news/2016/jul/18/hillary-clinton-running-mate-vice-president-choices (accessed January 10, 2020).

Sides, John. 2011. "The Political Scientist as a Blogger." *PS: Political Science & Politics* 44 (2): 267–271.

Sides, John, and Lynn Vavreck. 2013. *The Gamble: Choice and Chance in the 2012 Presidential Election*. Princeton, NJ: Princeton University Press.

Sigelman, Lee, and Paul J. Wahlbeck. 1997. "The 'Veepstakes': Strategic Choice in Presidential Running Mate Selection." *American Political Science Review* 91 (4): 855–864.

Simien, Evelyn M. 2005. "Race, Gender, and Linked Fate." *Journal of Black Studies* 35 (5): 529–550.

Smith, Jean Edward. 2008. *FDR*. New York: Random House.

Tajfel, Henri, Claude Flament, Michael G. Billig, and Robert P. Bundy. 1971. "Social Categorization and Intergroup Behavior." *European Journal of Social Psychology* 1 (2): 149–178.

Tajfel, Henri, and John C. Turner. 1979. "An Integrative Theory of Intergroup Conflict." In *Social Psychology of Intergroup Relations*, edited by William G. Austin and Stephen Worchel, 33–47. Chicago: Nelson.

Taylor, Paul, and Helen Dewar. 1988. "Running-Mate Sweepstakes; Advice Abounds, Even From Top Candidates." *Washington Post*, August 16. Accessed via Lexis Nexis.

Terris, Ben. 2015. "Sherrod Brown: Why Aren't Progressives Begging Him to Run for President?" *Washington Post*, January 28. https://www.washingtonpost.com/life style/style/sherrod-brown-why-arent-progressives-begging-him-to-run-for-pres ident/2015/01/28/f8378d9c-a63c-11e4-a7c2-03d37af98440_story.html?utm_term= .ad5096f303f3 (accessed January 10, 2020).

———. 2017. "Sherrod Brown Thinks He Could Have Helped Democrats Win in 2016. But What about 2020?" *Washington Post*, July 24. https://www.washingtonpost .com/lifestyle/style/sherrod-brown-thinks-he-could-have-helped-democrats -win-in-2016-but-what-about-2020/2017/07/23/168ac16c-6b2d-11e7-b9e2-2056e768 a7e5_story.html?utm_term=.ffod101669d3 (accessed January 10, 2020).

"Text of GOP Candidates Debate in South Carolina." 1996. CNN, February 29. Accessed via LexisNexis.

Tubbesing, Carl D. 1973. "Vice Presidential Candidates and the Home State Advantage: Or, 'Tom Who?' was Tom Eagleton in Missouri." *Western Political Quarterly* 26 (4): 702–716.

Turner, John C., Michael A. Hogg, Penelope J. Oakes, Stephen D. Reicher, and Margaret S. Wetherell. 1987. *Rediscovering the Social Group: A Social Categorization Theory*. Oxford: Blackwell.

Ulbig, Stacy G. 2010. "The Appeal of Second Bananas: The Impact of Vice Presidential Candidates on Presidential Vote Choice, Yesterday and Today." *American Politics Research* 38 (2): 330–355.

———. 2013. *Vice Presidents, Presidential Elections, and the Media: Second Fiddles in the Spotlight*. Boulder, CO: First Forum Press.

Unger, Irwin, and Debi Unger. 1999. *LBJ: A Life*. New York: Wiley & Sons.

Wattenberg, Martin P. 1984. "And Tyler, Too." *Public Opinion* 7 (2): 52–54.

———. 1995. "The Role of Vice Presidential Candidate Ratings in Presidential Voting Behavior." *American Politics Research* 23 (4): 504–514.

Wattenberg, Martin P., and Bernard Grofman. 1993. "A Rational Choice Model of the President and Vice-President as a Package Deal." In *Information, Participation, and Choice: An Economic Theory of Democracy in Perspective*, edited by Bernard Grofman, 173–177. Ann Arbor: University of Michigan Press.

Weinraub, Bernard. 1984. "Mondale Outlines Job Qualities in Running Mate." *New York Times*, June 13. Accessed via LexisNexis.

———. 1988. "Jackson Says He Deserves Thought as Running Mate." *New York Times*, June 1. https://www.nytimes.com/1988/06/01/us/jackson-says-he-deserves -thought-as-running-mate.html (accessed January 10, 2020).

Wofford, Taylor. 2016. "Who Will Be Hillary Clinton's Running Mate?" *Newsweek*, May 7. https://www.newsweek.com/hillary-clinton-vice-president-picks-456908 (accessed January 10, 2020).

Woodward, Bob. 1996. *The Choice*. New York: Simon & Schuster.

———. 2010. *Obama's Wars*. New York: Simon & Schuster.

———. 2012. *The Price of Politics*. New York: Simon & Schuster.

Woodward, Bob, and David S. Broder. 1992. *The Man Who Would Be President: Dan Quayle*. New York: Simon & Schuster.

Ysseldyk, Renate, Kimberly Matheson, and Hymie Anisman. 2010. "Religiosity as Identity: Toward an Understanding of Religion from a Social Identity Perspective." *Personality and Social Psychology Review* 14 (1): 60–71.

Zaller, John. 1992. *The Nature and Origins of Mass Opinion*. Cambridge: Cambridge University Press.

Index

Numbers in italics represent pages with figures.